EX AUDITU

An International Journal for the Theological Interpretation of Scripture

VOL. 32   2016

Ex Auditu is published annually by Pickwick Publications, an imprint of
Wipf and Stock Publishers, 199 West 8th Avenue, Suite 3, Eugene, Oregon 97401, USA

SUBSCRIPTIONS

Individuals:
U.S.A. and all other countries (in U.S. funds): $20.00
Students: $12.00

Institutions:
U.S.A. and all other countries (in U.S. funds): $30.00

This periodical is indexed in the ATLA Religion Database, published by the American Theological Library Association, 300 S. Wacker Dr., Suite 2100, Chicago, IL 60606, Email: atla@atla.com, www: http://www.atla.com/; *Internationale Zeitschriftenshau für Bibelwissenschaft; Religious and Theological Abstracts;* and *Old Testament Abstracts.*

Please address all subscription correspondence
and change of address information to Wipf and Stock Publishers.

©2017 by Wipf and Stock Publishers
ISSN:
ISBN: 978-1-5326-1688-4

EX AUDITU

An International Journal for the Theological Interpretation of Scripture

Klyne R. Snodgrass, Editor
Stephen J. Chester, Associate Editor
D. Christopher Spinks, Associate Editor

North Park Theological Seminary
3225 West Foster Avenue
Chicago, Illinois 60625-4987
USA

Tel: (773) 244-6243
Fax: (773) 244-6244
email: ksnodgrass@northpark.edu
Web site: http://wipfandstock.com/catalog/journal/view/id/12/

EDITORIAL BOARD

Terence E. Fretheim, Luther Seminary, St. Paul, MN
Richard B. Hays, The Divinity School, Duke University, Durham, NC
Jon R. Stock, Wipf & Stock Publishers, Eugene, OR
Miroslav Volf, Yale Divinity School, New Haven, CT
John Wipf, Wipf & Stock Publishers, Eugene, OR

THE EDITORIAL BOARD MEMBERS AND CONSULTANTS represent various disciplines and denominations. Theological interpretation of Scripture is a task to be taken seriously by scholars who are committed to the Christian faith and tradition. However, as one editorial consultant stated: "Let people gradually get used to the idea that a sane hermeneutics is both oriented in advance toward agreement/consent and is simultaneously exigent, discriminating, critical."

EDITORIAL CONSULTANTS

Richard Bauckham
University of St. Andrews, Emeritus
St. Andrews, Scotland

M. Daniel Carroll R.
Wheaton College
Wheaton, Illinois

Jan Du Rand
Emeritus, University of Johannesburg
and Extraordinary Professor, North West University

Willie Jennings
Yale Divinity School
New Haven, Conn.

Robert Johnston
Fuller Theological Seminary
Pasadena, California

R. Walter L. Moberly
University of Durham
Durham, England

Kathleen M. O'Connor
Columbia Theological Seminary
Decatur, Georgia

Iain Provan
Regent College
Vancouver, B.C.

Anthony Thiselton
University of Nottingham
Nottingham, England

Augustine Thompson
University of Virginia
Charlottesville, Virginia

Marianne Meye Thompson
Fuller Theological Seminary
Pasadena, California

Kevin J. Vanhoozer
Trinity Evangelical Divinity School
Deerfield, Illinois

Geoffrey Wainwright
The Divinity School
Duke University
Durham, N. Carolina

Sondra Wheeler
Wesley Theological Seminary
Washington, D.C.

William H. Willimon
The Divinity School
Duke University
Durham, N. Carolina

N. T. Wright
St Mary's College,
University of St. Andrews, Scotland

EX AUDITU

CONTENTS

Abbreviations vi

Introduction vii
Klyne Snodgrass

On Bringing Home the Bacons: Reflections on Science, Faith, and Scripture 1
Iain Provan

Response to Provan 22
John Walton

Paul and the Person: Perspectives from Philosophy and the Cognitive Sciences 26
Susan Grove Eastman

Response to Eastman 45
A. Andrew Das

Evolutionary Psychology and Romans 5–7: The "Slavery to Sin" in Human Nature 50
Paul Allen

Response to Allen 65
Christopher Lilley

Multiverse: Philosophical and Theological Perspectives 69
Gerald B. Cleaver

Made As Mirrors: Biblical and Neuroscientific Reflections on Imaging God 94
Joshua M. Moritz

Response to Moritz 121
Tyler Johnson

Contents

Forming Identities in Grace: *Imitatio* and Habitus as Contemporary Categories for the Sciences of Mindfulness and Virtue   125
Michael Spezio

Knowing in Part: The Demands of Scientific and Religious Knowledge in Everyday Decisions or "She Blinded Me With Science!" and Deciding Whether to Wear Checks with Stripes   142
Johnny Wei-Bing Lin

Response to Lin   165
Linda M. Eastwood

"A Rock of Offense": The Problem of Scripture in Science and Theology   169
Hans Madueme

Response to Madueme   193
Matthew Maas

"I Believe; Help My Unbelief!" Mark 9:14–29   198
Kirk Wegter-McNelly

Annotated Bibliography on Science and Religion   203

Presenters and Respondents   246

ANNOUNCEMENT OF THE 2017 SYMPOSIUM

North Park Theological Seminary in Chicago, Illinois, is pleased to announce that the thirty-second Symposium on the Theological Interpretation of Scripture will take place September 28–30, 2017. The symposium will start at 7:00 p.m. on September 28 in Nyvall Hall and will extend through a Saturday afternoon worship service on September 30. The theme in 2017 will be Participation/Union with Christ. The following persons have agreed to make presentations:

>   Cynthia Peters Anderson, preaching, Batavia United Methodist Church
>   Ben Blackwell, New Testament and Patristics, Houston Baptist University
>   Julie Canlis, John Calvin scholar, adjunct at Regent College
>   Bruce Fields, Faith and Culture, Trinity Evangelical Divinity School
>   Michael Gorman, New Testament, St. Mary's Seminary and University
>   Grant Macaskill, New Testament, King's College, University of Aberdeen
>   Brent A. Strawn, Old Testament, Candler School of Theology, Emory University
>   Olli-Pekka Vainio, Theology, University of Helsinki
>   Ashish Varma, Theology, Moody Bible Institute

Persons interested in attending the sessions should write before September 1 to Mr. Luke Palmerlee, North Park Theological Seminary, 3225 W. Foster Avenue, Chicago, Illinois 60625, or e-mail him at lrpalmerlee@northpark.edu. Meals may be taken at North Park and assistance can be provided in finding nearby lodging.

ABBREVIATIONS

All abbreviations are as specified in Patrick H. Alexander et al., eds., The SBL Handbook of Style, 2nd edition (Atlanta: SBL Press, 2014). Bibliographical details and any abbreviations not listed here can be found there.

AB	Anchor Bible
ACW	Ancient Christian Writers
ANF	Ante-Nicene Fathers
Interp	Interpretation
JR	Journal of Religion
KJV	King James Version
LW	Luther's Works
NIGTC	New International Greek Testament Commentary
NPNF	Nicene and Post-Nicene Fathers

INTRODUCTION

If you ask most people the distance a light year represents, they have no idea. A light year is nearly six trillion miles. Our galaxy, one of the smaller ones, is about 100,000 light years across. Reportedly the Hubble telescope has recorded the farthest object in space as a galaxy 13.4 *billion* light years away. How did we get on this planet? Are we merely the result of mechanical forces, or was there an action of God that brought us into being? The people at the symposium assumed an action of God, but does the God who created such a vast entity answer the prayers of an individual on a tiny planet called earth?

Humility—if anything resulted from the symposium papers and the mind-blowing discussions represented in this journal, it is humility, whether the issue was cosmological, anthropological, historical, or theological. Yet in all these discussions the stakes are extremely high regarding how we live our lives. The larger our understanding of the universe/multiverse the smaller humans become. What justifies talking about the dignity of humans?

The main concern was the relation of science and religion, of course, but the papers approached the subject from a variety of angles. Underlying assumptions seemed to be that all truth is from God and is for our best spiritual good and that the same God religion seeks to honor is the God whose work science—or at least some scientists—seek to understand. Science is usually good at explaining how things happened but not why. Most at the symposium rejected the image of a warfare between science and religion as detrimental, and people lamented the failure of education both in science and theology for most of our society.

While the issue was the relation of science and religion, much of the focus was on the questions What is Scripture and What is it for? Simplistic and monolithic views of the nature of the sacred writings cannot serve the discussion of science and religion or anything else in life. Iain Provan especially focused on the purpose of Scripture, and this question needs much more attention in the church. Additionally the church needs to emphasize the diversity of Scripture and that not all of Scripture has the same purpose and does not all carry the same authority, even while we affirm the value of all Scripture.

There was also a troubling question under the surface. These were high-level discussions of an elite group, but much of the world is just trying to get enough to eat for today. What gives science a reason to care, and how can the Christian religion

Introduction

meet such needs much more effectively than it has? To discuss science and religion is to treat all of life, and all the questions are interrelated.

At the symposium twice as much time is given to discussion of the papers as to their delivery, and the journal cannot reproduce the character of those discussions, which are always stimulating and enriching and in my opinion the most important part of the symposium. People in attendance at the symposium include an interesting mix of faculty types, pastors, church leaders, students, and lay people. We are grateful to all who participated. Appreciation is especially expressed once again to all the presenters and respondents who made a significant investment in the life of North Park. The friendship of all the people involved is a gift we value deeply. The authors of papers were given a chance to edit their contributions after the symposium, but the responses are essentially as they were presented. As is obvious, the views expressed are those of the authors and not necessarily those of the journal or of North Park. Special gratitude is expressed to Jonathan Fogel, a student at North Park, for his work on the bibliography and especially to Guylla Brown and North Park's staff, without whom the symposium would be impossible.

This is a year of transition for the symposium and the journal. Guylla is now retired and will no longer be involved. Luke Palmerlee will take over her duties. This is also my last year to plan the symposium and edit the journal. I want to thank especially the people listed in the front pages of the journal who have served on the editorial board and as editorial consultants. I will not repeat their names here, but I am grateful for their contributions and for their friendship. They have honored the journal and North Park by their involvement. I also want to thank Chris Spinks of Wipf and Stock who has been an associate editor and a tremendous help. His presence at the symposia each year is a real benefit, to say nothing of his friendship and that of the other people at Wipf and Stock.

Chris will continue as associate editor, and this fall Stephen Chester, who has also been an associate editor, will take over the editorial and planning responsibilities. I want to thank Stephen as well, for he has been a constant help and is a valued friend. I have no doubt of Stephen's ability to continue the agenda of theological interpretation of Scripture for the church. That is where his heart is, and he brings significant gifts to the task. He will reconstitute the editorial board and the editorial consultants.

Finally I would like to thank the attendees at the symposia over the years and the friends and readers of the journal. To be involved in this project has been a gift.

Klyne Snodgrass
Emeritus Professor of New Testament Studies
North Park Theological Seminary

ON BRINGING HOME THE BACONS: REFLECTIONS ON SCIENCE, FAITH, AND SCRIPTURE

Iain Provan

Once upon a time, there were three little pigs. But that is beside the point. Much more importantly, once upon a time there were two major Bacons. The first was called Roger, and he lived in the thirteenth century (ca. 1214–1292). The second was called Francis (no relation) and he lived in the sixteenth century (1561–1626); we shall meet him briefly later.

Roger Bacon was an English Fransciscan monk on a mission, and between 1267 to 1268 he sends three essays to Pope Clement IV. These essays represent a sustained Baconian lament about the woeful state of education in his time. Some of his concerns pertain to Bible reading and preaching. He wants to see biblical exegesis given more weight and be much better executed in the contemporary curriculum. Few thirteenth-century scholars, he complains, have more than an elementary knowledge of Hebrew and Greek. They read the Latin texts of the Vulgate, usually in an exceedingly corrupt form. As a result, the literal sense of the biblical text has fallen into doubt, and there must also be doubt, therefore, about its spiritual meaning. Roger is also concerned about the remainder of the curriculum. His contemporaries (he claims) possess defective knowledge even of the subjects they value, precisely because they only read Latin. They need to be reading at least Greek, Hebrew, and Arabic as well, if they really want to understand the world properly. Worse than this, the "valued subjects" (grammar, logic, natural philosophy, and some aspects of metaphysics) are in any case not very important for theologians, in comparison to others that are being neglected: mathematics, alchemy, chemistry, physics, the experimental sciences, and moral philosophy. Bacon himself was an experimental scientist, interested in astronomy, the laws of gravity, agriculture, and medicine. He researched such things as the reflection of light, explained the composition and effects of gunpowder, and discussed the possibility of inventions of later centuries such as steam vessels, microscopes, and telescopes. He was interested in new knowledge, i.e, in discovery. His contemporaries, he claims, are not. What does he advocate for, then, in these essays? He advocates for a better reading of both of God's "books"—both Scripture and creation. His plea is for a renewed commitment to genuine scholarship within a Christian frame of reference, in which science, faith, and the Scripture are all seriously engaged and contemplated in relation to each other, and sure knowledge of all kinds emerges from that process.[1]

One wonders what Roger Bacon would have to say about our own contemporary situation. I suspect that he would be driven, again, to lament. On the one hand, he would be far from impressed by the lack of interest in, and ignorance of, science among many Christians in our time—perhaps most especially among church leaders who have the duty of instructing the flock. On the other hand, he would certainly be critical of the lack of serious commitment to intelligent Bible reading in our churches, and increasingly in our seminaries as well, which appear in general to be fast abandoning their heritage, typically for poor reasons when it comes to the teaching of biblical languages (among other things). He would certainly, then, be appalled by the way in which contemporary Christian faith so typically keeps science and Scripture at arm's length from each other, and indeed frequently at war with each other, as if Scripture and creation were not the two books of God at all. He would insist on serious engagement with both, individually and in relation to each other, on the ground that all truth is God's truth, and all of it must be embraced by genuine seekers after truth. He would be right to do so, for Scripture and creation cannot coherently be conceived of, within the Christian tradition, as being at odds with one another in speaking about what is true. Biblical exegesis cannot be allowed to reside in a state of war with the scientific "reading" of creation, or vice versa. Indeed, although it is common for modern people both inside and outside the church to assume that the "warfare model" of faith and science to which they presently adhere is *the* model that has characterized the history of Christian reflection on such matters, this is not actually true. Roger Bacon has many important friends in the tradition, who like him have combined a high view of Scripture and its reliability as God's Word to us with a resolute commitment to integrating scriptural teaching with truth that has been discovered from creation.

Augustine of Hippo

The church fathers, for all that they sometimes disagreed on how to read Scripture, were united in the apostolic conviction that all Scripture is God-breathed and "useful for teaching, rebuking, correcting and training in righteousness, so that the man of God may be thoroughly equipped for every good work" (2 Tim 3:16). Augustine was certainly of this view: "Sacred Scripture was written under the inspiration of the

---

1. See especially Roger Bacon, *The Opus Majus of Roger Bacon*, trans. R. B. Burke (Philadelphia: University of Pennsylvania Press, 1928) Part III (75–115).

one Spirit of truth."[2] It possesses "paramount authority," and to it "we yield assent in all matters of which we ought not to be ignorant, and yet cannot know of ourselves."[3] The Scriptures certainly do not mislead us in the matters about which God wishes to address us through them; rather, they unerringly point us in the right direction. They are to be regarded as "sacred and infallible" when they teach, for example, "that in the beginning God created the heavens and the earth."[4]

What does this divine inspiration imply? At times the fathers can use the Latin verb *dictare* ("dictate") of the process of inspiration, implying an analogy with a master dictating a letter to a servant; Augustine uses this verb, for example, in his *Harmony of the Gospels*.[5] We might easily take such language as indicating a high degree of passivity on the part of the biblical author. Yet this is certainly not the kind of implication that the fathers typically draw, especially when it comes to the foundationally important literal sense of biblical texts. Throughout their writings, to the contrary, we find a governing assumption that the words of Scripture, albeit truly inspired by God, are nevertheless truly human words as well. They reflect the time and place in which they were uttered and written, including the linguistic and rhetorical forms available to the authors, who clearly wrote each in their own distinctive styles. This is certainly what Augustine assumes: "[He] clearly rejected the idea of a purely mechanical inspiration."[6] Therefore, to discover the will of God in Scripture, we must discover the thought and will of the human authors who wrote it. One implication of this co-existence of the divine and human word in Scripture is the reality of divine accommodation. This theme is explored in some depth by John Chrysostom, whose view can be summarized as follows: "The Bible owes its very existence to the condescension of God. . . . As in the historical Incarnation the Eternal Word became flesh, so in the Bible the glory of God veils itself in the fleshly garments of human thought and human language."[7]

If the fathers believed that, in the matters about which God wishes to address us, Scripture does not mislead us, which matters *are* these? Their most fundamental answer to this question is that Scripture has been gifted to us so that "we men [humans], each and all of us, as if in a general hospital for souls, may select the remedy

---

2. Augustine, *Literal Meaning of Genesis*, 4.34.53 (ACW 41.143).
3. Augustine, *City of God*, 11.3 (*NPNF* 1, 2.206).
4. Ibid., 11.6 (*NPNF* 1, 2.208).
5. Augustine, *Harmony of the Gospels*, 1.35.54 (*NPNF* 1, 6.101).
6. Andries D. R. Polman, *The Word of God According to St. Augustine* (Grand Rapids: Eerdmans, 1961) 50–51.
7. Frederic H. Chase, *Chrysostom: A Study in the History of Biblical Interpretation* (Cambridge: Deighton, Bell, 1887) 41–42.

for his own condition."[8] We are spiritually sick, and we need to be healed; Scripture is given to us as medicine. It is most especially knowledge about *such* matters that Scripture is intent on communicating; and the fathers can be strongly critical of Christians who do not attend to *this* knowledge, but "are fond of contention . . . and full of zeal about things which do not pertain to salvation."[9] They can be critical, indeed, of Christians who read Scripture itself in order to *subvert* what Augustine calls "the knowledge of present objects" that we already possess on account of "the testimony of our own senses."[10] So now we come directly to the proper relationship between the reading of Scripture and the reading of creation, about which Augustine holds some strong views:

> Usually, even a non-Christian knows something about the earth, the heavens, and the other elements of this world, about the motion and orbit of the stars and even their size and relative positions, about the predictable eclipses of the sun and moon, the cycles of the years and the seasons, about the kinds of animals, shrubs, stones, and so forth, and this knowledge he holds to as being certain from reason and experience. Now, it is a disgraceful and dangerous thing for an infidel to hear a Christian, presumably giving the meaning of Holy Scripture, talking nonsense on these topics; and we should take all means to prevent such an embarrassing situation, in which people show up vast ignorance in a Christian and laugh it to scorn. The shame is not so much that an ignorant individual is derided, but that people outside the household of the faith think our sacred writers held such opinions, and, to the great loss of those for whose salvation we toil, the writers of our Scripture are criticized and rejected as unlearned men. If they find a Christian mistaken in a field which they themselves know well and hear him maintaining his foolish opinions about our books, how are they going to believe those books in matters concerning the resurrection of the dead, the hope of eternal life, and the kingdom of heaven?[11]

There is such a thing as knowledge that is common to all educated people, Christian and non-Christian, and it is known by way of "reason and experience." Augustine does not believe that anyone should cite "the sacred authors of Scripture" in order to overturn such empirically and rationally grounded knowledge, not least because it will undermine the credibility of what the biblical authors have to say about their matters of central concern, namely "the resurrection of the dead, the hope of eternal life, and the kingdom of heaven." Indeed, Augustine goes on to refer

---

8. Basil of Caesarea, *Exegetic Homilies*, trans. A. C. Way; Fathers of the Church (Washington, DC: Catholic University of America Press, 1963) 151.
9. Clement of Rome, *The First Epistle of Clement*, 45 (ANF 1.17).
10. Augustine *City of God*, 11.3 (NPNF 1, 2.206).
11. Augustine, *Literal Meaning*, 1.19.39, (ACW 41.42–43).

to Bible readers who fail to observe the important distinction between what we can and cannot know "of ourselves" as "[r]eckless and incompetent expounders of Holy Scripture [who] bring untold trouble and sorrow on their wiser brethren," because they seek "to defend their utterly foolish and obviously untrue statements" by calling "upon Holy Scripture for proof." *Competent* expositors, in contrast, pay attention (among other things) to what we would now call "science" (although most people before us have referred to this as "philosophy"). Augustine was not the only church father who considered this important. Various patristic writers develop the same theme, using the language of God's "two books," Scripture and creation, in doing so. Both books must be carefully read in order to get at the whole truth of things.

Augustine's words themselves reveal, of course, that by no means all Christians in the patristic period agreed with him about what Scripture was designed, in the purposes of God, infallibly to teach. There *were* apparently those who believed that a Scripture that was "perfect" must at the same time comprise a kind of God-breathed encyclopedia of all knowledge. They cited Scripture, then, to dismiss and even to deride the kind of commonly shared scientific knowledge of their time that Augustine references. It was generally accepted in Late Antiquity, for example, that the earth was spherical, and not flat. The Christian apologist Lactantius (ca. AD 240–320) however, ridicules this idea in his *Divine Institutes*, placing the notion that "the world is round like a ball . . . like a globe" among various of the "marvellous fictions" created by those who "discuss philosophy for the sake of a jest, or purposely and knowingly undertake to defend falsehoods, as if to exercise or display their talents on false subjects."[12] Yet on the whole, writers of the patristic age did not take this all encompassing view of what Scripture was intended to reveal. By and large, the church fathers acknowledged that inspired, perfect Scripture was designed only to answer infallibly certain kinds of questions and not others. This was certainly true of Augustine, who cautioned that "one must not claim more for the Scriptures than they really teach," and specifically that "the sacred authors did not have the construction of a natural philosophy as their aim, even when they spoke about nature."[13]

The Magisterial Reformers

The magisterial Reformers—and here I follow only the Protestant part of the story of faith and science, for reasons of space and expertise—agreed with the church

---

12. Lactantius, *Divine Institutes*, 3.24 (ANF 7.94–95).

13. Kenneth J. Howell, "Natural Knowledge and Textual Meaning in Augustine's Interpretation of Genesis: The Three Functions of Natural Philosophy," in *Nature and Scripture in the Abrahamic Religions: Up to 1700*, ed. Jitse M. van der Meer and Scott Mandelbrote; Brill's Series in Church History 36; 2 vols. (Leiden: Brill, 2008) 1:117–45, at 128 and 144.

fathers, and those who followed them during the Middle Ages, when it came to the authoritative nature of Scripture as a God-inspired text. They also agreed with them in closely connecting Scripture's inspiration with its *usefulness*, which implies its *reliability*. Scripture is "the very sure and infallible Word of God," affirms Martin Luther.[14] Like the fathers, the Reformers too can sometimes give the impression that divine inspiration completely overwhelms the human author, to such an extent that the latter does not possess any real agency. God, John Calvin writes on one occasion, "dictated to the four Evangelists what they should write, so that, while each had his own part assigned to him, the whole might be collected into one body."[15] Yet the whole body of the Reformers' writings makes clear the extent to which they *in fact* presupposed that the human authors were thoroughly and actively involved in the processes by which Scripture came into being. For Luther, "the Scriptures have been 'written by men' *and* they are 'from God.'"[16] For Calvin, "the inspiration of scripture did not occur at the expense of the personalities of the human writers,"[17] and in his exegesis he used "the best tools of his days" to get at what these writers intended, "establishing historical contexts and background, searching for the precise meaning of terms in the original Hebrew or Greek, worrying over geography and chronology, and so on."[18]

As in the church fathers, one of the implications of the co-existence of the divine and human word in Scripture for the Reformers was the reality of divine accommodation. There are truths that need to be communicated, but the communication must attend to the capacities of the recipients. Luther writes, for example, of God lowering himself "to the level of our weak comprehension" and presenting himself to us "in images, in coverings, as it were, in simplicity adapted to a child."[19] This is a particularly important theme in Calvin's thought, such that "[a]ny study of Calvin as scriptural exegete would be incomplete which failed to examine his frequent appeal to the principle of accommodation."[20] Genesis 1 is one of the passages in which he

---

14.. Martin Luther, *Lectures on 1 Timothy* (1528) LW 28.239.

15. John Calvin, "Argument to the Gospel of John," in *Commentary on the Gospel According to John, Volume First*, Calvin's Commentaries 17; trans. William Pringle (Grand Rapids: Baker, 1981) 22.

16. Mark D. Thompson, *A Sure Ground on which to Stand: The Relation of Authority and Interpretive Method in Luther's Approach to Scripture*, Paternoster Biblical and Theological Monographs (Carlisle: Paternoster, 2004) 68.

17. David L. Puckett, *John Calvin's Exegesis of the Old Testament*, Columbia Series in Reformed Theology (Louisville: Westminster John Knox, 1995) 27.

18. John L. Thompson, "Calvin as a Biblical Interpreter," in *The Cambridge Companion to John Calvin*, ed. Donald McKim (Cambridge: Cambridge University Press, 2004) 58–73, at 61.

19. Martin Luther, *Lectures on Genesis Chapters 6–14*, LW 2.45.

20. Ford L. Battles, "God Was Accommodating Himself to Human Capacity," *Interp* 31 (1977) 19–38, at 19.

notably appeals to it. Acknowledging that astronomers understand that Saturn is larger than the moon, he explains that when Genesis 1:16 speaks of the sun and the moon as the two "great lights" in the sky, we must understand Moses as speaking of the heavens as they appear to ordinary people, and not as they really are:

> Moses does not here subtilely descant, as a philosopher, on the secrets of nature, as may be seen in these words. First, he assigns a place in the expanse of heaven to the planets and stars; but astronomers make a distinction of spheres, and, at the same time, teach that the fixed stars have their proper place in the firmament. Moses makes two great luminaries; but astronomers prove, by conclusive reasons, that the star of Saturn, which, on account of its great distance, appears the least of all, is greater than the moon. Here lies the difference; Moses wrote in a popular style things which, without instruction, all ordinary persons, endued with common sense, are able to understand; but astronomers investigate with great labour whatever the sagacity of the human mind can comprehend.[21]

This leads us directly to the question of the Reformers' view of what Scripture is useful *for*. It should already be clear from the above passage in Calvin that their answer to this question is not "everything." Calvin does not believe, for example, that Scripture is useful for understanding many aspects of the heavens. When dealing with Genesis 1:6–7, he explicitly advises: "He who would learn astronomy, and other recondite arts, let him go elsewhere."[22] Genesis treats only of "the visible form of the world," and not its essential reality, and to believe otherwise would create a conflict with what Calvin accepts as already known.[23] Like Augustine, then, Calvin believes that there is such a thing as knowledge that is common to all educated people—Christian and non-Christian alike—and it is known by way of reason and experience. For example, astronomers have proved, "by conclusive reasons, that the star of Saturn, which, on account of its great distance, appears the least of all, is greater than the moon."[24] Like other Christian thinkers before him, he pays serious attention to this knowledge as he engages in his exegetical and theological work; he is "extremely appreciative of scientific work."[25] He knows (as Augustine knew) that by no means all his contemporaries take the same approach—indeed, that some condemn astronomy. He robustly defends the discipline, however:

---

21. John Calvin, *Commentaries on the First Book of Moses Called Genesis*, Calvin's Commentaries 1; ed. and trans. John King (London: Calvin Translation Society, 1847; repr., Grand Rapids: Baker, 1981) 86.

22. Calvin, *Genesis*, 79.

23. Ibid., 79–80.

24. Ibid.

25. Davis A. Young, *John Calvin and the Natural World* (Lanham: University Press of America, 2007) 2.

> This study is not to be reprobated, nor this science to be condemned, because some frantic persons are wont boldly to reject whatever is unknown to them. [For] astronomy is not only pleasant, but also very useful to be known: it cannot be denied that this art unfolds the admirable wisdom of God. Wherefore, as ingenious men are to be honoured who have expended useful labour on this subject, so they who have leisure and capacity ought not to neglect this kind of exercise.[26]

"Reading the heavens" counts as "useful labour," and it "unfolds the admirable wisdom of God" within its own sphere, which pertains to the physical universe. Reading the Bible is also useful labour, and it too unfolds the wisdom of God in its own sphere, which pertains much more centrally to metaphysical matters like sin, repentance, and salvation. "It would have been lost time for David to have attempted to teach the secrets of astronomy to the rude and unlearned," Calvin comments on Psalm 19:4; "therefore he reckoned it sufficient to speak in a homely style, that he might reprove the whole world of ingratitude, if, in beholding the sun, they are not taught the fear and the knowledge of God."[27] This is what really concerns the psalmist: to teach the fear and the knowledge of God. Elsewhere Calvin identifies the primary function of Scripture as directing sinful people to Christ.[28] The two spheres of knowledge must not be collapsed into one; indeed, "the Bible should not be considered as the sole source of all knowledge and truth, infallible though it might be."[29] As the contemporary English *Edwardian Homilies* put it, "the perfection of holy scripture" consists in its containing every truth "necessary for our justification and everlasting salvation," yet "other sciences be good, and [are] to be learned."[30]

Martin Luther agreed. In fact, he was notably open to many of the scientific advances of his day—mechanical, medical, and others.[31] Looking ahead, he believed that the reform of religion, and in particular the retrieval of truer versions of the doctrines both of creation and incarnation would lead people to take nature more seriously and appreciate it more fully than had been possible under the "rule" of either the medieval scholastics or (unreformed) humanists like Erasmus of Rotterdam.[32]

---

26. Calvin, *Genesis*, 86–87.

27. John Calvin, *Commentary on the Book of Psalms, Volume 1*, Calvin's Commentaries 4; trans. James Anderson (Grand Rapids,: Baker, 1981) 315.

28. Calvin, *Commentary on the Gospel According to John, Volume First*, 218.

29. Young, *John Calvin and the Natural World*, 3.

30. Peter Lillback and Richard B. Gaffin Jr. (eds.), *Thy Word Is Still Truth: Essential Writings on the Doctrine of Scripture from the Reformation to Today* (Philadelphia: Westminster Theological Seminary, 2013) 283–89, at 284 and 287.

31. Lewis W. Spitz, *The Renaissance and Reformation Movements, Volume 2: The Reformation* (Chicago: Rand McNally, 1971) 583.

32. Ibid., 582.

Reformation thinking, he believed, enabled Protestants to see the world of "external objects" more clearly, and to comprehend them more fully. Recovery of true knowledge about "the external world" was indeed an important aspect of what the Reformation would accomplish, laying as it did the intellectual foundation for the scientific revolution that followed it.[33] This revolution occurred in a Protestant environment where it was emphasized that specifically religious vocations were not superior to secular ones, but that all should work to the glory of God. So it was that an enthusiastic band of Protestant "priests" soon emerged who dedicated themselves specifically to the acquisition of scientific knowledge. The famous Johannes Kepler regarded himself in exactly this priestly way: "I wanted to become a theologian, and for a long time I was restless. Now, however, observe how through my [scientific] effort God is being celebrated in astronomy."[34] There was in all of this an *openness* to the world that God has made, and what it has to offer humanity in terms of both teaching and blessing, that has all too often not been replicated in subsequent Protestant theology and practice. The main example often cited by advocates of the "warfare model" in favor of a *closed* Reformed attitude toward the reading of creation, pertaining to the sixteenth-century reception of the Copernican theory about the universe, is poorly chosen and does not in reality contradict the overall picture.[35]

Scripture and Science: The Scientific Revolution

The Reformation occurred towards the end of a long period in Europe during which the entire civilization had been Christian. Its citizens inhabited a "culture of the Book," in which it was widely assumed that it was the Bible, at root, that provided the authoritative reference point when it came to all human knowledge—albeit that philosophy had its own important role to play, especially when it came to questions about the natural world. Science, politics, art, architecture, literature, and music all

33. Michael B. Foster, "The Christian Doctrine of Creation and the Rise of Modern Natural Science," *Mind* 43 (1934) 446–68.

34. Cited in Gerald Holton, "Johannes Kepler's Universe: Its Physics and Metaphysics," *American Journal of Physics* 24 (1956) 340–351, at 351.

35. We cannot reasonably expect of Luther, Melanchthon, or Calvin in the middle of the sixteenth century that they should simply have accepted the new theory without demur, when "it is safe to say that even had there been no religious scruples whatever against the Copernican astronomy, sensible men all over Europe, especially the most empirically minded, would have pronounced it a wild appeal to accept the premature fruits of an uncontrolled imagination, in preference to the solid inductions, built up gradually through the ages, of men's confirmed sense experience." Edwin A. Burtt, *The Metaphysical Foundations of Modern Physical Science: A Historical and Critical Essay*, 2nd ed. (London: Routledge & Kegan Paul, 1932) 25. For an extended discussion of the point, see my forthcoming book, *The Reformation and the Right Reading of Scripture* (Waco, TX: Baylor University Press, 2017) chapter 13.

reflected the Great Story, as Christian thinkers attempted to unite in one domain, in various medieval syntheses, all human knowledge. A mere three centuries later, by the end of the nineteenth century, the same cannot be said. An entire premodern world defined by and organized in terms of the biblical narrative had all but disappeared, and a new, modern world had emerged. In Hans Frei's terminology, an "eclipse of biblical narrative" had occurred.[36] Why?

One popular, contemporary Christian answer to this question is to characterize the "eclipse" largely as a story of unjustifiable apostasy. Once there was a Reformed Christian culture founded on the inerrant Word of God. Then there arose what Norman Geisler has referred to as "an inductive scientific method [that] was assumed to be a means of obtaining all truth," and a materialism and a naturalism that were antithetical to orthodox Christian faith.[37] After this came an "Age of Enlightenment," in which a modern alternative to orthodox faith (Deism) was developed. In due course other problematic philosophies appeared, like Darwinian evolutionism. The eclipse of biblical narrative, on this view, is the plain and simple consequence of sinful people turning away from God and his inerrant Word, for no defensible reason, in order to embrace very wrong ideas and attendant practices. It "did not result from a discovery of factual evidence that made belief in an inerrant Scripture untenable. Rather, it resulted from the unnecessary acceptance of philosophical premises that undermined the historic belief in an infallible and inerrant Bible."[38] The church contributed to the eclipse insofar as theologians themselves "capitulated to alien philosophical presuppositions."[39] It is this kind of analysis that underlies, for example, *The Chicago Statement on Biblical Hermeneutics* (1982). It stands to reason that, if this is our view, then our response to modernity and postmodernity is going to be resolutely negative. Christian faith has essentially been at war with both modernity and postmodernity for some time—and not least with modern science. The nature of the solution offered, which is essentially to go on fighting the good fight, is bound up directly with the analysis of the nature of the problem.

While there are important elements of truth in this "Chicago Story," it does not provide us with anywhere near an adequate overall account of historical reality in the seventeenth through the nineteenth centuries, especially when it comes to understanding the modern relationship between Christian faith and science. One

---

36. Hans W. Frei, *The Eclipse of Biblical Narrative: A Study in Eighteenth and Nineteenth Century Hermeneutics* (New Haven: Yale University Press, 1974).

37. Norman L. Geisler, "Inductivism, Materialism, and Rationalism: Bacon, Hobbes, and Spinoza," in *Biblical Errancy: An Analysis of its Philosophical* Roots, ed. Norman L. Geisler (Grand Rapids: Zondervan, 1981) 9–22, at 10.

38. Ibid.

39. Ibid.

of its most glaring weaknesses is that it sees no role for the church itself, other than "capitulating" to falsehood, in causing the eclipse. Surrender, in Chicago-speak, is always a negative. Yet Christian "capitulation" to falsehood has only been part of the problem in the church's engagement with modernity (and now postmodernity). Also important has been a Christian refusal to surrender to truth (including "factual evidence") when surrender was required. The consequence of the flawed Chicago analysis is inevitably an entirely unhelpful and wrong-headed response. It is a response that, among other things, is not nearly as Reformed as it thinks it is, precisely because its understanding of the true nature of Reformed thinking about "an infallible and inerrant Bible" and its implications are confused.

This kind of confusion is not new; it is rooted in certain aspects of seventeenth-century Protestant thought that was already confused about the depth of its connection with the Reformers. The Reformation was *the* great catalyst in Europe in freeing intellectual life from the undue influence of the dominant streams of Greek natural philosophy, without which empirically based modern science could not have arisen at all—one of its various contributions to the dethronement of Aristotle as "'the pope in philosophy' . . . along with the other Pope," as Thomas Culpepper put it in the middle of the seventeenth century.[40] Luther had earlier opined that "nothing can be learned [from Aristotle's writings] either about nature or the Spirit."[41] The question that soon faced thoughtful Christians, of course, was how far to integrate into their Bible reading and their theology the claimed results of empirical enquiry that Reformed theological perspectives had played such a part in encouraging. What was to be done when evidence was unearthed by the new science that was, or appeared to be, inconsistent with settled, traditional interpretations of Scripture? How far could this be allowed to go?

Certainly some seventeenth-century Protestants took a very defensive position when it came to such questions, the kind of writers that often feature in modern accounts of the inevitable state of war that exists between science and faith. Certainly we find Protestants (as well as Roman Catholics) who clung desperately to what Alister McGrath has described as a "rigid Aristotelianism . . . which seriously held up advances in the fields of mechanics and astronomy" and other disciplines[42] and attempted to suppress the new knowledge that undermined their current convictions. The pro-Copernican Galileo is usually remembered as having been assailed by

---

40. Peter Harrison, *The Bible, Protestantism, and the Rise of Natural Science* (Cambridge: Cambridge University Press, 1998) 104. For an extended discussion of the point, see Provan, *The Reformation and the Right Reading of Scripture*, chapter 14.

41. Luther, *To the Christian Nobility*, LW 44.200.

42. Alister E. McGrath, *The Science of God: An Introduction to Scientific Theology* (Grand Rapids: Eerdmans, 2004) 159.

Rome specifically, and his heresy trial in 1633 has become emblematic of intolerant religious prejudice when confronted with scientific data. It is not so readily remembered that "[t]he first anti-Copernican monograph to appear in the Lutheran sphere ... that of Danish mathematician and theologian Peter Bartolinus," had already appeared in 1632.[43] The Utrecht professor Gisbert Voetius (1588–1676) later specifically rejected the arguments both that Scripture does not set out to teach science and that the Holy Spirit accommodates himself to the common people; the Copernican theory lay, he said, "in flat contradiction to the text and the intention of the Bible."[44]

However, two things are significant here. The first is that these "Reformed" writers are clearly out of step with both Luther and Calvin in their approach to matters of faith, science, and Scripture; and the second is that we find many *other* important seventeenth-century Protestant figures who clearly stand in *line* with Luther and Calvin on such matters—many who agreed with Galileo, for that matter, when he himself referenced divine accommodation in Scripture in relation to the Copernican issue. The idea that the correct way of proceeding was to set aside the emergent natural science with respect to cosmology and instead to adopt a "Mosaic" or "biblical" cosmology "found no general acceptance among the adherents of the Reformation" in the seventeenth century, just as it had not been accepted by influential writers in the sixteenth like Peter Ramus (1515–1572).[45] In fact, Ramus's criticisms of Aristotelian thought made a particularly strong impact on seventeenth-century English Calvinists, who were confronted by the Aristotelian-Thomistic scholastic theology of their Anglo-Catholic colleagues in the Church of England. Just a few years after Galileo's trial, for example (in 1640) John Wilkins (1614–1672) one of the founders of the Royal Society, insisted on the importance of allowing creation to speak in its own terms alongside Scripture, recognizing that the latter is not intended to provide us with the kinds of information in which science is interested:

> It were happy for us, if we could exempt Scripture from philosophical controversies; if we could be content to let it be perfect for that end unto which it was intended, for a rule of our faith and obedience, and not stretch it also to be a judge of such natural truths as are to be found out by our own industry and experience.[46]

---

43. Klaus Scholder, *The Birth of Modern Critical Theology: Origins and Problems of Biblical Criticism in the Seventeenth Century,* trans. John Bowman (Philadelphia: SCM, 1990) 53.

44. Reijer Hooykaas, *Religion and the Rise of Modern Science* (Grand Rapids: Eerdmans, 1972) 130–31, with further examples of anti-Copernican Protestants on pp. 131–38.

45. Hooykaas, *Religion*, 116–17, and see further 122–24, 126–30.

46. Cited in Hooykaas, *Religion*, 116.

This illustrates the way in which Wilkins and other seventeenth-century Protestants like him had come to disregard Scripture "as a source of factual information for [scientific research]."[47] Scripture does not set out to teach of "natural things . . . in accordance with the exact truth," affirms the Dutch theologian Christoph Wittich (1625–1687) but "often speaks . . . according to the view of the people."[48]

This same acceptance of a legitimate place for the new natural philosophy in the life and faith of the church is hinted at in *Westminster Confession of Faith* (1647) where it is important to note what it does and does not say about Scripture and knowledge. The knowledge that Scripture is said to teach in its infallible nature is "the whole counsel of God, concerning all things necessary for his own glory, man's salvation, faith, and life"—what is "either expressly set down in Scripture" or deducible from Scripture. There are various matters, however, which although they might be expected to fall within this remit, in fact do not. In these, "the light of nature" must help us arriving at right judgments: "There are some circumstances concerning the worship of God, and government of the church, common to human actions and societies, which are to be ordered by the light of nature, and Christian prudence, according to the general rules of the Word, which are always to be observed."[49] Unsurprisingly given the positive attitude toward science often evidenced in the Puritan context,[50] *Westminster* says nothing at all about how we should read Scripture in relation to the questions raised by natural philosophy.[51] However, individual participants in the Westminster assembly, like Samuel Rutherford, are quite explicit on the matter. Scripture is *not* our rule "in things of Art and Science, as to speak Latine, to *demonstrate conclusions of Astronomie*. . . . But it is our Rule . . . in fundamentalls of salvation . . . [and] in all morals of both first and second table [i.e., the Ten Commandments]," as well as in church government and worship.[52]

---

47. Hooykaas, *Religion*, 116.

48. Cited in Scholder, *Birth*, 125.

49. *Westminster Confession of Faith*, 1.6.

50. It is worth noting in this context that "among the group of ten scientists who during the Commonwealth formed the nucleus of the body that was to become the Royal Society, seven were strongly Puritan." Hooykaas, *Religion*, 98.

51. Nor do the earlier *Irish Articles of Religion* (1615) or the *Canons of the Synod of Dort* (1618–1619). See Lillback and Gaffin, *Word*, 189–215.

52. Samuel Rutherford, *The Divine Right of Church-Government and Excommunication* (1646) 99, cited in Jack B. Rogers, *Scripture in the Westminster Confession: A Problem of Historical Interpretation for American Presbyterianism* (Grand Rapids: Eerdmans, 1967) 366–67. Note also Rogers's summary comment on p. 442: "The Westminster Divines were open to the results of empirical science in its own realm . . . the Bible was a book to teach man of salvation, not, e.g., astronomy."

Scripture and Science: The Enlightenment

Two quite distinct approaches emerged in the Protestant churches, then, in response to the new scientific ideas of the seventeenth century. The "first way" (as we shall call it) involved the attempt to integrate new knowledge into the framework of Christian truth-claims, revisiting older interpretations of the Bible that were problematic in this pursuit and appealing as necessary to the ancient idea of divine "accommodation" in communication. Those who took this approach could be appropriately cautious about new ideas until they at least crossed the threshold between "a most probable theory" and "the theory that is likely on the basis of accumulating evidence to be true." Once convinced that they were dealing with genuine knowledge, however, they were committed to integrating it into their understanding of the Christian story as derived from Scripture. The "second way," conversely, involved a determination to dismiss new knowledge, in order to avoid any disturbance either to older ways of understanding Christian truth claims or to the interpretations of the Bible that supported them. The "first way" is truly Reformed (and Augustinian); it stands in line with the teaching and practice of the magisterial Reformers. The "second way" is not and does not.

The fork in the road of Protestant hermeneutics just described propelled its "ways" onwards in a manner that can be clearly traced throughout the "Age of Enlightenment" in the eighteenth century. For the moment let us allow the second path to wind its way out of our sight, since this is the one that is all too visible to many already, and let us follow only the first and focus on just one important figure. Jonathan Edwards was born in Connecticut in 1703, in what would soon be the United States of America, and died in 1758. He is probably best remembered for his role as a Puritan pastor in the religious revival known as the First Great Awakening (ca. 1730–1755). More important for our present purposes, however, is Edwards' upbringing among New Englanders who "had long been friendly to scientific advances and were confident that discoveries of God's ways of governing the natural world would only confirm what they knew from Scripture."[53] Isaac Newton (1642–1727) was known there "as thoroughgoing an empiricist as he was a consummate mathematician,"[54] combining in an extraordinary way mathematical calculation, empirical enquiry and reasoned deduction in the pursuit of scientific truth. So were other figures on the leading edge of the new scientific enterprise. From a young age Edwards himself was fascinated and profoundly influenced by the work of Newton. He was a keen observer of the natural world and wrote on various topics in natural

---

53. George M. Marsden, *Jonathan Edwards: A Life* (New Haven: Yale University Press, 2003) 60.
54. Burtt, *Foundations*, 208.

philosophy, including spiders, light, and optics. All of this he integrated with his Christian faith. The universe represented the complex language of God, and science was interpreting some of it. All in all, Edwards' "fundamental outlook was strikingly akin to that group of late seventeenth- and early eighteenth-century thinkers who have been characterized as 'theocentric metaphysicians' . . . [who] asserted that the new science was fully compatible with God's most intimate involvement with every moment of existence."[55] In Edwards then we see the continuation of the Puritan stream of scholarship already described above, with its openness toward considering how the reading of creation might inform the reading of Scripture, and vice versa.

In all of this Edwards was above all concerned to respond to Enlightenment Deism.[56] In responding, however, Edwards was quite "willing to acknowledge the epistemological and perceptual limitations of the biblical narratives and to transform his interpretation of them accordingly."[57] Such appropriate reinterpretation was indeed an important aspect of resolving the problem of "the growing conflict between Scripture texts and science," and he set about this task with optimism and enthusiasm. He was by no means alone in the English-speaking world, as the closing decades of the eighteenth century gave way to the opening decades of the nineteenth. English-speaking scholarship in this period remained broadly convinced, as did Edwards, that "the truths discovered in the empirical study of the natural world would tend to confirm the theological truths revealed in the study of Scripture" that was responsibly conducted with due attention to the latter's time-conditioned aspects. Leading figures of the English evangelical movement of the eighteenth century, for example, while suspicious of pure (and as they saw it, speculative) Cartesianism, certainly accepted and worked within the broad parameters of the Newtonian science of their time, with its commitment to empirical method and its delivery of practical, beneficial results. From their point of view—whether they were theologians, hymn writers, poets, or artists—what modern science revealed about the natural world simply confirmed the truths of special revelation and provided one further set of good reasons to worship the Creator.[58] It was by no means a problem in the eighteenth century, then, to combine heartfelt religious devotion and orthodox Protestant belief with intellectual openness to the world around about—the "first way" of many Christians before them.

55. Marsden, *Jonathan Edwards*, 73–74.

56. Robert E. Brown, "Jonathan Edwards and the Discourses of Nature," in *Nature and Scripture in the Abrahamic Religions: 1700–Present*, edited by Jitse M. van der Meer and Scott Mandelbrote; Brill's Series in Church History 37; 2 vols. (Leiden: Brill, 2008) 1.83–114, at 109–110.

57. Brown, "Jonathan Edwards," 110.

58. Bruce Hindmarsh, *The Spirit of Early Evangelicalism* (New York: Oxford University Press, forthcoming) chapters 3–4.

Scripture and Science: The Nineteenth and Twentieth Centuries

In the sixteenth century during the time of the Reformation, "very few people were engaged in systematic study of the Earth. Geology as a science did not yet exist.... Significant developments in the scientific investigation of the Earth lay ... in most cases, at least two centuries in the future."[59] At the beginning of the nineteenth century, however, "old-earth cosmology" was widely perceived as credible,[60] and by the middle of the century—after Charles Lyell (1797–1875) had published his three-volume *Principles of Geology* (1830–1833) and his *Elements of Geology* (1838)—we find ourselves well on the way to the contemporary situation, in which for two further centuries "thousands of geologists from around the globe have examined in astounding detail dozens of lines of evidence that bear on the antiquity of the Earth ... the fact that the Earth is extremely old with an age that is measurable in hundreds of millions to billions of years has been established."[61]

As to the relevance of the Bible to this question, already by the end of the nineteenth century it was widely understood all over the world that the earth was the product of a very long historical process. How did educated Protesant Bible-readers in the nineteenth century respond to this changing situation?

Especially as the new ideas first begin to impinge on people's consciousness, we find significant resistance to them in many quarters with strong affirmations of traditional "young earth" cosmology. Unsurprisingly, many people needed to be convinced that these ideas were valid, and that they really did need to make fresh adjustments to the way in which they had been reading Scripture in order to account for new evidence. For much of the nineteenth century, there was lively debate in Britain and in the United States on this question of the age of the earth and how it had come to be as it is now—about the correct way to read both creation and Scripture. What is significant, however, is that as the strength of the new scientific evidence came to be more widely accepted, the wisdom of continuing to argue for "Mosaic geology" was more widely questioned, and we find more and more recourse to popular proposals for reading Gen 1 in new ways that are still with us in some quarters today. For example, people read a huge chronological "gap" into Gen 1:1–3 or interpret the Hebrew word *yōm* ("day") throughout Gen 1 as referring to an "age" rather than a twenty-four hour day. The latter idea, in particular, was often presented in the nineteenth century in an "accommodationist" manner in line with classical Reformed exegesis. Either because they accepted such specific proposals, or simply

---

59. Young, *John Calvin and the Natural World*, 77.

60. Ralph O'Connor, "Young-Earth Creationists in Early Nineteenth-Century Britain? Towards a Reassessment of 'Scriptural Geology,'" *History of Science* 45 (2007) 357–403.

61. Young, *John Calvin and the Natural World*, 199.

because they had now come to recognize that the Bible was not designed to speak reliably about natural history, many Protestant Bible-interpreters by the century's end—including the notable Princeton theologian Benjamin Warfield—had come to accept the great age of the earth. This remains the majority Protestant and indeed evangelical view, albeit that some have steadfastly continued to hold to a young earth cosmology in the teeth of much evidence to the contrary.

Close on the heels of Lyell's work came the publication of Darwin's *On the Origin of Species by Means of Natural Selection* (1859). In this book he presented the biological theory upon which he had been working ever since returning from his famous sea journey on the *HMS Beagle* (1831–1836). Against a background in nineteenth-century Britain in which Christians, including the great majority of evangelical Protestants, were generally interested in and open to new scientific ideas,[62] many in that country took the new evolutionary ideas very seriously, and they sought to account for the data in ways that were congruent with a Christian worldview. The theory of biological evolution could indeed be seen as a welcome development in the world of science, for its "organicist paradigm" was more congruent with Christian faith than the mechanistic one that had dominated the immediately preceding centuries. Evolution *could* be interpreted in terms of growth toward the fulfillment of a divine purpose. Among Darwin's more "forgotten defenders" in this period were many Protestants of evangelical persuasion, not just in Britain, but also elsewhere—"forgotten" now precisely because the popular contemporary "warfare model" of science and faith can find no place for them.[63] The story told in that model tends to "talk up" other figures like Edward Pusey in Britain (1800–1882) Charles Hodge in the United States (1797–1878) and John Dawson in Canada (1820–1899) who were uncomfortable with recourse to the idea of divine accommodation in Scripture when it came to the new biology, even if they were happy to deploy the argument in other respects. However, in the European context the Darwinian hypothesis increasingly came to be seen as explaining coherently a very large number of data, and doing so much more successfully than the competing theory of non-evolutionary creation.[64] While Darwinianism steadily gained support in public discourse as a true hypothesis, Pusey's work on science and faith was destined to be of little lasting impact in England. Dawson's thoughts on science and faith were likewise generally discounted in his native Canada after his death. It is Charles Hodge, not only in his

---

62. Aileen Fyfe, *Science and Salvation: Evangelical Popular Science Publishing in Victorian Britain* (Chicago: University of Chicago Press, 2004) 3–9.

63. David N. Livingstone, *Darwin's Forgotten Defenders: The Encounter Between Evangelical Theology and Evolutionary Thought* (Grand Rapids: Eerdmans, 1987).

64. McGrath, *Science of God*, 215–16.

opposition to the atheism that he understood to be integral to Darwin's work, but also in his insistence that evolution had not in any case occurred, who has had the greatest ongoing influence in the United States down to the present time. Yet a very great number of orthodox Protestant people from the nineteenth century down to the present have not adopted a "Hodgian" stance on this issue, but rather—and it is quite right to put it in this way—a Reformed stance. They stand with Luther and Calvin and their "first way" Protestant successors, not in what they thought about the *issue* (obviously, since they did not *think* about the issue as such) but in what the hermeneutical principles are that we should bring to bear on such questions as we seek to read God's two books well in their unified truthfulness.

Conclusion

What contemporary Protestants should learn from all of this is, first, that we should not continue to deploy a generalized "warfare model" of the relationship between science and Christian faith when we are thinking about the past. Such a model does considerable violence to a much more complicated historical reality. This is now widely accepted by scholars. "While conflicts between science and religion have occurred in the past," Deborah Haarsma concedes, "warfare is not the primary interaction between religion and science."[65] For Lisa Stenmark, "this model simply does not bear up under scrutiny."[66] Then, secondly and as a consequence of learning about the "complicated historical reality," we need to realize that we, like our forebears, are confronted with a choice. We can certainly adopt a fighting stance if we want to, when it comes to Scripture and creation, faith and science, but if that is our decision, we cannot take refuge while trying to justify ourselves behind either the Reformers and most of their immediate Protestant successors or church fathers like Augustine. They do not commend such a stance. The question then is Why would *we* want to choose it? Why would we want to depart from the practice of so many of our significant Christian forebears in taking seriously the evidence for what is true that comes to us from outside the Bible? Why would we want to wrestle afresh with what that means for how we understand Scripture on particular points? In Facebook terms, why would we want to "friend" Norman Geisler and his small band of chums (historically speaking) when Roger Bacon and his much larger, weightier group would very much enjoy our company? Are we really so very sure of our entire infallibility as Scripture readers that we can afford to ignore the warning of those who have

---

65. Deborah B. Haarsma, "Science and Religion in Harmony," in *Science and Religion in Dialogue*, ed. Melville Y. Stewart; 2 vols. (Oxford: Wiley-Blackwell, 2010) 1:107–19, at 108.

66. Lisa L. Stenmark, *Religion, Science, and Democracy: A Disputational Friendship* (Lanham: Lexington, 2013) 13.

gone before us on this very point? "One should adhere to a particular explanation [with respect to Scripture]," advised Thomas Aquinas, "only in such measure as to be ready to abandon it, if it be proved with certainty to be false."[67] If we are not open to evidence, how shall we ever come to consider even the *possibility* that our current interpretation of Scripture is to some degree mistaken?

If love of self is not sufficient to persuade us, then perhaps we need to consider our neighbors. That is actually where Aquinas himself alights as he finishes the above sentence: "lest Holy Scripture be exposed to the ridicule of unbelievers, and obstacles be placed to their believing."[68] (There are clear echoes of Augustine in the background.) Historically the "second way" of biblical hermeneutics with respect to science has only ever provided stumbling blocks for those observing its pilgrims' journey. This was already true in the seventeenth century. In Europe many influential people were increasingly impressed by what the new natural philosophy was capable of delivering, and it was generally agreed that "after Kepler and Galileo, no informed man could continue to support the 'common-sense' observation of the rising sun, and it took a dedicated obscurantist to carry on opposition to the new theory."[69] In such a world it did the church no good at all when it allied itself stubbornly with Ptolemaic cosmology. If the Christian story could not be shown to be capable of absorbing new truth and making sense of it, what were they supposed to do? A choice had to be made. One could adhere to the official teaching of the church and ignore the science, *or* one could embrace the science and detach oneself from the official teaching of the church. A gap began to open between those who believed the story and those who believed the science. There can be no doubt that Christians who walked the "second way" greatly contributed, historically, to this reality. It was precisely their view of faith, hostile to science, which helped to produce its mirror-image, a science that was hostile to faith. This hostility was pursued by people whose experience had convinced them that many religious persons were "obscurantists" who stood in the line of succession from the medieval, scholastic theologians to whom that label had first been attached by largely Christian, Renaissance humanists. This is still happening now.

If even love of neighbor cannot persuade us to join the happy Baconian band, let us consider for a moment the needs of God's creation at large. Here we return at last to the other Bacon, the English philosopher, Francis. Modern science arose in the harbor of distinctively Christian thought; it was initially a Christian idea. Already in the seventeenth century in Francis Bacon's writings, however, we see

---

67. Aquinas, *Summa theologiae*, 1.68.1.
68. Ibid.
69. Spitz, *Renaissance*, 587.

science beginning to slip its moorings and sail off in its own direction.[70] For *this* Bacon, "reason exploring nature," unencumbered by any previous form of tradition, philosophy, or religion, is everything. Rigorous empirical enquiry into the nature of this world, with experimentation at its heart, is the method; total knowledge of nature, not in order to live in *agreement* with it but in order to *master* it, is the goal. It is an approach to "nature" that was inevitably in its time still influenced by some biblical ideas. They were now recontextualized within a thoroughly this-worldly, utopian story about reality that justified (as biblical faith does not) the bending of everything in nature to human ends. This approach was exceedingly optimistic about the ability of human power to reach these ends.

With this we see foreshadowed the development of science as a totalizing worldview in principle independent of the doctrinal and ethical constraints of Christian religion. We are still dealing today with the consequences of the birth of this autonomous, modern scientific monster, with its profound and negative effects not just on humanity but on the whole of creation. How did it gain so much traction? Part of the answer lies precisely in the seventeenth-century Christian failure or refusal to stand in the line of succession of many of their Christian forebears in seeking an integrative approach to knowledge, and in the ongoing popularity of this kind of obscurantism with respect to science in the succeeding centuries. We shall never know how differently the modern world might have turned out, had emerging modern scientific knowledge been fully integrated as it arose—and much more than it was—into an authentically biblical and Christian worldview. All that we do know is that it was not, and that part of the reason was that Christian faith came to be seen incapable of the integration.

The more-than-unfortunate consequence has been the substantive, modern bifurcation of Protestant Christianity and science, the latter slowly sinking into reductionistic scientism that has lost its metaphysical and ethical bearings. This was often in overt reaction to what is perceived as anti-scientific Protestant fundamentalism that is quite unable to accept scientific progress. To a significant extent, this is our corporate, Christian fault. We cannot expect to be taken seriously when we object to this or that particular aspect of "progress" as a negative step, if in general we are "known" always to be against progress. It is a little like a politician expecting a speech opposing a particular war to be taken seriously, when it is known that he is a principled, lifelong pacifist. So it is that the church has not been able to offer as much guidance as it should have in the recent development of science in modern societies. To that extent, the world of science has been deprived of crucially important input

---

70. John Channing Briggs, "Bacon's Science and Religion," in *The Cambridge Companion to Bacon*, ed. Markku Peltonen (Cambridge: Cambridge University Press, 1996) 172–99.

and guidance on matters that cannot be decided within its own parameters of operation, questions, for example, about what to do, and not do, with scientific discoveries, and why. The continuing eclipse of biblical narrative means that the Christian ability to supply such answers is compromised, assuming of course that Christians are even interested any longer in offering them. All too often in the present moment they seem oblivious to the really important scientific questions, such as what is to be done or not done with respect to robotics and genetic engineering. Instead, they are distracted still by quite old and trivial questions that do not really matter very much in the whole scheme of things, like the age of the earth and the processes by which life came to be the way it is now.

It would be easy, if space allowed, to provide further examples to illustrate the importance of retrieving biblical narrative for the life of the world.[71] Modernity is not doing as well in adulthood as it might have expected when it first began to make off with its Christian parents' wealth in its prodigal adolescence back in the seventeenth century, and it needs some ongoing family support—and rebuke.[72] Space does not, in fact, allow. I close immediately with this. We need to bring home both the Bacons. We need to own Roger's vision of integrated knowledge gleaned from both of God's books and to corral Francis's vision of dominion over nature once again within a more authentic version of the Christian Story, where love of God, neighbor, *and* creation at large directly informs our understanding of what dominion means and what it is *for*. That is the need of the hour when it comes to science, faith, and Scripture.

---

71. I have borrowed this phrase from Alexander Schmeeman, *For the Life of the World*, 2nd ed. (Crestwood: St. Vladimir's Seminary Press, 2002).

72. See, e.g., Brad S. Gregory, *The Unintended Reformation: How a Religious Revolution Secularized Society* (Cambridge, MA: Belknap, 2012) 365–87.

RESPONSE TO PROVAN

John Walton

As Provan observes, the complaint of Roger Bacon to the pope rings a familiar bell in our modern world. It is commonplace in many of our churches that science and its discoveries are viewed with suspicion and considered dangerous—threatening to people of faith and contrary to the historic traditions of the faith.

Provan has restored to us our footing in history by clarifying the perspectives that respected theologians have promulgated throughout the history of the church. Consequently, we have recovered our identity in them and can now be confident that we stand in solidarity with them as we think about science and Christianity. Today we join with them in sorrow that Christianity is so often ridiculed by the world around us, not for the stumbling block of the cross, but for adopting an anti-scientific perspective. It should affect us deeply to realize that so many in the world around us believe that an anti-scientific posture is characteristically Christian and intrinsic to Christian belief. We have misrepresented the nature of the Bible and the focus of the Bible, and as a result people misconstrue Christianity and are driven away from it.

In contrast to the anti-scientific perspective, I resonate with Provan's insistence that God's two books need to be read together and that the warfare model should be utterly rejected. As he has reviewed for us the tradition of integrating faith and science attested in a number of the worthy and respected theologians of the past, he helpfully reminds us of a heritage that is often forgotten or neglected in contemporary conversations.

In Provan's conclusion he opines that part of the answer to the rise of what he calls the autonomous scientific monster, "lies precisely in the seventeenth-century Christian failure or refusal to stand in the line of succession of many of their Christians forebears in seeking an integrative approach to knowledge, and in the ongoing popularity of this kind of obscurantism with respect to science in the succeeding centuries." It is a sensible assessment and helps us to recognize that the flawed premises that led some in the church to adopt their obscurantist, bifurcated positions were driven by 1) a failure to recognize what Scripture was and how it worked, and concomitantly 2) a failure to acknowledge that Scripture was given in a particular cultural context and needed to be read as an embedded, situated text.

Though often today we may find cause to distance ourselves hermeneutically from some early Christian writers, we can at the same time identify overlapping objectives in Augustine's claim that "to discover the will of God in Scripture, we must discover the thought and will of the human authors who wrote it." Unlike Augustine and most other theologians over the last 2,000 years, however, we actually have the means to achieve those objectives that they never could have imagined due to the archaeological recovery of the literature of the ancient world. These texts give us the unprecedented opportunity to actually understand the "will of the human authors" armed with invaluable information about the world in which they lived.

God used Israelite human communicators who addressed an audience that shared their culture and language. This communication is therefore inevitably embedded in the ancient world. It does not mystically incorporate subtle but specific information about other cultures in other times, whether that of medieval Japan, Stone Age Borneo, pre-Enlightenment Spain, the Cherokee of the fifteenth century, or post-modern American culture today. Its form and content are *always* governed by the Israelite context. Truly, even though it is written for us and for everyone, it is only written *to* Israel of the Iron Age. This is what Chrysostom refers to as "fleshly garments of human thought and human language."[1] What we and the early Christian writers referred to as "accommodation" must be viewed as an essential element of any effective communication.

Despite these fleshly garments, the revelation of God is sufficient, not only to discover the remedy for our human condition, but on the positive side of the ledger, to learn of God's plans and purposes that supersede our desperate plight and help us to comprehend what God is up to enough to participate with him in the great enterprise that he has undertaken—not just to redeem us, but to invite us in as partners in his kingdom work.

When I speak to audiences today presenting proposals about how the Israelites would have viewed the origins accounts in Genesis quite differently than we do today, one objection that is frequently raised concerns how God could have left us in the dark for so long. Am I really suggesting that all through the history of the church we have gotten it wrong? I believe that this tension is alleviated when we are made aware that even from the earliest discussions it was recognized that, as Provan summarizes it, "Scripture was designed only to answer infallibly certain kinds of questions and not others." Armed with that knowledge, we can see that even though all interpreters will always be hampered by their lack of information about the cultural

---

1. Quoted by Provan; see his n. 7.

context in which Scripture is given, the kinds of questions that Scripture ultimately answers, the information that we desperately need, has never been in doubt.

Our current knowledge of the ancient world serves to help us recognize when we are anachronistically imposing our modern perspectives on the text. We can succeed in at least setting those off to the side in our reading, even if we cannot fully recover the perspectives of the ancient audiences. Despite the challenge of penetrating the ancient world, we are fully in a position to understand, as Calvin indicates, what Scripture is useful for. In our contemporary use of Scripture, we too often casually commandeer it for use in all sorts of capacities that were never intended. It does not offer us scientific knowledge covertly woven between the lines of the ancient biblical text and cryptically addressing the sophisticated issues of today. It does not propose a systematic theology; it does not establish a moral code; it does not help us unravel how to interact with social media; it does not provide a "how to" handbook.

When we turn our attention to science specifically, we recognize that the scientific method as practiced today, as well as the larger enterprise of scientific investigation, is based on exploration of the natural world as it can be perceived through what we classify as natural laws. We are inclined to differentiate that sharply from what would be classified as "supernatural"—that is, events that defy natural laws or at least admit of no natural explanation. In contrast, in the biblical world they had no such categories; God was involved in all events as agent without differentiation of levels of agency. He was just as involved in what we refer to as natural cause and effect as he was in the extraordinary events that continue to defy our attempts to explain as achievable through natural causes. If this is true, then the Bible *cannot* weigh in on whether anything it discusses should be categorized today as natural or supernatural. If they have no category "natural," then the designation "supernatural" would be meaningless. To draw the fine point , if science is only engaged in what is deemed "natural" and Scripture does not have the category "natural," then Scripture cannot disagree with science when it claims something is "natural" (e.g., Big Bang or human origins). When Scripture insists on God's active involvement, it is saying nothing different from it would say for anything that happens (e.g., "You knit me together in my mother's womb"; Ps 139:13).

I am in full agreement with Provan's conclusion: "we should not continue to deploy a generalized 'warfare model' of the relationship between science and Christian faith to characterize the situation in the history of the church's engagement." This can be accomplished by fine-tuning our expectations of the Bible. To cite an example, how we label texts can make a difference. What if we started referring to Genesis 1 as a "Cosmic Identity Account" rather than a "Cosmic Origins Account?"

Likewise we could refer to Genesis 2 as a "Human Identity Account." As such it concerns anthropology more than biology.

Many other strategies might help us turn away from the warfare model with the precedent of respected theologians of the church throughout history to lead us. Nonetheless, we still must address what we *should* do; how *should* we interpret the origins accounts (Identity Accounts) of Scripture. Granted that the Bible does not teach us science and that what it intends to be useful *for* is not related to the scientific issues of our contemporary world, we can gladly and freely focus on that for which the Bible *is* useful. Even as we do that, we also must continue to work together to interpret the early chapters of Genesis responsibly, in full recognition of their embeddedness in their particular cultural context. Proper reading of what the text *is* saying will still result in very important theological insights that will contribute to that for which the Bible *is* useful.

PAUL AND THE PERSON: PERSPECTIVES FROM PHILOSOPHY AND THE COGNITIVE SCIENCES

Susan Grove Eastman

What does it mean to be a person? In the movie *You've Got Mail*, Meg Ryan plays an independent bookseller named Kathleen, who is up against a new corporate bookstore just around the corner. The executive of the megastore, played by Tom Hanks, is named Joe. Joe and Kathleen have a budding online romance, without Kathleen knowing that the person to whom she pours out her thoughts on the internet is the same man who is shuting down her beloved store. Joe defends his own actions with the mantra, "It's not personal; it's business." As long as he keeps the virtual and the embodied realities separate, he can continue to fool himself with this mantra. But the careful distinction between "personal" and "business," and even the illusion that any action can avoid being personal, comes crashing down in a face-to-face encounter between Joe and Kathleen. After putting her out of business, Joe takes her flowers and tries to explain—or rather defend—his business decisions:

> "It wasn't personal—" he begins.
>
> Kathleen completes his sentence:
>
> "—It was business. What is that supposed to mean? I am so sick of that. All it means is it's not personal to you, but it's personal to me, it's personal to a lot of people."
>
> (She shrugs helplessly)
>
> "What's wrong with personal anyway?"
>
> A bit lamely, he replies, "Nothing."
>
> She continues: "I mean, whatever else anything is, it ought to begin by being personal."[1]

What makes something "personal"? One answer would be to say that something is personal when it involves a personal agent, but that just shifts the question to the qualities of the agent. Is it action done by an "individual substance of a rational nature," to use the classic definition of Boethius?[2] In that case all Joe's actions are

---

1. Nora Ephron and Delia Ephron, *You've Got Mail*, 1998.
2. Boethius, *Liber de persona et duabis naturis contra Eutichen et Nestorium*, cap. ii, in *Patrologia Latina*, ed. J. P. Migne (Paris, 1841–61) 64, 1342–43. Cf. Henry Chadwick, *Boethius. The Consolations*

"personal," but the definition does not seem to get at his use of the word. Does personhood simply denote the existence of a self-conscious self-relation, the capacity to watch ourselves and narrate what we think and do? Then Joe's business dealings are indeed personal, but that also does not catch the implied understanding that Joe and Kathleen share about what it means to be "personal." No, for both of them, "personal" implies "interpersonal"—a personal action is something that affects other people as persons. Furthermore, when Kathleen says, "It ought to *begin* by being personal," she implies something more: human actions are always done by personal agents, who are such agents precisely in and through their interpersonal connections. She is reminding Joe that he also is a person who needs to take responsibility for his actions and their effects on other people. Within the human economy, at the least, all actions are personal, and indeed interpersonal. Kathleen knows this, but Joe only begins to face it when he moves out of the virtual reality of internet connections into an embodied encounter with the woman he is beginning to love and has just put out of business. Here "personal" implies the embodied face to face encounter of whole persons.

You've Got Mail came out in 1998. Fast forward to the present, to the world of Match.com on the one hand and burgeoning neurobiological discoveries about the essential embodiment of human identity on the other. Never have so many people sought a sense of personal connection via the internet rather than meeting "in person"; never have scientific discoveries so compellingly established the links between the self, the body, social relations, and the larger physical environment in which the person is embedded. What is going on? Who are we, and are we in danger of losing our personhood in an age dominated by technology?

To illustrate the point in another way, I reference two very different works of art. The first is a medieval wooden carving of the Virgin Mary and her mother, Saint Anne.[3] It depicts an animated discussion between a youthful Mary, with her abundant hair flowing down her back, and Anne in her matronly wimple. Anne holds a book, presumably the Bible, in one hand, and both women gesture and smile as they talk, indeed reaching out toward each other. They sit facing each other at a wooden desk strewn with papers: two women enjoying conversation.

The second work of art is a painting of a brain by a contemporary Canadian artist, Edmund Alleyn.[4] It could be taken from an anatomy book. Attached to the painting is a small video screen on which the viewer can see movies of people doing

---

of Music, Logic, Theology, and Philosophy (Oxford: Oxford University Press, 1981) 192–93.

3. In the permanent collection of the Montreal Museum of Fine Arts.

4. Part of an exhibit entitled "In my studio I am many" at the Montreal Museum of Contemporary Art, which ran from May to September, 2016.

ordinary activities. The people in the video are much smaller than the brain itself, which dominates the field of vision. But as I took the photo of the painting of the brain, a young woman moved into my field of vision, looking at the painting and then looking at me taking her picture. There is so much more to that young woman, and to the split-second look between us, than can be portrayed by the disembodied brain on the wall; she is mystery incarnate.

These two very different images convey sharply contrasting preconceptions about what it means to be a human being. The first presents a lively face-to-face dialogue between two embodied people. The second presents a disembodied brain, which somehow is supposed to get at the mysteries of human consciousness. Yet the painting of the brain illustrates very well a mechanical model of the person that has dominated much philosophical and scientific discourse in the West in the past century. Consider the metaphors that abound in common speech: we are "wired for relationship," we speak of "reprogramming" our mental habits and actions, we push the reset button on relationships, and so forth.

As we shall see, many contemporary philosophers of mind and scientists working in neurobiology and developmental psychology reject such a disembodied and mechanistic model of the person. In so doing, they are reshaping some long-standing assumptions about the self that date back at least to the Enlightenment. Not so long ago the core self, the essential self, was thought to reside in an incorporeal mind, detached from the vicissitudes of the body. Personhood was defined in terms of the autonomy, rationality, self-awareness, and self-determination of this incorporeal mind or core self. Such thinking is still extant today in popular culture, evident, for example, in widespread belief in a nonmaterial soul that transcends the death of the body. The flip side of such body-soul dualism can be a kind of escapism accompanied by a pernicious denigration of the body. Such dualism and denigration are often laid at the feet of Christian theology, and more specifically, at the feet of the apostle Paul.

Is this indeed the case? Or does Paul in fact have a more integrated understanding of persons as both embodied and socially embedded? If so, what might their agency look like and signify for an understanding of what it means to be a person? Does Paul's view bear any resemblance to current findings in neurobiology about the relationship between the body and the mind? These are big questions, far exceeding the time limit for today's talk! My brief here is—well—brief. In a short foray into these larger questions, I propose to juxtapose the theory of mind of one eminent neuroscientist, Vittorio Gallese, with the puzzle of personal agency in Paul's thought. Along the way we will find surprising resonances between Paul's views and contemporary notions of the person as an intersubjective agent and the body as mediating relationships between the self and others.

Gallese: The "Shared Manifold Hypothesis" of Intersubjective Identity

Vittorio Gallese is an Italian neuroscientist who was involved in the early discoveries of "mirror neurons," and who has become one of the major spokespersons for the importance of neuroscience in our concept of persons and our theories of mind. Here I will briefly outline his theory of intersubjectivity, which he calls the "shared manifold hypothesis."[5]

Gallese grounds his theory on research in two areas: experimental psychology, particularly the studies of infant imitation done by Andrew Meltzoff in the 1970s and thereafter; and neuroscience, particularly studies of neural activity in the premotor cortex (area F5) of monkeys' brains and in fMRI studies of human brains. Because the latter is Gallese's own area of expertise, I will focus on it. As is now well known, the "discovery" of "mirror neurons" occurred in a lab in Parma, Italy, when Gallese noticed that certain wired neurons in a monkey's brain were activated by the sight of the scientist eating a gelato (or drinking a cup of coffee; there are variations on this story) without the monkey actually performing a parallel action.[6] The activated neurons were also ones that would be engaged were the monkey to actually eat a gelato—that is, they were neurons that fired both for *performing* an action and for *observing* someone else performing the same action.[7] This surprising discovery has led to a storm of further research, including research on human beings through fMRI techniques and to a flurry of new theories about ways the brain functions to link us with other agents. How many TED talks have there been celebrating the discovery that human beings are "wired for relationship"?

---

5. Vittorio Gallese, "The 'Shared Manifold' Hypothesis: From Mirror Neurons to Empathy," in *Between Ourselves: Second-Person Issues in the Study of Consciousness*, ed. Evan Thompson (Exeter: Imprint Academic, 2001) 33–50; Vittorio Gallese, "'Being Like Me': Self-Other Identity, Mirror Neurons, and Empathy," in *Perspectives on Imitation: From Neuroscience to Social Science*, vol. 1 of *Mechanisms of Imitation and Imitation in Animals*, eds. Susan Hurley and Nick Chater (Cambridge, MA: MIT, 2005) 101–18.

6. I use scare quotes because not all neuroscientists are convinced by the ascription of "mirroring" properties to these particular neurons, let alone by the theories of mind that are based on such properties. See in particular Raymond Tallis, *Aping Mankind: Neuromania, Darwinitis, and the Misrepresentation of Humanity* (London: Routledge, 2014); Robert A. Burton, *A Skeptic's Guide to the Mind: What Neuroscience Can and Cannot Tell Us about Ourselves* (New York: St. Martin's, 2013); Gregory Hickok, *The Myth of Mirror Neurons: The Real Neuroscience of Communication and Cognition* (New York: Norton, 2014).

7. Subsequent experiments with congenitally blind people have demonstrated that the corresponding visuomotor neurons "light up" at the sound of an action being performed, so this neural activity is not limited to vision.

Gallese delineates three classes of neurons in the premotor cortex: simple motor neurons that are activated in the successful performance of an action, and two subcategories of so-called "visuomotor" neurons, which he dubs "canonical neurons" and "mirror neurons," respectively.[8] "Canonical neurons" fire when the person sees an object; they are the neurons that would be needed to grasp the object or do some other activity with it. That is, through generating an "as if" neurological feedback loop within the body, they supply information about what would be required to perform an action with an external object. Gallese calls this feedback loop a "multimodal semantic node"; according to his theory it creates a model or simulation of a possible action.[9] In this way, *canonical neurons map action for the actor*.[10] "Mirror neurons," on the other hand, link the actor and the observer, because they fire for both performance and the observation of an action.[11] That is, there is a proto-motor neuronal activity (in contrast with simple motor activity) that generates an inner simulation or representation of the other's behavior, which in turn (perhaps) potentially guides imitative actions. *Mirror neurons map action for the observer.*

I should note that this interpretation of the available data is contested. Not everyone, for example, buys Gallese's simulation theory—that is, the idea that the activity of the "visuo-motor" neurons generates an inner map or simulation of action. Some scientists and philosophers think that the existence of such a representational neural map is not supported by the data and is not necessary to explain the phenomena of mimetic interaction. For example, philosopher Shaun Gallagher accepts Gallese's findings in regard to mirror neurons, but rejects his simulation theory because the theory presumes "The subject seemingly reads off the meaning of the other, not directly from the other's actions, but from the internal simulation of *the subject's own* 'as if' actions. . . . Here second-person interaction is reduced to a first-person internal activity."[12] Instead Gallagher proposes an "interaction theory" that even more strongly posits the primacy of intersubjective, immediate bodily interaction and shared cognition between human agents.[13] Describing the personhood of very young children in terms of "primary intersubjectivity," he argues, "In most intersubjective situations we have a direct understanding of another person's intentions because their intentions are explicitly expressed in their embodied actions, and

---

8. Gallese, "'Being Like Me,'" 105.
9. Ibid., 109.
10. Ibid., 111.
11. Ibid.
12. Shaun Gallagher, *How the Body Shapes the Mind* (Oxford: Clarendon, 2005) 222.
13. Ibid., 223–30.

mirrored in our own capabilities for action."[14] This is a fully embodied and embedded, non-mentalist picture of the person as constituted in interaction with others.[15]

It is beyond the scope of this paper to adjudicate between Gallese and Gallagher regarding the correctness of simulation theory. I do note in passing the different philosophical perspectives implicit in their theories. Gallese's theory is first-personal, by which I mean that in his theory the experience of the self is primary and mediates the experience of others. This is what Gallagher means when he says "second-person interaction is reduced to a first-personal internal activity." I understand others through an internal map of my own experience. Gallagher's theory is explicitly second-personal in its standpoint; he says that intersubjectivity is so foundational, so primary in the constitution of the self that my experience of my self is mediated primarily through my experience of others. Some theories of infant development would say something similar by claiming the infant first knows she exists when she sees herself mirrored in her parents' eyes.

So there are real differences in the ways in which the data is interpreted. Nonetheless, my focus here is on what Gallese and Gallagher share, which is a thoroughly intersubjective notion of the person as always already constituted in relationship with others. In this respect, the discovery of "mirror neurons" is of most interest for theories of how human beings come to know others and themselves as intentional agents who are both similar to, and different from, themselves. Because the same class of neurons "fires" in both the observer and the actor, Gallese posits that a "shared space" of embodied experience opens up between them. The activity of mirror neurons maps a "multimodal representation across different spaces inhabited by different actors. These spaces are blended within a unified common intersubjective space, which paradoxically does not segregate any subject. This space is *"we-centric."*[16] Gallese further identifies this "we-centric space" with a "shared implicit semantic content." Through the actions of both classes of neurons, a "shared informational space" is established that acts as a "control model" for behavior and relationship, not only with objects but also with other agents.[17]

What does this mean? It seems to mean that, within such a "space," persons share cognitive experience through the parallel actions of their neural systems. In the process they experience a self-other identity that grounds an intersubjective

---

14. Ibid., 224–25.

15. Gallagher's work on the body provides a basis for the embodied, relational model of the person proposed here, and it is not subject to some of the criticisms of Gallese's theories about mirror neurons, which Andrew Das rightly outlines in his response to my paper.

16. Gallese, "'Being Like Me,'" 111, emphasis original.

17. Ibid., 105.

"certitude" that other people are intentional agents like oneself.[18] That is, they have a sense of similarity with other people, even a sense of oneness.

Gallese is among the scientists who have engaged such neurological theories philosophically as well as scientifically. His claims are bold: "Anytime we meet someone, we do not just perceive that someone to be, broadly speaking, similar to us. We are implicitly aware of this similarity because we literally embody it."[19] Such certitude about other people in turn grounds Gallese's remarkable optimism about the human capacity to "mind-read"—not only to experience other people's behavior and "understand its content and predict its consequences," but also to "attribute intentions to other individuals."[20] These are astounding assertions, raising questions not only about potential distinctions between understanding and projection, but also about the boundaries of the self and the negotiation of difference as well as similarity.

To be sure, Gallese does not dispute the importance of difference as well as similarity in interpersonal interaction and knowledge, but he claims, "Self-other identity preexists and further parallels the self-other dichotomy."[21] In other words, at the very beginning of life, prior to our experience of ourselves as "conscious subjects" of our own lives, there is a "primitive self-other space, a paradoxical form of intersubjectivity without subjects."[22] This self-other space, instantiated by the activity of canonical and mirror neurons, and further mediated by other sensory input, constitutes the "shared manifold of intersubjectivity." Consequently, "intersubjective relations play a *major* and *constitutive* role in shaping our cognitive capacities and in providing the shared database required to establish meaningful bonds with other individuals."[23] If this is what we are in the foundations of our being, all human beings are "personal" in an "interpersonal" sense.

---

18. Ibid., 102.

19. Ibid., 104.

20. Ibid., 101. For evidence to the contrary, see Nicholas Epley, *Mindwise: Why We Misunderstand What Others Think, Believe, Feel, and Want* (New York: Vintage, 2015).

21. Gallese, "'Being Like Me,'" 111. Regarding the importance of difference as well as similarity, Gallese adds a caveat at the end of his essay, in which he says, "Self-other identity is not all there is to intersubjectivity.... If that were the case, others could not be experienced as others. On the contrary, the *alterity* of the other grounds the objective character of reality. The quality and content of our own self-experience of the external world are constrained by the presence of other subjects who are intelligible while preserving their character as other. This alterity, as we have seen, is present also at the subpersonal level instantiated by the different neural networks coming into play when *I* act versus when *others* act." (p. 117, emphasis original)

22. Ibid., 105. In this regard Gallese and Gallagher are in complete agreement. It is worth pondering whether there can be real "intersubjectivity" without distinct subjects; I will return to this at the end of the paper.

23. Ibid., 103, emphasis original.

Gallese has much more to say, notably positing that the activity of mirror neurons provides the neural substrate for empathy, but my interest here is limited to this picture of the human agent as constituted intersubjectively in a "we-centric space." Through links between observation, action, and the relational network in which the person exists, "body action" is "essentially relational."[24] Conversely, then, personal action is not individualistic, autonomous, self-directed, or removed from its effects on others; the person who acts is foundationally, essentially a subject constituted in relationship to other subjects.

All of this raises immense questions about personal identity, freedom and responsibility, the limits of empathy and mind-reading, and so on. Two questions come to the fore. First, what is the difference between a genuinely empathic understanding of other people and a presumed understanding that really is the projection of our own experience? The second and related question concerns the necessity of both similarity and genuine difference for true intersubjectivity: if the other person is basically an "other self," how can there be a self-other identity? In other words, is it possible for there to be an "intersubjectivity without subjects," as Gallese puts it? At the end of this paper I will return to these questions, but first we will move on to Paul's depiction of the acting human subject, a depiction that turns out to be every bit as paradoxical as that of Gallese.

Paul: "I yet not I but another"

At two key places in his letters Paul uses an odd grammatical formulation to depict a kind of construction of the self. It goes like this: "It is no longer I who [verb] but [subject plus verb] in me."

The first instance of this paradoxical grammatical construct concerns Paul's relationship with Christ; the second concerns his relationship with what he calls "Sin," which is most often a noun, not a verb, in Paul's letters. So, first:

> I have been crucified with Christ; *I no longer live, but Christ lives in me*; and [the life] I now live in the [realm of the] flesh, I live in the [realm of trust] generated by of the Son of God, who loved me and gave himself for me. (Gal 2:20)

And second:

> I do not know (or understand) what I'm doing. For I do not do what I want, but I do what I hate. Now if I do what I do not want, I agree that the law is good. So then *it is no longer I who does it, but sin dwelling in me*, that is, in my flesh. . . . Now if I do what I do not want, *it is no longer I who does it, but sin dwelling in me*. (Rom 7:17, 20)

24. Ibid., 109.

Despite their respective influence and massive importance in Paul's thought, the parallel structure of these two passages is rarely noted.[25] In each case, the speaker says, "I no longer am acting, but someone or something else inhabits my person as the subject of my actions." The difference between the constructions of the self in the two passages consists in the difference between distinctly other and yet personally indwelling actors—in the first case, "Christ who lives in me," and in the second, "Sin that dwells in me."[26] Sin and Christ are diametrically opposed to one another, but the constructions of the self in these texts are striking in their similarity. In both cases the self is a self-in-relation-to-another, undermining any notion of the person as a bounded, isolated, self-determining individual agent.

It is worth noting that this notion of the self-in-relation-to-another is very ancient, and in some ways it permeated Paul's own context. As Dale Martin observes, for people in the Hellenistic era, "Innards . . . are constituted of the same stuff as the rest of the cosmos."[27] Martin asks his readers "to try to imagine how ancient Greeks and Romans could see as 'natural' what seems to us bizarre: the nonexistence of the 'individual,' the fluidity of the elements that make up the 'self,' and the essential continuity of the human body with its surroundings."[28] Nonetheless, one would be hard-pressed to find another Hellenistic author speaking of a distinctly other agent indwelling the speaker in quite the way that Paul describes.

---

25. The identity of the rhetorical "I" in Romans 7 is hotly debated, whereas few doubt that Paul is speaking personally in Galatians, even if he also is using himself as an example for his readers in Galatia. To many interpreters, if not to all, it seems impossible that the anguished self in Romans 7 could be the same person as the confident speaker in Gal 2:20. In fact, they seem antithetical to one another: one is full of confidence, the other of despair. One paradoxically "lives" even after "co-crucifixion" with Christ, while the other will shortly cry out for deliverance from "this body of death" (Rom 7:24).

26. In distinction from the more common use of "sin" as a verb with human beings as its subject, Paul more typically personifies "sin" as a noun that is the subject of active verbs. "Sin" enthralls human beings, who unwillingly find themselves acting contrary to their own intentions. See Susan Eastman "The Shadow Side of Second-Person Engagement: Sin in Paul's Letter to the Romans," *European Journal for Philosophy of Religion* 5.4 (2013) 125–44.

27. Dale Martin, *The Corinthian Body* (New Haven, CT: Yale University Press, 1995) 16. As the preceding paragraphs of this paper demonstrate, these ancient claims are no longer "bizarre" in modern discourse.

28. Martin, *Corinthian Body*, 21. Other classicists, such as A. A. Long and Troels Engberg-Pedersen, contend that there was very much a notion of the self as a discrete and self-determining agent, at least in Stoicism. On the one hand, the Stoics saw all of existence, including the agent that speaks of herself in the first person singular, as on a continuum of being; in that sense there is no self, and there is a constant traffic between the "inner" and the "outer" world. On the other hand, perhaps precisely because there is such a traffic, the Stoics in particular taught the importance of maintaining an evaluative boundary between the "inner citadel" of correct judgments about all data and everything else. Engberg-Pedersen discusses his disagreement with Martin on this issue in "A Stoic Concept of the Person in Paul? From Galatians 5:17 to Romans 7:14–25," in *Christian Body, Christian Self: Concepts of Early Christian Personhood*, ed. Clare K. Rothschild and Trevor W. Thompson (Tübingen: Mohr Siebeck, 2011) 85–112, at 85–86.

This structured subjectivity is what interests me. Notably, in both texts there is still an "I" that is the subject of active verbs, despite the radical claims, "I have died . . . I no longer live," and "It is no longer I doing the action, but another." In Galatians the "I" who "no longer lives" nonetheless immediately reappears as the subject of the verb "to live"! Furthermore, this personal agent "lives" simultaneously in two contrasting realms: "in the flesh" and "in the faith" generated by the self-giving action of the Son of God.[29] In Romans the "I" appears as the subject of verbs of perception and appraisal: "I don't understand," "I agree," "I hate," "I want." This acting subject both does and does not do what it hates, the doing of which also is ascribed to "Sin" as another acting subject.

In both cases the ascription of continuing action to the human subject suggests that the person is not absorbed into or fully melded with the other "subjects" that perform its actions, whether that be Christ or Sin. Paul seems to assume a "self-other identity" in which the distinction between the self and the other is maintained, and yet their actions are fused. This is not precisely an "intersubjectivity without subjects" or a "we-centric space" in Gallese's terms; in fact, I cannot think of any biblical examples where the divine and human actors are collapsed into a plural first person "we" as the subject of personal action. Yet there is a puzzling "overlay of subjects" in the action depicted in each passage.[30]

In what follows I will focus on Galatians, where Paul's astounding self-description is all about death and life: "I died to the law"; "I have been crucified with Christ"; "I no longer live." Despite what I have just said about the perseverance of the ego as an acting subject, the extremity of the metaphor implies a full extinction and complete reconstitution of the human agent. Here is no partial deadening of one part of the self, or exercising of mastery over undesirable passions, or simply cutting oneself off from a law-observant past. Rather, as Beverly Gaventa puts it, "It is the whole of the *ego* that is gone."[31] How can we make sense of such language? Commentators refer to the "real and total demolition of the self, as previously constituted," or the "execution of [Paul's] own identity."[32] Accurate as these restatements of Paul's

---

29. Rightly noted by A. Andrew Das, *Galatians* (St. Louis: Concordia, 2014) 273 n. 221: "Paul is contrasting two overlapping spheres of existence: the bodily flesh and the realm of faith." My only quibble is the implication that faith does not also take place in bodily existence.

30. Pauline scholars use this language to talk about the "I" and Christ in Galatians and in other places in Paul's letters under the rubric of "participation in Christ"; such analysis is distinctly lacking in regard to Paul's account of sin in Romans 7.

31. Beverly Gaventa, "The Singularity of the Gospel Revisited," in Mark Elliott et. al, ed., *Galatians and Christian Theology: Justification, the Gospel, and Ethics* (Grand Rapids: Baker, 2014) 193.

32. The first quotation comes from John M. G. Barclay, "Paul's Story: Theology as Testimony," in *Narrative Dynamics in Paul: A Critical Assessment*, ed. Bruce W. Longenecker (Louisville: Westminster John Knox, 2002) 133–56, at 143; the second is from Douglas Campbell, *The Deliverance of God:*

language are, they leave us wondering what this crucifixion of the self looks like in practice (and what keeps it from being a masochistic rejection of one's personhood, or a case of schizophrenic personality disorder).

If Paul's paradoxical and visceral imagery of death is shocking, the imagery of life is equally paradoxical: "That I might live to God"; "Christ lives in me"; "I live in the flesh"; "I live in the faith of (or in) the Son of God."[33] Apparently the "I" has been put to death and no longer lives, but rather Christ lives "in me." This language in turn leads commentators to say such things as, "Paul is provocatively denying his own role as the acting 'subject' of his own life and claiming that he has been supplanted in this capacity by Christ," and "Christ becomes the acting subject of Paul's life, apparently replacing Paul himself as the agent of his own life."[34] Such interpretations imply a competitive relationship between God's action and human action: either Paul acts, or God acts, but they do not act at the same time. Such an account might follow from the passive voice of the Greek verb, "I have been crucified"; Paul certainly was not the agent of his co-crucifixion with Christ.

Yet immediately preceding this self-depiction Paul claims that his death to the law was precisely so that *he* might "live to God." As I have noted, in the next breath Paul again employs the verb "to live" with himself as the acting subject. "I live in the flesh" and simultaneously, "I live in the faith." Is this the same "I" that was put to death? Paul's extreme language would seem to forestall such an interpretation. What notion of the human agent underlies Paul's radical and puzzling language?

In Pauline scholarship, answers to that question may be grouped according to two different accounts of Paul's body language. The first emphasizes the autonomous individual and the body as the mode of *self*-relation. We may take the work of Rudolf Bultmann as an example of such an approach. The second emphasizes the interpersonal constitution of the self and the body as the mode of *other*-relation. We may take Bultmann's student, Ernst Käsemann, as an example of this approach. I will summarize their views very briefly, and then turn back to Paul and Gallese.

Rudolf Bultmann (1884–1976) was one of the most important NT scholars of the early twentieth century. He is best known for his attempt to "de-mythologize" the NT, which he believed was necessary in order to appropriate its message for his contemporaries in the European academy. He began his explication of Paul's theology with a discussion of Pauline anthropology; indeed, he famously claimed that in

---

An Apocalyptic Rereading of Justification in Paul (Grand Rapids: Eerdmans, 2009) 848.

33. The translation of this short clause is a matter of significant debate among Paul scholars.

34. Richard Hays, *The Faith of Jesus Christ: The Narrative Substructure of Galatians 3:1—4:11*, 2nd ed. (Grand Rapids: Eerdmans, 2002) 154; J. Louis Martyn, *Galatians: A Commentary* (AB 33A; New York: Doubleday, 1996) 258.

doing theology we must do anthropology because the only level on which we can know or say anything about God is God's involvement with human beings. As he put it famously, "Every assertion about God is simultaneously an assertion about man *and vice versa.*"[35]

Bultmann thought that, for Paul, the body is the capacity for self-relation. Through the body we become aware of ourselves; we gain self-consciousness. We are fully embodied and self-aware individuals; in contemporary terms we could call this bodily self-relation a proprioceptive feedback loop. Yet ironically, the language of self-awareness effectively invokes a self that watches itself, perhaps floating somewhere above the body. There is a subject self and an object self, so to speak, paradoxically instantiating the mind-body dualism that Bultmann explicitly sought to avoid through his totalizing conception of the body as the whole person. "Personal" action can be conceptualized only as essentially autonomous, self-determining action because "persons" are presumed to be isolated individuals in their essence. In a nutshell, "the will to selfhood is the presupposition for genuine communion; for only those who are persons, that is, each a self, can join in true communion."[36] Borrowing language from the philosopher Timothy Chappell, we may call this "individualism about persons," in which "relationality presupposes individuality."[37]

Ernst Käsemann was Bultmann's student and critic. Contrary to Bultmann, Käsemann claimed that Paul's "anthropological terms" do not refer primarily to the individual at all, but rather, "existence is always fundamentally conceived from the angle of the world to which one belongs."[38] Furthermore, Käsemann insisted on the centrality of physical embodiment for Paul's thought: "For Paul all God's ways with his creation begin and end in corporeality," and that embodied existence necessarily means connection with the rest of the cosmos in particular, concrete, and historical ways.[39] To be a body is to be embedded in one's world and inextricably shaped by it.

In Käsemann's interpretation of Paul, the body is all about connection and communication. Bodies are what connect us to the wider world and to other people, for good or for ill. They function exteroceptively, receiving external stimuli that are

---

35. Rudolf Bultmann, *Theology of the New Testament*, 2 vols. translated by Kendrick Grobel (Waco: Baylor University Press, 2007) 2:191.

36. Rudolf Bultmann, *Glauben und Verstehen: Perspektiven hermeneutischer Theologie* II (Neukirchen-Vluyn: Neukirchener, 2000) 264. The translation here is by Wayne Meeks, "The Problem of Christian Living," in *Beyond Bultmann: Reckoning a New Testament Theology,* edited by Bruce W. Longenecker and Mikeal C. Parsons (Waco: Baylor University Press, 2014) 211–29.

37. Timothy Chappell, "Knowledge of Persons," *European Journal for Philosophy of Religion* 5.4 (2013) 3–28.

38. Ernst Käsemann, "On Paul's Anthropology," in *Perspectives on Paul*, translated by M. Kohl (Philadelphia: Fortress, 1971; repr. Mifflintown, PA: Sigler, 1996) 1–31, at 26.

39. Ibid., 18.

fundamental to the persons we are. As bodies we are participatory beings, never autonomous individuals, but neither absorbed into a collective whole; the relationship between individual and communal existence is never an either/or. This means that the actions of the body are unavoidably *inter*personal actions. They are done by complex, relationally constituted acting subjects, always impacted by and affecting others in a constant interchange in which God also is involved as the primary personal and genuine "Other." It is not the "will to selfhood" that is the presupposition for communion but exactly the reverse: communion is the presupposition for a self that is capable of self-knowledge and action. This is "relationalism about persons" in which "individuality presupposes relationality."[40]

What happens when we juxtapose these two different interpretations of Paul's body language with the theories of Gallese regarding the existence of neurological substrate for shared cognition and a "we-centric space"? It is fairly clear that Käsemann's understanding of Paul's anthropology is considerably closer to Gallese's hypothesis. Indeed, Käsemann was remarkably prescient; writing in the 1960s he argued, "We must draw attention to the change in our horizon," which emphasizes "the interdependence of all humankind," not isolated individuals.[41]

I suggest that if we put Käsemann's reading of Paul together with Gallese's theory of intersubjectivity, we discover a helpful mode of discourse for interpreting Paul's language in contemporary terms. There are significant caveats, of course. I will come to those at the end of the paper, but first, here is the payoff: What Gallese and Käsemann give us is a picture of the person as constituted fundamentally in relationship with others. Even more, personal action is the action of such intersubjectively constituted persons. The "I" that acts is a "person-in-relationship-to-another."[42] As Shaun Gallagher puts it, intersubjectivity "is the ubiquitous setting of human behavior."[43]

Such a model of the person, in which the body mediates "other-relation" or "self-other identity" prior to, and as a basis for, "self-relation" or "self-identity," suggests fresh categories for interpreting Paul's structured self. These categories are needed, for as Bultmann demonstrates, interpretation of Paul's central theme of participation has long been hampered by anthropological assumptions premised on the notion that human beings are essentially autonomous, isolated, and self-directing individuals. Given such a notion of personhood, it follows naturally that "we each

---

40. Chappell, "Knowledge of Persons," 4.
41. Käsemann, "On Paul's Anthropology," 11.
42. This formulation comes from Peter Hobson, *The Cradle of Thought* (London: MacMillan, 2002) 183.
43. Gallagher, *How the Body Shapes the Mind*, 247.

understand our self to be a closed inner unity that is not open to the interference of supernatural powers."[44]

But if the self is always a "system of self-in-relation," then in theory the self can also be open to divine powers as well as the influence of other people. This notion of an intersubjective self suggests new ways to interpret Paul's metaphors of death and life in Galatians. If there is no *a priori* individual prior to or apart from the intersubjective engagement within which the person is constituted, there is no need to posit some abstract, essential, self-reflective, and continuous "I" over against the body. Rather, bonded with its relational matrix, the whole self lives or dies with that matrix. In Galatians then the "I" that has died to the law through the law and been crucified with Christ is a relationally constituted system of self-in-relationship to the Mosaic law, including its practices and the community formed by and in those practices. Similarly, when "those who belong to Christ have crucified the flesh with its passions and desires," as Paul says later in Gal 5:24, they have moved from an old identity constituted in relationship to "the flesh" as a systemic holding environment to a new identity constituted "in Christ." This radical remaking of the person is not, therefore, a splitting off of one part of the self designated as "flesh." It is the integration of the whole person within a new intersubjectively constituted self that is given and sustained by Christ as the relational partner, instantiated and mediated through other persons in embodied and socially embedded ways. That new intersubjectivity, like the old one "in the flesh" and "under the power of sin," takes place in human bodies, entwined in and constituted by interpersonal social bonds. The cognition of self and other is relationally mediated within a new "shared informational space," to use Gallese's terms. Metaphorically speaking, members of the body of Christ share neural "circuitry" in worship through joint attention to the one Lord.

---

44. In his provocative essay, "New Testament and Mythology: The Problem of Demythologizing the New Testament Proclamation," in *New Testament and Mythology and other Basic Writings*, edited and translated by Schubert M. Ogden (Philadelphia: Fortress, 1984) 1–44, Bultmann outlined "our self-understanding as modern persons": "We ascribe to ourselves an inner unity of states and actions"; "we look upon [dependence] as our true being, over which we are able to take dominion by understanding, so that we can rationally organize our life"; we distinguish our "true selves" from our physical bodies. Furthermore, "We know ourselves to be responsible for our own existence and do not understand how through water baptism a mysterious something or other could be communicated to us that would then become the subject of our intentions and actions." According to our modern world-view, says Bultmann, "We each understand our self to be a closed inner unity that is not open to the interference of supernatural powers." Knowing guilt only as "a responsible act" by individuals, "we cannot understand the doctrine of substitutionary atonement through the death of Christ," nor can we "understand Jesus' resurrection as an event whereby a power to live is released that we can now appropriate through the sacraments." In other words, as essentially isolated individuals who require a revised *self*-understanding before they can relate to others, how can human beings be touched by others, even by God, and reconstituted in new relationships?

All of this suggests that discoveries in the cognitive sciences are opening up new opportunities for a fresh articulation of Paul's gospel in contemporary terms. Of course, that is not to say that Paul's thought can be *explained* neurologically.[45] Rather, several caveats come into play in such a juxtaposition of Paul's theology with contemporary theories of the person. I will name three.

In the first place Paul's language is metaphorical, and he uses it to denote a construction of the self as co-constituted with "subjects" that are neither simply other human beings nor are they simply objects. They are suprahuman agents. Gallese, to the contrary, limits his investigation to the activity of visuo-motor neurons in the physical bodies of individual human beings. He has no stated theological or indeed metaphysical agenda; insofar as such matters are left completely out of his account, his method is functionally naturalistic. Second, therefore, insofar as the claims Gallese makes and the claims Paul makes are—by their very structure as interpersonal accounts of the person—embedded in distinctive communities of discourse and practice, are they simply incommensurable? Third, how does the radical otherness of God permit the kind of intersubjective divine-human engagement that Paul depicts? Can such engagement be in any way elucidated by an account of the person that derives from neurobiological analysis and theories? Or will any attempt at such elucidation simply reduce Paul's language by squeezing it into a naturalistic framework from which divine causality is excluded?

I begin with the first caveat. Yes, Paul's language is metaphorical, and unavoidably so, because metaphors are necessary to point to realities that exceed human comprehension. But Gallese's language is also metaphorical. "Mirror" neurons, "we-centric space," "shared semantic field," even the posited interior "simulation" or "representation" generated by neurons—all of this is metaphorical language, and also unavoidably so. As Janet Martin Soskice has argued, both scientific and religious discourses require metaphors to denote realities that are not yet fully defined.[46] The danger of such language lies in a collapse of the gap between the signifier and the thing signified, but the great promise and usefulness of metaphors is that they allow us to speak of what we do not, and in the case of God, cannot fully understand. They function as pointers without which the discourse cannot proceed.

This brings us to the second caveat—the question whether scientific discourse and Paul's radical vision are simply irreconcilable. The answer is yes and no. It depends on what the goal of the conversation is. If I think I can *explain* the meaning of "crucified with Christ" and "Christ lives in me" by talking about mirror neurons,

---

45. For an attempt to do just that, see Colleen Shantz, *Paul in Ecstasy: The Neurobiology of the Apostle's Life and Thought* (Cambridge: Cambridge University Press, 2009).

46. Janet Martin Soskice, *Metaphor and Religious Language* (Oxford: Clarendon, 2002) 134, 148.

then I do run the danger of reducing Paul's thought, sheering it of supernatural causality in the name of some mistaken notion of modernity and scientific credibility. I also equally run the danger of misusing scientific discourse against its own explanatory goals. In fact, attempting to explain Paul's language in terms of Gallese's theories would be making a category mistake for the reason stated above: both Paul and Gallese are speaking metaphorically, using metaphors to denote realities that exceed full description. The difference is that religious metaphors point to realities that never will be explained or understood fully; scientific metaphors point to realities on the way to being explained or at least being more fully described. The goal of scientific investigation is, in this sense, quite different from the goals of Paul's letters.

That said, there is another way in which both Paul's language and Gallese's investigations are deeply commensurate, insofar as both involve the understanding of human beings. Paul points to the mystery of God's gracious and transforming action with and in human beings in their embodied, historical, social, temporal embeddedness; divine-human interaction will always be a mystery exceeding explanation. Gallese's metaphors point to a level of human connection at a subpersonal, neurobiological level that renders human beings deeply vulnerable to deforming, lethal influences on the one hand, and yet open to life-giving relationships on the other. In contrast to Bultmann's "closed inner unity that cannot imagine interference from a supernatural power," this profoundly embodied, interpersonally structured self is porous, interconnected, and therefore in principle open to "interference" from God as well.[47] People may *feel* that they are closed inner unities. They may say, with Simon and Garfunkel, "I am a rock, I am an island, I touch no one and no one touches me."[48] But both Gallese and Paul would say they're fooling themselves. Rather, the poet John Donne had it right. "No man is an island, entire of itself; every man is a piece of the continent, a part of the main."[49] From a neurobiological perspective that is how every person starts out—in utero, at birth, in the earliest formation of the self. From a theological perspective every human being is in the image of the Triune God. Specifically from Paul's christological perspective, the worth of every

---

47. I put "interference" in scare quotes because, theologically speaking, the God who made and sustains the universe cannot be spoken of as interfering. God doesn't "interfere" in a cosmos that could not exist independently of God.

48. Paul Simon and Art Garfunkel, "I am a Rock," from their album, "Sounds of Silence," Columbia, 1966.

49. John Donne, *Devotions upon Emergent Occasions*, edited by Anthony Raspa (Montreal: McGill-Queen's University Press, 1975) 87. Timothy Chappell elaborates in "Knowledge of Persons," 3–4: "[N]o human *starts out* as an island. Each of us at least begins as a piece of the continent, a part of the main. Insofar as we ever come to be anything like 'entire of ourselves,' this is a learned and socialized achievement; an achievement, moreover, which is necessarily built upon our prior status as parts of the main. In a word, *individuality presupposes relationality*."

person is evident from the fact that Christ assumed human form and died on our behalf. Contemporary intersubjective accounts of personhood in the cognitive sciences are amenable to this claim. As Wayne Meeks said in comments about Bultmann's project, "The fundamental issue turns on the question of how we construe personal identity."[50] He added, "The most interesting turn in moral philosophy of the past several decades is the growing persuasion, from a variety of quarters, that the modern individualist self is an illusion."[51] There is a major shift going on in ways of conceptualizing what it means to be a person, and that shift opens up a rich new language for articulating Paul's gospel.[52]

But what about the third caveat? The methodological framework of Gallese's work is naturalistic; he is not looking at matters of divine action at all, whereas at the heart of Paul's preaching is the intimate and yet qualitatively other reality of a God who acts in human history but in no way is derived from it. How then does the radical otherness of God permit the kind of intersubjective divine-human engagement that Paul depicts when he says, "It is no longer I who lives but Christ lives in me"? Can such a reality be in any way elucidated by an account of the person that derives from neurobiological analysis and theories? Or will any attempt at such elucidation simply reduce Paul's language by squeezing it into a naturalistic framework from which divine action is excluded?

I suggest we turn the question around: how can we conceptualize a truly intersubjective account of the person *without* the radical otherness of God as the relational partner? Implicit in this reframing of the question is the tension between similarity and difference that I noted in Gallese's theory. Gallese's primary interest is in the way we know that other people are like us, but he does suggest that the differences between ourselves and other people alert us to "objective realities" over against our projections of our own experience. In fact, both similarity and alterity are necessary for genuinely intersubjective engagement. If I see another person simply as "another self," am I not in danger of simply imposing a projection of myself onto him or her?

It is not always clear that Gallese's overriding concern for finding a "we-centric space" in which we know that others are like us provides the necessary conditions for

---

50. Meeks, "The Problem of Christian Living," 222.

51. Ibid.

52. This shift involves not only neuroscientists but others working in cognitive sciences. For example, Peter Hobson is a psychoanalyst who depicts self-other identity in participatory terms: "There is a sense in which one 'participates in' the other person's state, yet maintains awareness of 'otherness' in the person with whom one is sharing, while also being affectively involved from one's own standpoint." Peter and Jessica Hobson, "Joint Attention or Joint Engagement? Insights from Autism," in *Joint Attention: New Developments in Psychology, Philosophy of Mind, and Social Neuroscience*, edited by Axel Seemann (Cambridge, MA: MIT, 2011) 115–36, at 117.

the recognition of difference.⁵³ Intersubjective constitution of the person requires a relational partner who both assimilates to the self and remains distinct from it. It requires, that is, what Rowan Williams describes as the "soul" in the sense of "a whole way of speaking, of presenting and 'uttering' the self, that presupposes *relation* as the ground that gives the self room to exist, a relation developing in time, a relation with an agency which addresses or summons the self, but is in itself no part of the system of interacting and negotiating speakers in the world."⁵⁴ Such an agency can only be that of God who is both outside creation and immanent in it, with a mimetic likeness but not equivalence to human beings.⁵⁵ This mimetic correspondence finds even fuller expression in the incarnation, death, and resurrection of Jesus, in whom God enters fully, bodily, temporally, and historically into human experience. Christ assimilates to the human "other" and "participates" in the human state, yet without losing his divine identity. Perhaps such radical similarity and difference opens the space for a mode of intersubjectivity that is truly non-competitive, in which one actor does not override the actions of another, nor project his or her own image on the other.

Theological Interpretation: Closing Thoughts

In this essay I juxtapose some aspects of Pauline interpretation with current work in neuroscience on the intersubjective constitution of the self. Is this theological interpretation? I think that it is in the following sense: this is an attempt to interpret (and not simply repeat) Paul's thought with the presumption that his letters have something to say to contemporary readers. For Bultmann historical reconstruction of the NT context is "in the service of the interpretation of the New Testament writings under the presupposition that they have something to say to the present."⁵⁶ That is, it is an attempt to read Paul's letters as a word of address to us, today, in our context. As such, it follows a trajectory shared by Rudolf Bultmann and Karl Barth,

---

53. For criticism along these lines, see Vasudevi Reddy, *How Infants Know Minds* (Cambridge, MA: Harvard University Press, 2008) 13–21.

54. Rowan Williams, *Lost Icons: Reflections on Cultural Bereavement* (London: Continuum, 2003) 196.

55. This interplay between similarity and difference obtains in theological discussions of the relationship between divine and human agency. On the one hand, in both Jewish and Christian traditions the notion of a mimetic correspondence between God and humanity underwrites the creation in the image of God. For extensive survey of the ancient texts, see George H. van Kooten, *The Image of God, Assimilation to God, and Tripartite Man in Ancient Judaism, Ancient Philosophy and Early Christianity*, WUNT 232 (Tübingen: Mohr Siebeck, 2008).

56. Bultmann, "Epilogue," in *Theology of the New Testament*, 2:251. For the notion of "interpretation, not repetition," see John M. G. Barclay, "Interpretation, Not Repetition: Reflections on Bultmann as a Theological Reader of Paul," in *Journal of Theological Interpretation* 9.2 (2015) 201–9.

for both of whom the living voice of Scripture was of primary importance. Above all, Bultmann wanted to avoid interpreting biblical texts as "an objectifying kind of thought cut loose from the act of living," because genuine theological interpretation "is real only in the act of existing and not in the isolated reflection of thought."[57] Karl Barth introduced the first edition of his monumental commentary on Romans with the bold claim, "Paul, as a child of his age, addressed his contemporaries. It is, however, far more important that, as Prophet and Apostle of the Kingdom of God, he veritably speaks to all men of every age."[58] May it be so even now.

---

57. Bultmann, *Theology of the New Testament*, 2:241.

58. *The Epistle to the Romans*, trans. E. C. Hoskyns (Oxford: Oxford University Press, 1977, repr. from 1933) 1. For Barth's and Bultmann's shared commitment to missional exegesis, see now David Congdon, *The Mission of Demythologizing: Rudolf Bultmann's Dialectical Theology* (Minneapolis: Fortress, 2015).

RESPONSE TO EASTMAN

A. Andrew Das

Professor Eastman offers in her paper the rich, suggestive fare that is the hallmark of her work as she brings the first-century Apostle Paul into conversation with the last twenty-five years of research on mirror neurons. She begins with the definition of a "person" and eventually stresses that a person is shaped and defined by *interpersonal relationships*. A person is also *embodied*, which enables these relations.

Pauline specialists have indeed criticized anthropologies that stress humans as autonomous, isolated, self-directed individuals apart from relationships in a larger world, inclusive also of suprahuman agents. James D. G. Dunn's 1998 *The Theology of the Apostle Paul* defines the Greek *soma* as "embodiment," since the body is not just a matter of corporeal or physical existence but is also the instrument by which a person experiences and relates to the world.[1] This does not deny, of course, that Paul often speaks of the body primarily in terms of physical function or presence,[2] but bodies also participate in a wider web of relationships. Sexual relations with a prostitute jeopardize bodies that are also members of Christ.[3] The Romans are to offer their bodies as a living sacrifice.[4] Paul's stress on the resurrection and a spiritual body simultaneously underscores that an embodied existence is God's ultimate intention for the human being.

What is less clear in Eastman's paper is where she ultimately falls in the monistic/dualistic anthropologies debate.[5] Some specialists contend that Paul also distinguishes the soul from the body, and that the soul may temporarily exist apart from the body—perhaps even after the body dies prior to the resurrection. Paul imagines a presence "by the Spirit" rather than "by the body" in 1 Cor 5:3, and he wonders about an experience that may well have been out of the body in 2 Cor 12:2–3.[6]

---

1. James D. G. Dunn, *The Theology of Paul the Apostle* (Grand Rapids: Eerdmans, 1998) 56.
2. E.g., Rom 1:24; Gal 6:17; 2 Cor 4:10.
3. 1 Cor 6:13–18.
4. Rom 12:1; Dunn, *Theology*, 57–58.
5. One must still account for the raw data in Robert H. Gundry, Soma *in Biblical Theology: With Emphasis on Pauline Anthropology*; SNTSMS 29 (Cambridge: Cambridge University Press, 1976).
6. Whether hypothetical or not, Paul *envisions* an out-of-body experience, which speaks to his anthropology, as commentators have recognized; e.g., Murray J. Harris, *The Second Epistle to the Corinthians*; NIGTC (Grand Rapids: Eerdmans, 2005) 839.

The contribution of this paper, however, is in the conversation Eastman broaches with neuroscience. To her credit she closes the paper with careful qualifications about the danger of reductionism. Carl Hempel, the renowned twentieth-century philosopher of science, questioned whether biological processes may simply be reduced to chemical reactions.[7] How much more would Hempel's questioning of reductionism apply to a soul designed to survive the death of the current body, only to enjoy resurrection to a new, spiritual body? This issue remains a live one, unless one denies any non-embodied personal existence, and one must still question whether the laws governing the future "spiritual" body will be the same as for the current body. In other words, a discussion of mirror neurons in relation to Paul's *soma* may, in fact, involve reductionism.[8]

As a conversation partner, Eastman has chosen Vittorio Gallese.[9] She also mentions Shaun Gallagher's disagreements with Gallese but notes that Gallagher has accepted Gallese's findings with regard to mirror neurons.[10] The choice of Gallese as a conversation partner is questionable. Mirror neurons, the foundation of Gallese's shared manifold hypothesis, have in the last few years come under increasing scrutiny and skepticism with respect to their potential explanatory value. A brief response permits only a few, initial lines of critique.

First, monkey mirror neuron experiments have not proven as useful as was initially hoped for understanding the development of language, mind reading, and empathy in humans.[11] Monkey and human mirror neuron systems are simply different. For instance, in human transcranial magnetic stimulation experiments causing and tracking excitability in motor systems—in effect, twitching hand muscles—human

---

7. Carl G. Hempel, *Philosophy of Natural Science*; Foundations of Philosophy Series (Englewood Cliffs, NJ: Prentice-Hall, 1966) 101–10.

8. Certainly Hempel would question the analogy made in note two of Eastman's paper whether human relationships may be usefully reduced to or compared to quantum physics or electrons.

9. Vittorio Gallese, "The 'Shared Manifold' Hypothesis: From Mirror Neurons to Empathy," in *Between Ourselves: Second-Person Issues in the Study of Consciousness*, edited by Evan Thompson (Charlottesville, VA: Imprint Academic, 2001) 33–50; Gallese, "'Being Like Me': Self-Other Identity, Mirror Neurons, and Empathy," in *Mechanisms of Imitation and Imitation in Animals*, vol. 1 of *Perspectives on Imitation: From Neuroscience to Social Science*, ed. Susan Hurley and Nick Chater (Cambridge, MA: MIT Press, 2005) 101–18.

10. Shaun Gallagher, "The Practice of Mind: Theory, Simulation, or Interaction?" in *Between Ourselves: Second-Person Issues in the Study of* Consciousness, edited by Evan Thompson (Charlottesville, VA: Imprint Academic, 2001) 83–108; Gallagher, *How the Body Shapes the Mind* (Oxford: Oxford University Press, 2005).

11. J. Grezes et al., "Objects Automatically Potentiate Action: An fMRI Study of Implicit Processing," *European Journal of Neuroscience* 17 (2003) 2735–40; G. Rizzolatti et al., "Localization of Grasp Representation in Humans by PET: I: Observation versus Execution," *Experimental Brain Research* 111 (1996) 246–52; V. Gallese and A. Goldman, "Mirror Neurons and the Simulation Theory of Mind-Reading," *Trends in Cognitive Sciences* 2 (1998) 493–501; V. Gallese and A. Goldman, "Mirror Neurons and the Simulation Theory of Mind-Reading," *Trends in Cognitive Sciences* 2 (1998) 493–501.

mirror systems also respond to pantomimed gestures tracing shapes in the air whereas monkey mirror neurons respond only to object-directed actions, such as reaching for a raisin.[12] Also, positron emission tomography studies have detected mirror systems in Broca's area in the brain that correspond to the mirror neurons in the monkey F5 region for *observing* grasping actions.[13] Unfortunately, unlike monkeys, the human Broca region does not show any activity during the *execution* of grasping actions. Subsequent experiments have failed to find activity in Broca's area during grasping, but they did for complex actions. Furthermore, the monkey F5 region is homologous to the human posterior *pars opercularis* in Broca's area and not the *pars triangularis* region, where human action observation triggered neural activity. Even in *imagining* actions, it is the *pars triangularis* region that is active and not the expected *pars opercularis*.[14] Finally, the one study that found some direct overlap in Broca's area involved the imitation of meaningless hand gestures, something that macaques do not do—again, indicating that the human system is functioning very differently from the monkeys'.[15] Thus there is no direct evidence from monkeys that mirror neurons support action understanding.

Second, mirror neurons were supposed to be a neurophysiological mechanism for the development of language as humans perceive not only speech but the vocal tract gestures that make those sounds. The problem is that in the language disorder of Broca's aphasia, damage to motor speech areas in the brain, including Broca's area, does not diminish the individual's comprehension of speech. Speech perception is possible without the motor speech system, contrary to what the mirror neuron theory of action understanding would predict.[16]

Third, humans are able to understand actions that they cannot perform such as the meaning of a dog wagging its tail when happy, a dog's tail tucked between the legs when scared, or a cat's purr for receptivity or a hiss when not receptive to human contact. The brain can understand actions apart from the mirror neuron system. So what is the selection value of the mirror neuron system if those capacities already exist elsewhere in the brain? In an experiment the mirror neuron system provided sighted individuals with no advantage in discerning the meaning of the

---

12. L. Fadiga et al., "Motor Facilitation during Action Observation: A Magnetic Stimulation Study," *Journal of Neurophysiology* 73 (1995) 2608–11.

13. Rizzolatti et al., "Localization of Grasp Representation in Humans."

14. S. T. Grafton et al., "Localization of Grasp Representations in Humans by Positron Emission Tomography. 2. Observation Compared with Imagination," *Experimental Brain Research* 112 (1996) 103–11.

15. M. Iacoboni et al., "Cortical Mechanisms of Human Imitation," *Science* 286 (1999) 2526–28.

16. Gregory Hickok, *The Myth of Mirror Neurons: The Real Neuroscience of Communication and Cognition* (New York: W. W. Norton, 2014) 42–43.

barks of Hungarian sheepdogs over people who had *become* blind or those congenitally blind.[17]

Fourth, in limb apraxia caused by stroke or a neurodegenerative disease such as Alzheimer's, an individual understands a command but is not able to perform the task or movement. Patients with limb apraxia that affected their movements were shown videos of actors performing correct and incorrect object-directed actions like a hitch-hiking gesture or strumming a guitar. The patients had to identify which were correct and incorrect actions. One-third of the apraxic patients had no trouble at all.[18] In other words, the ability to understand actions does not require the ability to do them as predicted by the mirror neuron theory of action understanding.[19]

Fifth, the mirror system is malleable. In one experiment, subjects' index fingers were twitchier when watching videos of index fingers moving. The subjects then practiced moving their pinky fingers when they saw index fingers moving, and then the pinky fingers became twitchier in the experiments.[20] The subjects certainly did not misunderstand that an index finger was moving. This is stimulus-response associative learning and indicates, rather crucially, that action understanding and action execution are dissociate. The motor response is not the basis of the perception since the motor response can be changed without affecting perception. Indeed, the standard mirror effect can be reproduced, after a short period of training, with pinky twitching at seeing just a picture of a cloud and not even any action observation.[21] Even the original mirror neuron experiment with monkeys took place only after the monkeys observed the experimenter's hand grasping and placing objects that the monkey would then grab.[22]

Sixth, mirror neurons' hypothesized function in both object and speech recognition and production is contrary to the structure of the brain. Damage to Broca's

---

17. C. Molnar, P. Pongracz, and A. Miklosi, "Seeing with Ears: Sightless Humans' Perception of Dog Bark Provides a Test for Structural Rules in Vocal Communication," *Quarterly Journal of Experimental Psychology* 63 (2010) 1004–23.

18. M. Passaglia et al., "Neural Underpinnings of Gesture Discrimination in Patient with Limb Apraxia," *Journal of Neuroscience* 28 (2008) 3030–41.

19. For the two-thirds, *both* parts of the brain may have been damaged, one controlling action and one controlling action understanding.

20. C. Catmur, V. Walsh, and C. Heyes, "Sensorimotor Learning Configures the Human Mirror System," *Current Biology* 17 (2007) 1527–31.

21. Jonathan Venezia's experiment, reported by Hickok, *Myth*, 54–55.

22. On the role of associative learning in activating mirror neuron responses, see especially the work of Cecilia Heyes, including her essay in the volume to which Gallese also contributed: "Imitation by Association," in *Mechanisms of Imitation and Imitation in Animals*, vol. 1 of *Perspectives on Imitation: From Neuroscience to Social Science*, edited by Susan Hurley and Nick Chater (Cambridge, MA: MIT Press, 2005) 157–76. See also Heyes's "Where Do Mirror Neurons Come From?" *Neuroscience and Biobehavioral Reviews* 34 (2010) 575–83.

area and the surrounding regions causes speech production deficits, but not speech understanding deficits, as would be expected if mirror neurons were involved in both. Undemonstrated ad hoc hypotheses are necessary to explain away this problem. The loss of speech production but not speech understanding, however, makes sense in view of the structure of the brain. The brain has distinct regions that identify *what* a sight or sound is as opposed to *how* to grasp an object or respond to the sound. Patients with visual agnosia cannot recognize objects but still can grasp and interact with those objects. Patients with optic ataxia can recognize objects but are unable to grasp them.[23]

Seventh, mirror neurons do not likely contribute to any "understanding" of an action. Simulating a movement is not necessary to "understand" an action. A dog observes an owner throwing a ball in a game of fetch on the basis of observation and association and not by mirror neurons, since a dog cannot throw. Also, mirror neurons do not fire for an action itself but only when the object of that action has been made clear. If the target of an action is there, then there is simulation. In other words, understanding of the action and its goal has preceded the simulation itself.[24]

Eighth, Christopher Nolan has been a quadriplegic since birth with no motor control and yet has become a celebrated poet, inspired by images of people in motion.[25] Cerebral palsy patients with no bodily control can understand and contribute to the world.

Ninth, it is the non-motor regions of the temporal lobes that have now been identified by functional imaging studies as the site of object concept understanding, and this has been confirmed in stroke patients and in instances of lesions.[26] If the mirror neuron systems are not involved in object recognition and understanding, how are they helpful as a supposed basis for language or empathy?[27] Cognition is not a low-level sensory, motor-activation scheme without higher level abstraction and information processing. These problems are only the tip of the iceberg. If the shared manifold hypothesis is a house built on sinking sand, its value for interdisciplinary work is questionable.

23. Hickok, *Myth*, 60–61.

24. Ibid., 66–67.

25. Retrieved (2016) from: http://www.publishersweekly.com/pw/by-topic/authors/interviews/article/19743-pw-christopher-nolan-against-all-odds.html; http://www.publishersweekly.com/978-1-55970-511-0.

26. S. Kalenine et al., *Brain* 133 (2010) 3269–80.

27. A point stressed by Greg Hickok in personal e-mail correspondence with the author; Sept. 29, 2016.

EVOLUTIONARY PSYCHOLOGY AND ROMANS 5–7: THE "SLAVERY TO SIN" IN HUMAN NATURE

Paul Allen

One of the most powerful trends in contemporary social life is the tendency to abandon the idea that there is a single human nature by which we can all be understood and judged. The cultural landscape of the contemporary university magnifies this tendency. Disciplines are increasingly oriented to radically different accounts of specialized phenomena, rather than a universe in which human beings are understood as a unity. One reason for the abandonment of the idea of a single human nature is that, judged according to the past, some human beings have been left out of the picture altogether.

The natural sciences have played a dual, contradictory role in this trend. On the one hand, the discovery of the human genome underpins the unity of the human species. Not only does genetic research relativize the historic classifications of human beings according to such artificial divisions as race, but also it deepens the understanding of the nature of our species as individuals in possession of an inherent dignity by virtue of being alive. In public references human dignity is spoken about, yet it remains undefined. For instance, article 1 of UNESCO's 1997 statement on the human genome states: "The human genome underlies the fundamental unity of all members of the human family, as well as the recognition of their inherent dignity and diversity. In a symbolic sense, it is the heritage of humanity."[1]

The evolutionary scientific portrait of human beings somehow informs human dignity. According to this well-known narrative, human beings are the latest (and not necessarily the last) descendant species in a long line of mammals, stretching back through our immediate hominid ancestors to more distantly related species of primates. Paleoanthropology is a less well appreciated aspect of evolutionary biology and the branch of biology that deals with human origins, specifically the study of the variety of capacities and dispositions that human beings possess. The anthropic toolbox of capacities is clearly marked by a contingent set of evolutionary predispositions that were tried and tested by our evolutionary ancestors for the purpose of survival

---

1. UNESCO, "Universal Declaration on the Human Genome and Human Rights." http://portal.unesco.org/en/ev.php-URL_ID=13177&URL_DO=DO_TOPIC&URL_SECTION=201.html.

and reproduction in accordance with the theory of natural selection. From within the processes explained by natural selection and in keeping with the broad conditions set by God's creative purposes, human beings evolved from ancestor species with the capacity for language, art, rationality, and love. Combined, these capacities, which some evolutionary psychologists describe as byproducts of evolution, make it possible to evaluate comprehensively our evolutionary inheritance itself. Marking a new sophistication in this process of evaluation is evolutionary psychology, a field that has come into its own over the past fifty years as various behavioral traits are studied in terms of statistical outcomes of trait distribution and the evolutionary etiology of these traits. Yuval Hariri summarizes what the field studies in this way:

> Our eating habits, our conflicts and our sexuality are all the result of the way our hunter-gatherer minds interact with our current post-industrial environment with its mega-cities, aeroplanes, telephones and computers [which] gives us more material resources and longer lives than those enjoyed by any previous generation, but it often makes us feel alienated, depressed and pressured. To understand why, evolutionary psychologists argue, we need to delve into the hunter-gatherer world that shaped us, the world that we subconsciously still inhabit.[2]

Hence, at its best, we have a paradoxical view of human creatures that is given to us by contemporary science. While the unity of human nature is affirmed by the new found unity of our shared genetic heritage, our ability to act in dignified ways is marred by the unevenly distributed, mixed inheritance of evolutionary behavioral predispositions, which in turn have the capacity to create disunity.

I want to explore a few passages in Paul's Letter to the Romans for its diagnosis of this very portrait of human nature. When I say "this" very portrait, I do not mean to suggest that Paul was mindful of the genetics of DNA sequencing or studies into the mechanism governing the inheritance of genes that are partially responsible for alcoholism or violent outbursts. I mean to suggest that Paul understands well the implications of thinking of the human person as a paradoxical creature. In other words, what is really astounding is the fact that scientific research is *supporting* a theological reading of the Bible in our day rather than serving as a narrative around which a reading of the Bible has to be organized.

I will proceed by examining some of the methodological aspects of the theological interpretation of Scripture, the perspective that informs this annual symposium. The first question is a simple one: can science inform a genuinely theological approach to Scripture? Second, I will discuss the way in which Rom 5–7 addresses

---

2. Yuval Noah Harari, *Sapiens: A Brief History of Humankind* (Toronto: McClelland and Stewart, 2014) 40.

perennial questions about human nature, such as the relationship between virtue and vice, between unity and disunity, and between dignity and monstrosity. Of course, Paul treats these issues in relation to the person and work of Christ, but he does not force us to choose between a Christian reading of human nature and a biologically oriented reading of human nature. Rather, Paul offers a key to mutual interdependence of discourses about human nature: faith and natural law. Third and finally, I will show how a Christian reading of human nature, building on Paul's view of sin, can engage with contemporary scientific interpretations of human nature. Correctly understood, Rom 5–7 offers a view of human nature that avoids three perils common in our day:

1. A naturalism of popular interpretations of science, e.g., "I was born this way"

2. A historicism which would read NT texts as pertinent only to Jews and followers of Jesus in the first century

3. An ethical relativism that spurns natural law theory either on grounds of faith or naturalism.

Theological Interpretation of Scripture Informed by Science?

It has become typical for theological interpreters of Scripture to think of their enterprise in contrast to historical-critical methods of exegesis, since the latter are rooted in the scientific milieu of nineteenth-century Germany. For many it would seem odd to think of the theological interpretation of Scripture as informed by science. The theological interpretation of Scripture, after all, is supposed to offer a deeper view of the relationship between the biblical text and the character of biblical interpretation, giving emphasis to the intentions of the biblical writers where at all possible and seeing in their inspiration meaning and truth for Christian discipleship.

In its struggle with the exactitudes of historical-critical methods of biblical interpretation, the theological interpretation of Scripture has pulled away from the confines of strict exegesis without meaning to wander into the territory of pure eisegesis. However, there is a problem with this status quo. The problem consists in thinking of exact historical information and interpretive imagination as two entirely separate matters. As students of the history of science well know, the pride of place given to the human imagination in the practice of science is legion.

In the hermeneutics of biblical interpretation, it is now well established that claims to strict neutrality governing the reading of texts are empty. While objectivity cannot be denied within a particular set of parameters, we all bring some context to bear on the interpretation of Scripture and take hints from the text as to the relevant parts of its context that need to be related to the text. Contrary to the more excessive sentiments of historical criticism, there is no Archimedean point from which to survey and understand the Bible.

A classic figure in the context of biblical studies and a scientific hermeneutic is Rudolf Bultmann. He was fond of critiquing the three-story universe that he thought rendered a biblical cosmology obsolete. Bultmannian exegesis was intended to be motivated by a love of modern science in order to extract theological meaning from the text in terms strictly of existential meaning. Yet, it has had the effect of using science in the service of working against the plausible meanings of the text, especially in the case of miraculous events. The case of the bodily resurrection of Jesus is the most obvious case. The point to make in response to Bultmann is that every reading of the Bible is attended by a cosmology, including his own cosmology which owes a great deal to a form of empiricism.

Bultmann certainly took it for granted that science excludes miracles, in contrast to the biblical text's allowance for God's special action in the world, including the world of nature. In the contemporary scientific setting in which quantum physics and a more complex relationship between mind and matter occurs, miracles seem more plausible. Specific questions such as this one raise the more general, methodological question about the stature of the theological interpretation of Scripture and science. Karl Barth certainly seemed to seal the fate of this discussion by reviving the theological interpretation of Scripture because of his refusal of natural theology. This stance is echoed by contemporary advocates of a theological interpretation of Scripture such as J. Todd Billings, who states that while the book of nature yields insight into what humans may understand, it does not offer an explicit knowledge of Jesus Christ, for which Scripture is necessary.[3] Yet, is it that simple?

I think it is valid to see how the questions to which Jesus Christ is an answer are themselves formulated on the basis of human understanding. What I mean is that if, as Scripture attests, Jesus Christ was sent into the world to save us from sin, we ought to probe what this condition of sin is to which the possibility of salvation is a response. That is, while I agree with Billings that Scripture provides a necessary testimony to the saving mission of Christ, it is inadequate in helping us understand how this could be so. A theological interpretation of Scripture therefore needs to incorporate a structure of questions that pertain to the human condition. One example of how this transpired in the Christian tradition is through the motif operative in the patristic period (based on Exod 12:36) of plundering the gold of the

---

3. See his *The Word of God for the People of God: An Entryway to the Theological Interpretation of Scripture* (Eerdmans, 2010) 82–83.

Egyptians in order to establish stronger theological claims. And so Origen, in a letter to Gregory Thaumaturgos, advocates that he

> extract from the philosophy of the Greeks what may serve as a course of study of a preparation for Christianity, and from geometry what will serve to explain the sacred Scriptures, in order that the sons of the philosophers are wont to say about geometry and music, grammar, rhetoric and astronomy as fellow-helpers to philosophy, we may say about philosophy itself, in relation to Christianity.[4]

This view of an interdisciplinary support for a theological approach to Scripture is prized as normative in the patristic period and comes to full fruition in Augustine's *De Doctrina christiana*, where the seven liberal arts, including the more scientific disciplines of astronomy and geometry, are deemed to support the Christian dispensation. I think it could be argued that this work of Augustine's is the most undervalued of all his works, and perhaps its focus on methodological questions explains why it is insufficiently well appreciated outside circles of Augustinian scholarship. Nevertheless, method is the key question that dogs the theological interpretation of Scripture (as distinct from biblical theology[5]). I think it is both conceivable and desirable for there to be a scientific "component" to a theological interpretation via philosophy in which the worldview of the interpreter engages with and is engaged by the Word of God. The problem with twentieth-century theological hermeneutics was a problem with one way interpretive strategies: either Scripture reigned over science (Barth) or science reigned over Scripture (Bultmann). Against this false dichotomy, the theological interpretation of Scripture is both interdisciplinary and properly theological. This is not a contradiction in terms.

Romans 5–7 and Sin

In 1987 *Harper's Magazine* ran a fun feature on the question of how one might "sell" the seven deadly sins. On the possibility of sloth the tagline read: "If the original sin had been sloth, we'd still be in Paradise."[6] As intentionally humorous as this is, Rebecca Konyndyk DeYoung makes the point in her book *Glittering Vices* that sin

---

4. Origen, "Letter to Gregory," *ANF* 4.393.

5. Stephen Fowl discusses the important difference between theological interpretation and biblical theology with reference to the problem of the fragmentation of theology and indeed all knowledge, to which the movement of theological interpretation is partly intended as a remedy. See Stephen Fowl, *Engaging Scripture: A Model for Theological Interpretation* (Oxford: Wiley Blackwell, 1998).

6. See Rebecca Konyndyk DeYoung, *Glittering Vices: A New Look at the Seven Deadly Sins and Their Remedies* (Grand Rapids: Brazos, 2009) 12. See "You Can Have it All! Seven Campaigns for Deadly Sin," *Harper's* (November, 1987) 43–50.

is perceived to be a less serious problem now compared with what it once was. The mouthpieces of our culture have done much to situate sin as a peculiar fixation of a harried, religious minority.

However, Christian theologians are the ones who excised sin from the theological anthropology of the modern period. The reduction of references to sin came about for several reasons, not least of which was a need felt by some to correct an overly punitive soteriological framework. Some of the reduction of scientific references to sin was a reaction to a perception of what science implied about the human condition. Friedrich Schleiermacher (1768–1834) initiated a "thoroughly developmental theological anthropology" with the hopes of rendering a picture of sin as a "failure to integrate one's higher self-consciousness and God-consciousness with one's sensible self-consciousness."[7] Apart from being an individualistic interpretation of sin, Schleiermacher took the Augustinian accent on sin as privation and interpreted it as a matter of what is lost or missing in conscious human activity. The sense of sin's power and its tendency to evil are relativized in Schleiermacher's work and, as a consequence, in liberal Protestantism and secularized western culture. Yet, Paul and Schleiermacher share the view that sin is at least a matter for individuals to deliberate.

Unlike proponents of a more social view of sin, in Romans Paul proposes that both individual disciples and the church of Rome itself avoid sin's dominion. In contrast with Schleiermacher, we find in Rom 5–7 that sin is not a matter of the orientation of one's consciousness per se. Romans is structured according to a classic theological hermeneutic that sees a treatment of the doctrine of justification in Rom 1–4/5 and the doctrine of sanctification in 5/6–8. Chapter 5 is a bridge chapter between these "doctrinal" foci. Within chapter 5, however, a significant distinction exists between the individual and collective objects of Paul's treatment, with vv. 1–11 foreshadowing the individual focus of chapters 6–8, and the collective focus of vv. 12–21 foreshadowing the section on Israel in chapters 9–11.[8]

In 5:13, according to Paul, "Sin is not counted where there is no law." The association of sin with law is one of the more perplexing aspects of Paul's thinking. The meaning of "law" shifts dramatically. In 2:12, "All who sin apart from the law will also perish apart from the law, and all who sin under the law will be judged by the law." In 2:14–15 Paul seemed to elevate the role of law: "When Gentiles, who do not have the law, do by nature the things required by the law, they are a law for

---

7. Derek R. Nelson, *What's Wrong with Sin: Sin in Individual and Social Perspective from Schleiermacher to Theologies of Liberation* (T & T Clark, 2009) 180.

8. James D. G. Dunn, *Romans 1–8*, Word Biblical Commentary 38 (Nashville: Thomas Nelson, 1988) 242.

themselves, even though they do not have the law, since they show that the requirements of the law are written on their hearts, their consciences also bearing witness, and their thoughts now accusing, now even defending them." By 7:7 Paul says, "If it had not been for the law, I should not have known sin." Paul's personal interest in sin's relationship to the law is meant to assert Adam's responsibility for sin, the ability of the Torah to identify the global consequences of sin, and Christ's ultimate victory over it.

Yet, Paul's understanding of sin is much wider than its link with the Torah. Sin is also associated in Paul's mind with the (famously sexual) "unnatural" of Rom 1 and 2. The grace of Christ, in contrast to the law, acknowledges the full power of sin by disclaiming its power. Grace thus offers conversion and life over death. In Christ, we are free from sin, whereas in accordance with the law, we are only sinless.[9] Law recognizes only moral impropriety and calls on the human will only to live within the parameters of the law, a situation in which we are still not wholly free. In order to go beyond morality and law, Paul locates sin not as a deprivation of consciousness, but in association with the flesh. He sees its physicality, its real existence:

> I am of the flesh, sold into slavery under sin. I do not understand my own actions. For I do not do what I want, but I do the very thing I hate. Now if I do what I do not want, I agree that the law is good. But in fact it is no longer I that do it, but sin that dwells within me. For I know that nothing good dwells within me, that is, in my flesh. I can will what is right, but I cannot do it. For I do not do the good I want, but the evil I do not want is what I do. Now if I do what I do not want, it is no longer I that do it, but sin that dwells within me. (Rom 7:14a–20)

The important thing to note about what Paul is saying is that he locates sinfulness not in the will but in one's body. This association of sin and embodied flesh has come under sustained criticism in modernity, but I am unsure whether the plain sense of his words can be denied. For Paul, Christ exposes the nature of sin, not as an infraction of the natural law or the Torah per se, but rather as something that enslaves the body to the point of being the harbinger of death, a negation of self.

The point of this summary is not to nuance the textual support for the doctrine of original sin or the hermeneutical considerations of those critics who do not think Romans supplies enough conceptual support for that doctrine. My aim here is to emphasize the fact that *Paul sees human nature, and by implication human embodiment, as morally ambivalent, fatally open to the power of sin*. The body, while good, is marked by privations that manifest in the form of predispositions to sin. On the

---

9. This language stems from Anders Nygren, *Commentary on Romans* (Philadelphia: Fortress, 1949) 242.

one hand, human nature is a function of enslavement through bodily desire and yet, human nature is simultaneously the awareness of enslavement through conscience. Conscience is a created, emergent evolutionary capacity of our complex brain that is sufficiently good to provide Gentiles—people who lack the explicit moral law revealed by God—with criteria to do what is right. So, doing what is right may emerge from within our inclinations, but it likely will not.

The process of deliberating over what is right is sheer anxiety, as Paul notes in 7:15: "I do not understand my own actions. For I do not do what I want, but I do the very thing I hate." Doing the good also presupposes assumptions of a natural law such as those that pervade Judaism's Wisdom literature where the wise ordering of creation is a kind of foundation of knowledge that is available to all, Jews and Gentiles alike.[10] Thus, it is not as though human nature is either inherently evil or inherently designed to resist evil successfully. Both are true of human nature. Because it is fleshly, it seems to possess a peculiar disposition both to produce the capacity to sin and carry out sinful deeds and yet circumvent sin at least in some meaningful measure, at least potentially.

Paul is thus providing a cosmic interpretation of sin's scope, subject as it is to the victory of Christ, but nevertheless sufficiently powerful to exercise influence and rule over human nature as a whole. Sin is not only a sundering of relations with God on account of human choice; sin makes an entrance. It "came into the world" (Rom 5:12). The typological contrast of Adam and Christ establishes a duality that has broad implications not only for moral deliberation but for how we understand ourselves. Human nature is thus not only the will. On a moralistic account of sin, the law is sufficient. Paul is interested in a broader defeat of sin's power, which is a power not only over the moral will but also over human cognition and human embodiment as a whole.

Evolutionary Psychology, Sin, and Human Nature

In this last section of the paper I will briefly touch on some of the most relevant research that correlates with Paul's understanding of sin as something that is rooted more deeply in the human body than the will. I think one of the reasons why philosophers and scientists dismiss Christian theology's talk of sin is because sin is perceived to be an entirely subjective interpretation of the will and its disobedience towards God. Sin is seen as a superfluous category because it has no traction with the world of embodied beings. The will is, of course, essential in an understanding of

---

10. See Markus Bockmuehl, "Natural Law in Second Temple Judaism," *Vetus Testamentum* 45 (1995) 17–44.

sin, but it is insufficient in a theological interpretation of Paul. This is where contemporary evolutionary biology can play a fascinating role in elucidating the meaning of sin.

Philosophy has its own problematic history in its understanding of the relationship between human embodiment, human weakness, and failure. Alastair MacIntyre has an extended interpretation of this history that he makes clear in his book *Dependent Rational Animals*:

> We human beings are vulnerable to many kinds of affliction and most of us are at some time afflicted by serious ills. How we cope is only in small part up to us. It is most often to others that we owe our survival, let alone our flourishing, as we encounter bodily illness and injury, inadequate nutrition, mental defect and disturbance, and human aggression and neglect. This dependence on particular others for protection and sustenance is most obvious in early childhood and in old age. But between these first and last stages our lives are characteristically marked by longer or shorter periods of injury, illness or other disablement, and some among us are disabled for their entire lives.
>
> These two related sets of facts, those concerning our vulnerabilities and afflictions and those concerning the extent of our dependence on particular others are so evidently of singular importance that it might seem that no account of the human condition whose authors hoped to achieve credibility could avoid giving them a central place. Yet the history of Western moral philosophy suggests otherwise. From Plato to Moore and since, there are usually, with some rare exceptions, only passing references to human vulnerability and affliction and to the connections between them and our dependence on others. Some of the facts of human limitation and of our consequent need of cooperation with others are more generally acknowledged, but for the most part only then to be put on one side.
>
> And when the ill, the injured and the otherwise disabled are presented in the pages of moral philosophy books, it is almost always exclusively as possible subjects of benevolence by moral agents who are themselves presented as though they were continuously rational, healthy, and untroubled. So we are invited, when we think of disability, to think of "the disabled" as "them," as other than "us," as a separate class, not as ourselves as we have been, sometimes are now, and may well be in the future.[11]

Sinfulness is quite distinct from dependency and vulnerability of course, but one cannot have sinfulness without the forms of dependency that are associated with human relationships. Sinfulness can readily arise from nonintentional feelings of vulnerability that arise on account of dependence. This category of dependence

---

11. *Dependent Rational Animals: Why Human Beings Need the Virtues* (Chicago: Open Court, 2001) 1.

becomes particularly distorted in the case of addictions, but more mundane examples of these basic conditions of human living, which give rise to sin, are manifold. Even the dependency of an economic trading relationship is a form of vulnerability that can give rise to sinful tendencies, whether due to envy or rivalry. If philosophy has missed this massive area of human living in its efforts to deliver an ethics, then it is all the more urgent that theology map this conceptual territory clearly.

To my mind, the critical point that MacIntyre is making is that philosophy has gone out of its way to avoid seeing the situation of human beings as it really is. Adding sin to the picture of human nature, something philosophy neglects, is really a *necessary* step for getting at the truth. It is not a step that needs to be adopted simply because one has chosen to take a theological perspective of the anthropological constants of life. This is the methodological point of my argument: sin is not something that is imposed on anthropology for the sake of satisfying previously adopted theological presuppositions. The disobedient will and the judgment of God are necessary but insufficient grounds for the articulation of a concept of sin. The gap that science helps to fill in is the part about how the power of sin works with existing privations in human nature.

What is the portrait of those privations that is opened by evolutionary psychology? There are a number of fascinating aspects of contemporary research that deserve to be thoroughly grasped for what they reveal about human nature. We ought to begin with the predisposition to criminal behavior, a scientific enterprise that has an admittedly awkward history. In 1871 Cesare Lombroso, the (Jewish) father of modern criminology postulated a correlation between criminal behavior and a smaller sized cerebellum, the area of the brain that sits underneath the larger left and right hemispheres. Because Lombroso's theory was linked not only to certain physiological features such as a large jaw, sloping forehead and a single palmar crease, his thought became partly responsible for the rise in eugenics and is noted for a role played in the later persecution of Jews in Italy under Mussolini.[12]

In a strictly evolutionary perspective, aggression is typically assumed to be maladaptive, and this is particularly the case for in-group social evolution in which the various forms of cooperation, such as kin selection and reciprocal altruism, are seen to be as significant as competition for the growth and flourishing of human society. Two scholars associated with the emphasis on cooperation are Martin Nowak and Sarah Coakley, whose research has led them to affirm the idea that organisms engage in cooperation, "a form of working together in which one individual pays a cost (in terms of fitness, whether genetic or cultural) and another gains a benefit as

---

12. Adrian Raine, *The Anatomy of Violence: The Biological Roots of Crime* (New York: Pantheon, 2013) 12.

a result."[13] Altruism is then a form of cooperation in which one is motivated by love or good will toward another. Primatologist Frans de Waal, because of his work with chimpanzees, is another whose central role in highlighting cooperative behavior in human societies has been widely noted. De Waal has been an outspoken proponent of the extent to which human sympathies accounts for human nature. He is especially critical of accounts of human nature that accentuate competition or dualism between a genteel exterior and a nasty core that schemes to use superficial geniality for selfish purposes. De Waal calls this portrait of human beings the Veneer theory.[14]

However real cooperative behavior may be, and whatever its evolutionary origins, research into the genetic basis for violent (or antisocial) behavior has become well established. Studies comparing identical and fraternal twins appear to provide a particularly fertile way in which to demarcate a genetic predisposition to violence from cultural environmental causes. As Adrian Raine comments,

> A meta-analysis of 103 studies compared heritability of aggressive behavior with rule-breaking nonaggressive behavior. Nonaggressive antisocial behavior was 48 percent heritable, while aggressive behavior was 65 percent heritable. Yet again, shared environmental influences were small for nonaggressive antisocial behavior (18 percent) and minimal for aggressive behavior (5 percent). Genetics and non-shared environmental influences rule the roost when it comes to aggression.[15]

Other research has made precise the inverse relationship between genetic relatedness and homicide. If you are living with someone not genetically related to you, you are eleven times more likely to be killed by that person than by a person genetically related to you. Stepparents are "celebrated" in fairy tales in exactly these terms: Hansel and Gretel's stepmother tries to persuade their natural father to abandon the children in the woods. Sleeping beauty's stepmother orders her killing by a hunter, and Cinderella's stepmother is infamously cruel. In the United Kingdom 1 percent of babies live with a stepparent, yet 53 percent of baby killings in the United Kingdom are by a stepparent.[16] Then there is the compelling case of Jeffrey Landrigan, whose father and grandfather were all convicted murderers. Landrigan was adopted as an infant and raised in a loving home, yet he became criminal. The genetic predisposition to violence is not absolutely determinative, but as Raine notes in his study of the natural causes of violent behavior, "Identical twins, who by definition have all their

---

13. Sarah Coakley and Martin Nowak, eds., *Evolution, Games and God: The Principle of Cooperation* (Cambridge: Harvard University Press, 2013) 4.

14. See Frans de Waal, Stephen Macedo, and Josiah Ober, eds., *Primates and Philosophers: How Morality Evolved* (Princeton: Princeton University Press, 2006) xiv–xv.

15. Raine, *The Anatomy of Violence*, 42.

16. Ibid., 24.

genes in common, are much more similar to each other on crime and aggression than fraternal twins, who have only 50 percent of their genes in common."[17] Criminology's resistance to the idea that there are genetic causes to violence has been instrumental in the failure of imagination when it comes to ways and means of investigating how these genetic causes can be mitigated. Much of contemporary social science is in the peculiar position of affirming aspects of free will, while accepting many social factors that limit free will. While I cannot discuss the details of what evolutionary psychology research implies for free will generally, there are clearly some empirical constraints it imposes on it without coming close to eliminating free will. The interpretation of evolutionary psychology runs up against substantial narratives against what it suggests for an overall portrait of human nature. Certainly in its early days the research conducted by figures such as Robert Trivers indicated a positive assessment of human nature because of his theory of reciprocal altruism and its compatibility with Darwinian theory.[18]

Also relevant here is the case of substance abuse and addiction. Part of the reason why substance abuse does not figure prominently in the narrative about sin is the way in which it presents itself psychologically as though it were a "brain disease."[19] But, addiction, as pastors who are familiar with Alcoholics or Narcotics Anonymous know well, does not completely eliminate the free will that can arrest a bad habit or at least curtail a bad habit's overpowering effects. According to Kent Dunnington addiction defies a simplistic explanation. As a habit it is neither a disease, nor is it a course of action that is freely chosen. Addictive behavior can be addressed strategically if we think realistically about human action in terms of desire and especially habit. For Dunnington, as with Aquinas, habits are "strategies of desire."[20] Habits describe addictive behaviors themselves, and at the same time habits can successfully quash the addictive impulse to a significant degree because they capitalize on neuroplasticity. Addiction to a substance is not merely an inordinate desire for the particular substance in question. Addiction is thus not the same as intemperance. Addiction is a special case of inordinate desire, in which biological factors have ruled out free will to the point where normal functioning is impaired.

---

17. Ibid., 39.

18. See Robert L. Trivers, "The Evolution of Reciprocal Altruism," *The Quarterly Review of Biology*, 46.1 (March, 1971) 35–57.

19. Institute of Medicine, *Dispelling the Myths About Addiction: Strategies to Increase Understanding and Strengthen Research* (Washington, D.C.: National Academy, 1997) 13. Cf. Kent Dunnington, *Addiction and Virtue: Beyond the Models of Disease and Choice* (Downers Grove, IL: InterVarsity, 2011) 17.

20. See Dunnington, *Addiction and Virtue*, 61.

Addictive behaviors are habits, as Dunnington says, because they "mediate between instinct and disposition . . . between determinism and indeterminism [and] between the involuntary and the voluntary."[21] Environmental cues that correlate with stimulation are sought by various centers in the brain without the usual selective control of the prefrontal cortex. A rehabituation away from substance abuse involves a reformation of behavior that addresses two necessary conditions: "first the external act [of abstinence] must be repeated. Second, there must be appropriate attention to the interior quality of the acts."[22] As with the addiction itself, recovery from addiction means ensuring that "neurons wire together when they fire together"[23] in the cause of abstinence/sobriety. It is this second component that is key to the success of Alcoholics Anonymous and Narcotics Anonymous, in which the work on the interior, spiritual steps involved will likely aid recovery from addiction. Vigilant attention to habit reformation involves much more than acts of abstinence, though both are necessary.

According to Daniel De Haan,

> [I]n the majority of cases . . . addictions are initiated by non-compulsive decisions, yet they seem to result in motivations and cravings that undermine the person's ability to rationally deliberate and freely decide how to act . . . . addiction provides a clear case of what happens to the nervous system and psychological faculties of a human person who partakes in acts that are often deprived of moral goodness. The results are the numerous psychosomatic operational privations . . .[24]

The privations that result from acts that lack moral goodness do not mean that addiction is reducible to privation. Rather, addiction is the misdirected striving for cultural order and for the good amidst social chaos. According to Buchanan, Illes, and Reiner, the "brain disease" model of addiction is harmful: "Placing emphasis on the diseased brain may foster unintended harm by increasing social distance on the vulnerable group the term is intended to benefit."[25] This problem of ostracization means that both extremes of thinking about addiction avoid the possibility and the reality of habit reformation. Habit reformation is much more intense for addicted

---

21. Ibid., 63.

22. Ibid., 78.

23. First attributed to neuroscientist Donald Hebb, this saying is mentioned by Siegrid Löwel, in S. Löwel and W. Singer, "Selection of Intrinsic Horizontal Connections in the Visual Cortex by Correlated Neuronal Activity," *Science* 255 (January 10, 1992) 209–212.

24. Daniel D. De Haan, "Thomistic Hylomorphism, Self-Determination, Neuroplasticity, and Grace: The Case of Addiction," *Proceedings of the American Catholic Philosophical Association* 85 (2012) 99–120, at 100 and 102.

25. See Daniel Z. Buchman, Judy Illes, and Peter B. Reiner, "The Paradox of Addiction Neuroscience," *Neuroethics* 4 (2011) 65–77, at 66.

persons whose abstinence from acts of substance abuse has to be sustained through steady socialization and attentive reflection. The same is true for those who are not addicted as well.

Human nature is similarly ordered and disordered for addicts and non-addicts, though prophetically—I agree with Dunnington's use of the term "prophetic" here—addicts allow us to understand clearly the paradoxical nature of the human condition by virtue of their intense experience of the struggle between our human nature and the will. To suffer an addiction is to be in the thrall of the power of death, of service to the stifling of our own flourishing, to be seized from within by a power that is somehow paradoxically without. Therefore, freedom in Christ cannot mean anything unless sin is really experienced as a true slavery. To pass on a genetic predisposition to disease, violent behavior, or addictive impulses is to be prone to a slavery to sin and death. An adequate theological anthropology needs to take into account this aspect of nature, the roots of sin in naturally determined aspects of sin.

Conclusion

The theological interpretation of Scripture is too often seen as a complex hermeneutical reaction against historical-critical exegesis. True, it does offer a different and altogether more adequate way of framing the scriptural text, one that is more faithful to the Christian tradition. However, the theological interpretation of Scripture is also a much simpler set of tasks, perhaps best described as a modelling of the reading of Scripture that Jesus Christ himself offers. In Luke 15 Jesus asks his audience of sheepherders, those close to the land, a question: "Which one of you, having a hundred sheep and losing one of them, does not leave the ninety-nine in the wilderness and go after the one that is lost until he finds it?" In his appeal to their own sense of selflessness in order to speak of God's mercy toward the one lost sheep, Jesus draws on the experience of ordinary people and their common experience in order to interpret the tradition's view of salvation as it was understood through the Jewish Scriptures. The goal is to speak of God, not as an agent whose intentions are reducible to human forms of pastoral activity, but as an agent whose intentions are analogously understood from the most selfless example of love within the available frame of ordered desires of human living.

The idea here is that sheepherding is a livelihood that meets a set of self-interested desires that is the expression of human nature. This is given particular emphasis by evolutionary psychology in its determination that our interests are pre-set according to genetic proximity or perceptions of reciprocal exchange that assist our status. Yet, from within the set of tasks that a given livelihood such as this one implies, opportunities exist to offer mercy that would seem to contravene rational self-interest, notably in a case such as this where the pursuit of one sheep puts the herder at risk along with the herd. The point here is that Jesus himself accepts the limits and finitude of human existence, yet sees within those limits the episodes of natural living in order to speak of God's ordered love and God's inordinate justice.

The parable of the Lost Sheep affirms the idea that Jesus is concerned for the salvation of the individual. Our natural and cultural environments incline us to sinful behavior in the ways already spelled out, but even within the limits of those inclinations, Jesus manages to identify the kind of activity that suggests the exceptional concern God has for us. If sin is natural, it is also possible to see in natural terms the possibility of supernatural love that is a greater power than the sinful power that has befallen nature. A theological interpretation of Rom 5–7 ought not to downplay the genuine paradoxes or contradictions that lie both within human nature and between nature and God. Sin is real, and it is not simply a function of the will.

The modern tendency to see a narrative of progress in human affairs is both contradicted by the NT and evolutionary psychology, though it is a narrative that has a powerful hold on the western imagination, in part because it is inspired by the possibility of redemption from fallenness. This narrative of progress is contradicted in part by our evolutionary nature, since a pattern of predictable partiality in human affairs exists by human beings toward kin and toward those with whom we are engaged in reciprocal economic or social arrangements. Human nature is also irregularly distorted by inclinations toward addiction, compulsion, anxiety and hyperactivity that interact with a variety of vices that result in behavior that ill befits the body as it was created. It is ultimately contradicted by Christ, whose offer of freedom is a final "no," as Barth said, to a purely natural religious reconstruction of human desire. The "ordered desire" of Augustine's *City of God* is consistent with both a recognition of our fallen state and the eschatological tension that exists between this state and our final destination with God. It is fitting to end with Augustine, because as he was the proponent of the doctrine of original sin, he had a consistent, realistic view of the wretched tendency in human willfulness to disturb the ordering of desire. A theological interpretation of Scripture must also be a faithful, realistic interpretation of the human condition, both in all its natural goodness and its tendency to evil.

RESPONSE TO ALLEN

Christopher Lilley

I would like to thank Paul Allen for his stimulating and thought-provoking paper. In this brief response, I will call attention to a few of the claims Allen has advanced, as well as offer some potential questions for the discussion. This paper offers many opportunities for a fruitful discussion; however, in the short time that I have I will only focus on two areas, one methodological and one theological.

Allen has suggested that advances in contemporary science, specifically evolutionary psychology, are able to support what he terms a "theological" reading of Scripture. More specifically, the "paradoxical" nature of humans as both dignified and sinful, as reflected in the natural sciences, both supports and illuminates the Apostle Paul's discussion of sin in Rom 5–7. Behind Allen's proposal lies a key methodological assumption, which he notes right from the outset of his argument. His assumption is that the natural sciences are able to support a thoroughgoing theological interpretation of Scripture, where a theological interpretation of the biblical text is intended to provide a deeper view of the relationship between the text itself and the rich tradition of interpreting the biblical text, rather than focusing solely on the specifics of historical-critical exegesis.

Allen's contention that the natural sciences may be employed to support a theological reading of the biblical text is both promising and refreshing in an intellectual atmosphere where it is commonly assumed that theology must retreat in the face of advancing scientific discovery, or that science is an unmovable frame around which theology must be forced to fit. However, despite what I take to be a promising methodological avenue, there remain a few potential conceptual difficulties with this approach. Allen quite fittingly points out that there is no pristine, "objective" perspective from which to view and interpret the biblical text. From this, it is entirely fitting that a truly theological approach to Scripture incorporates the full spectrum of human experience, since all of us bring our own contexts to bear on textual interpretation. In this case, it means "plundering the gold" of the natural sciences in order to facilitate an interdisciplinary interpretation of Scripture. As Allen notes in his paper, there indeed *ought* to be a scientific component to the theological interpretation of Scripture.

My question concerning this approach does not challenge the potential benefits of incorporating the natural sciences into theological interpretation, for as Allen shows, there are many. Rather, my question concerns the potential theological hazards of such an interdisciplinary approach. Allen calls our attention to Rudolf Bultmann who, in his fondness for contemporary science, critiqued the "three-tiered" universe of biblical cosmology as hopelessly out of date for the contemporary reader of the text. Such a reductive reading of the biblical narratives is viewed as damaging to theological interpretation, for it employed science in a combative fashion *against* what Allen calls the most "plausible" reading of the text, and as rendering such theological fundamentals as the literal resurrection of Christ as naïve relics of a bygone era.

The response to Bultmann is to point out that we all bring our own cosmologies and worldview assumptions to the text, so it is illegitimate for Bultmann to "rule out" the biblical allowance for miracles or the resurrection on the basis of the particular prevailing science of his day. This point is well taken, and I think accurate. However, Allen makes a further interesting point. While the scientific perspective of Bultmann ruled out miracles and special divine action, contemporary quantum physics is thought by many to be far more amenable to God's miraculous intervention in the natural world. I take it that *this* scientific perspective would be understood as supporting, rather than contradicting, a plausible theological reading of the biblical text involving such miraculous events as the resurrection of Christ.

However, if we adopt this methodological approach, it would appear that we have two potentially conflicting narratives underlying a theological interpretation of the biblical text, both vying for our attention. On the one hand, we have what might be deemed the most "plausible" theological reading of the text which, although not limited by historical-critical exegesis, is certainly informed by it in order to ascertain the most reasonable assessment of the intentions of the biblical authors. Yet, on the other hand, we have the differing cosmologies and historically conditioned worldviews of ourselves as interpreters of the text which play into our theological interpretation. Rather than merely rehash the well-worn and frequently over exaggerated "conflict" narrative between science and religion, I simply ask how it is that we are to decide which scientific gold to "plunder" to support our reading of the text and which to discard as mere fool's gold that is detrimental to a proper theological understanding? Bultmann's scientific interpretation was harmful to plausible readings of the text, yet quantum physics offers a potential way to see how science supports a plausible interpretation of the text. As a manner of method, is the proper way to incorporate the natural sciences to adopt only those perspectives which are helpful to theological interpretation? Or, do we adopt Thomas Aquinas's approach and affirm that "it is impossible that the truth of faith should be opposed to those principles that the human reason knows naturally," where *in principle* discoveries in the natural sciences cannot contradict the core tenets of faith?

In sum, my question about Allen's promising methodological approach is not *whether* the natural sciences can be fruitfully incorporated into theological interpretations of the biblical text, but rather how to adjudicate this interaction going forward with the aim of arriving at a theological interpretation of the text that properly takes into account the full spectrum of human experience. Near the end of his paper Allen notes that both the NT and evolutionary psychology contradict the modern tendency to see a "narrative of progress" in human affairs. However, if evolutionary psychology were to *affirm* a "narrative of progress" contrary to Paul's treatment of the sinfulness of humanity, ought we to hold such a scientific perspective at arm's length as running *contrary* to a plausible reading of the text, or do we attempt to adjust our reading of the text to accommodate the science in the interest of producing a realistic interpretation of the human condition?

Aside from this methodological question, the second component of Allen's argument to which I would like to call attention is his discussion of the nature of sin in Paul. As he notes, Paul's treatment of the nature and destructive power of sin emphasizes the cosmic scope of sin's destructive power, with sin's insidious power affecting not only the "will" of a person but also the flesh. Sin destroys and consumes the whole person, which reflects well the nature of human embodiment in an evolutionary context. Allen marshalls a compelling argument for the fact that evolutionary psychology supports the notion that sin engulfs the "whole body," where we are by nature distorted by a genetic predisposition to disease and violence. From both Paul's perspective and from an evolutionary perspective, sin is not merely a disordered will, but a destructive power which affects the whole person. Or, as Allen suggests, sin has power "over human cognition as a whole."

I take Allen's emphasis on the cosmic scope of sin as affecting the whole embodied person to be a very helpful approach. He suggests that this "slavery" to sin and death, and therefore the necessity of Christ's salvific work, can be understood in terms of the "passing on" genetically of a disposition to disease, infirmity, and death. This suggestion aids in the task of clarifying what it means to have a "sin nature" and focuses on the nature and evolutionary development of humans as a whole, rather than on the contentious issue of whether or not a faithful interpretation of the biblical text necessitates a single originating pair, Adam and Eve, who somehow "passed on" this tendency to sin, a position that is extremely implausible from a scientific perspective.

However, while this approach is both theologically and scientifically strong, a concern may be raised as far as the proposed interpretation that Paul's understanding of sin "is more deeply rooted in the human psyche than the will." Certainly Paul considered sin to have sufficient power to "rule over human nature as a whole." However, where I would like to see more development is with the claim that sin is not merely the breaking of a relationship with God on account of human will, but has its own "agency" apart from human choice. As Allen notes, Paul argues in Rom 5:12 that sin "came into the world," which would seem to indicate that sin is not merely present on account of human "choosing." However, Paul further clarifies in 5:12 that way in which sin entered the world is "through one man." In 5:15 Paul contends that many have died "through the one man's trespass." So, even if death is not by any means *limited* to the human will, and does indeed engulf the whole person, the manner by which sin engulfs a person appears to be causally rooted in human choice. While Paul never actually spells out the manner by which "one man's trespass" subjects the whole of humanity to the power of sin, the universal subjection of humanity to sin, even the very embodied flesh of humanity, does indeed seem to be the result of a logically prior choice. This *choice* fatally opens the human body to the destructive power of sin.

In sum, Allen has offered a compelling account of how to understand the cosmic power of sin, which affects the whole person, in terms that are faithful to Paul's account in Scripture as well as contemporary scientific insights into human nature. Therefore, we have been offered a model for how genuine interdisciplinary work is able to be done involving both the natural sciences and theological interpretation.

MULTIVERSE: PHILOSOPHICAL AND THEOLOGICAL PERSPECTIVES

Gerald B. Cleaver

Perceptions of God

How does God interact with creation? How much control does God exert on the physical world or on individual lives? Theists have long sought to understand the answers. The relationship between the divine will of the Creator, the freedom of the natural world, and the free will of human beings continues to be debated. Scripture, traditions, and theology provide no clear answer to the divine will/free will dichotomy. Rather, opposing sides claim scriptural support for their views.

A 2006 survey conducted by the Institute for Studies of Religion at Baylor University and funded by the John Templeton Foundation revealed that 54 percent of Americans believe that God is "engaged in every creature's life and world affairs."[1] In contrast, 46 percent believe God does not (generally) intervene within his creation (the life of Christ being the most acknowledged exception, along with other possible biblical events).[2] Christians are closely divided between the two categories, with fundamentalists and evangelicals believing predominantly in an interventionist God and members of mainline Protestant churches and Catholics believing predominantly in a non-interventionist God.

Some views may overlap both categories, expressing belief in a God who acts within creation, while carrying out his will purely (or primarily) through processes obeying the physical laws of the universe. God is then understood as the *Primary Cause*, while the physical laws are deemed the *secondary cause*. Ian Barbour and John Polkinghorne are proponents of this view.[3] Further, divine primary cause

---

1. Of those who believe in an interventionist God, 57 percent view God as simultaneously "angry at humanity's sin . . . [and] ready to throw the thunderbolt of judgment down on the unfaithful or ungodly" while the remaining 43 percent perceive God primarily as forgiving.

2. Forty-five percent of this group also view God as personal, while the remaining 55 percent perceive God as distant, like a cosmic force or disengaged as in deism.

3. Ian G. Barbour, *When Science Meets Religion* (New York: Harper Collins, 2000); J. Polkinghorne, *Belief in God in an Age of Science* (New Haven, CT: Yale University Press, 1998).

activity may be, by its very nature, essentially impossible to identify, relating to the concept of the "hiddenness of God."[4]

The classical physics of Newton implied that physical laws, in combination with initial conditions of a system, prohibit any freedom in that system (i.e., that its future is fully determined from the past). However, quantum mechanics (QM) which supplants classical physics at short distances, removes this determinism. Through QM the future of a system is not inherently predictable; there is profound freedom in the physical universe, and future states of a system can only be predicted with probability. Chaos theory shows that even the futures of many large-scale classical systems can often be vastly altered by very slight changes to initial conditions. Through the uncertainties of QM and, at a more classical level though chaos theory, God, being transcendent to space-time, is understood to provide room for himself to act in our universe.

Unfortunately, a strong tension between science and theology has existed in the United States for approximately 120 years. As indicated in a recent five-year study by the Barna Group, nearly a third of today's young adults with a Christian background believe that "churches are out of step with the scientific world we live in," and a quarter of young adults believe that "Christianity is anti-science."[5] As telling, a recent survey conducted by the Associated Press/GFK of 1012 United States adults indicates that Americans have more doubt than acceptance of concepts that scientists accept as firmly established by overwhelming evidence.[6] The Big Bang, the 13.8 billion year age of the universe, the 4.5 billion year age of the earth, and the 3.5 billion year evolution of life on earth are disbelieved by 51 percent of the United States population. Reportedly only about 21 percent of Americans are confident or extremely confident that the universe began with the Big Bang 13.8 billion years ago.

Acceptance of scientific conclusions strongly supported by evidence decreases sharply with increasing theistic belief. Evangelical and fundamentalist Christians, in particular, express much greater doubts. Based on a recent Gallup poll of 1028 people, more than two-thirds of those who attend weekly religious services espouse belief in a young earth (defined as only around 10,000 years old) compared to just 23 percent of those who never go to church.[7] This is not surprising given that only 27

---

4. Brian Gerrish, "To the Unknown God: Luther and Calvin on the Hiddenness of God," *JR* 53 (1973) 263–92, at 263.

5. See www.barna.com/research/six-reasons-young-christians-leave-church/#. These findings of the Barna Group, a Christian polling organization, are discussed in David Kinnaman, *You Lost Me: Why Young Christians are Leaving the Church . . . and Rethinking Faith*, (Grand Rapids: Baker, 2011).

6. S. Borehstein and J. Agiesta, "Big Bang a Big Question for Most Americans," 21 April 2014. See http://ap-gfkpoll.com/featured/findings-from-our-latest-poll-2.

7. Tia Ghose, "4 in 10 Americans Believe God Created Earth 10,000 Years Ago," See livescience. com/46123-many-americans-creationists.html.

percent of evangelical pastors "strongly disagree" with the statement that the earth is 6,000 years old. A higher number "strongly agree" that the earth is just 6,000 years old. Seven in ten evangelical pastors "strongly disagree" that "God used evolution to create people."[8]

Indeed, as Polkinghorne laments, a large number of Christians hold "a very limited view of creation." When they "speak of the world, they often (only) mean planet Earth and not the vast universe with its 100,000 million galaxies. When they speak of the future, they often seem to mean at most the next 1,000 years."[9]

Paradigms of Creation

A re-unification of faith and science within the Christian community is deeply needed. A theology of nature (as coined by Barbour) is clearly fundamental to these issues. From studies of the natural world we can gain knowledge about the process(es) through which the transcendent God acts with and within creation. Scientific knowledge can contribute significantly to deeper theological understanding of God's interactions. It is time for a renaissance of a consistent theology of nature within more Protestant churches. Christians will thereby be encouraged to take a grander view of the scope of divine creativity.

Perception of the nature and modes of God's transcendent interaction with creation has advanced significantly over millennia through growing understanding of the natural world. Significant steps in theological aspects have often correlated strongly with paradigm shifts in our understanding of the physical world. Over the millennia, humankind has advanced in stages through *regionocentric* (pre-history to ca. 300 BC) *geocentric* (ca. 300 BC to seventeenth century AD) *heliocentric* (ca. seventeenth to eighteenth century) and *galactocentric* (ca. eighteenth century to 1920s) paradigms to the present *univercentric* paradigm (ca. 1920s to ?).

Each major paradigm shift of the natural world has led to a vaster, but simultaneously more ordered and unified perception of creation. Quite often significant discoveries have produced profound answers to fundamental questions, while simultaneously generating more profound questions. The search for answers to a scientific understanding and description of our universe continues, with advancement of knowledge driving deeper questions. The cycles continue until the total collection

---

8. Karl Giberson, "Creationists Drive Young People Out of the Church," See www.huffingtonpost.com/karl-giberson-phd/creationists-and-young-christans_b_1096839.html.

9. J. Polkinghorne, "Some Theological Reflections," in *Georges Lemaitre: Life, Science and Legacy*, ed. Rodney D. Holder and Simon Mitton; Astrophysics and Space Science Library (Berlin: Springer, 2013) 193–96.

of new knowledge forces adoption of a deeper, more over-arching paradigm for creation.

For theists the knowledge that science reveals, and the growth of paradigms this may generate, should be viewed as a deeper, richer content of God's Book of Nature. Each upward paradigm shift of understanding physical creation has simultaneously promoted growth in theological perception of nature's Creator. With each step the perception of God has increased in grandeur. Each paradigm advancement has shed brighter light on the general methods by which and through which the Creator interacts with all of creation.

The Observable Universe

For the past century humankind has contemplated its existence within a univercentric paradigm. The detailed characteristics of the volume of the universe we observe (a.k.a., "the observable universe") have been studied and measured to ever increasing precision. The history of the universe is well known. The birth of our universe produced both our space and time. Between time zero and $10-36$ seconds the universe was no larger than $10-33$ cm—that is a billionth of a trillionth of the size of an atomic nucleus. The latter is known as the Planck length and is the smallest possible scale at which length has any physical meaning. During the inflationary era (when the universe was expanding at a velocity faster than the speed of light) from $10-36$ seconds to $10-32$ seconds, the universe expanded in volume by a factor of over 1026. Since that infinitesimal fraction of a second, the universe has been expanding at a rate just slightly below the speed of light. The age of the universe has been pinned down to 13.798 ± 0.037 billion years.

The roughly fourteen billion years of expansion suggests the effective size of our observable universe should be approximately twenty-eight billion light years (ly) (since the universe is expanding in all directions). However, the long-term accelerating expansion from dark energy (discovered in 1997) has stretched the size of the universe much beyond twenty-eight billion ly to over forty-six billion ly. The three-dimensional spatial sphere with this radius defines our observable universe, which is also often referred to as the "Hubble volume or horizon volume."

The best fit of data from a combination of measurements of physical properties of the universe indicates our space-time is exactly flat (in contrast to a positive or negative curvature that "bends" space-time). While we cannot observe beyond our Hubble volume, the flatness of the space-time we observe implies a vast space-time beyond it. What might be the properties of space-time beyond the horizon?

While we cannot rule out the possibility that beyond our Hubble volume there is just more of the same, or even nothing at all, widely accepted theories suggest not only more of the same, but something else too. The Big Bang/Inflation (BBI) stage of our universe implies that, while there is much more space-time beyond our Hubble horizon that is like ours, even farther beyond is space-time that is not like ours. As chaotic inflation discussions in standard cosmology textbooks discuss, it is most plausible that the mechanism that gave rise to both the observable and non-observable components of our universe has been repeated a vast, perhaps infinite, number of times. The physics underlying a BBI stage within one universe, likely gives rise to a collection of countless universes, thereby generating a *multiverse*.[10]

The analogy of a large pot of boiling water is often called upon to understand this. One asks, "How many bubbles should one expect to appear (per unit volume) in a boiling pot of water?" At 100 degrees Celsius a large pot full of boiling water produces a vast number of bubbles, not just one bubble. Similarly, a volume of space-time at the inflation temperature of around 1032 degrees Celsius should produce much more than one inflating space-time bubble. That is, a pot of bubbling universes (a.k.a., a multiverse) appears inevitable.

Multivercentric Paradigm

With this realization humanity may be in the initial stage of another cosmological paradigm shift, from our existence within a universe to existence within a multiverse. This transformation from a univercentric to a multivercentric view of the whole of creation would be beyond anything conceived prior. This paradigm shift has spread beyond the scientific community,[11] as evidenced by the collection of bestselling mul-

---

10. The term "multiverse" was coined in 1895 by the American philosopher William James, while addressing the Men's Christian Association of Harvard University in a talk entitled "Is Life Worth Living?" James derived the term as an alternative to "universe" to convey an absence of order or unity. He used the term to express his thoughts regarding natural evil. In the twentieth century the meaning of the term was broadened to find application in a range of areas, including cosmology, physics, astronomy, religion, philosophy, transpersonal psychology, and fiction (particularly in science fiction and fantasy). In most of these contexts, including cosmology and physics, the universes composing a multiverse are generically referred to as alternative universes, quantum universes, parallel universes, alternative realities, alternative timelines, and bubbleverses, among others. Although "multiverse" as a term originated in the nineteenth century, the cosmological concept it invokes is much older—over 800 years older. One of the first in Western Europe to consider the possibility of multiple universes was Roger Bacon (ca. AD 1200). From his underlying assumption of symmetry of space, Bacon argued that the universe must be spherical. He also assumed that more than one spherical universe could exist. However, Bacon realized that two or more universes without a common center point would form a shape that when rotated could create a vacuum. From his belief that "nature abhors a vacuum," Bacon concluded that only one universe likely exists.

11. Bernard Carr, ed., *Universe or Multiverse* (Cambridge: Cambridge University Press, 2007).

tiverse books written for the general public. This is altering our vision of the vastness of creation and the totality of reality. It is revolutionizing our understanding of the fundamental laws and properties of nature.

The multivercentric paradigm has deep philosophical and theological implications.[12] A full paradigm shift from a single universe to a multiverse of universes would profoundly alter many theological perceptions, in particular our understanding of God as Creator and God's interaction with and within creation. The specific form of the multiverse, if determinable, would also have profound implications for our understandings of the nature of God. Simultaneously, the Judeo-Christian understanding of God may also suggest some constraints upon the form and properties of a multiverse. How a multiverse might alter our perceptions of God and, alternately, how theological beliefs regarding the nature of God might suggest constraints on the universes within a multiverse are mutually addressed.

The concept of multiverse and a popular multiverse taxonomy scheme used by many cosmologists will be reviewed first, and then the dominant scientific, philosophical, and theological controversies of multiverse will then be discussed. Several related theological aspects of a multiverse will be examined. Ultimately I will suggest that a multiverse implies that freedom is the greatest gift of God. Though the "fingerprint" of God can likely be found in some aspects of the multiverse, God has probably given the multiverse the freedom of indeterminacy. Relatedly, I suggest a more deistic nature of God than is usually considered: a God who wills the multiverse to be, who may impose constraints on the realized universes within, and who allows each realized universe to follow its own path (possibly multiply copied by others). I also suggest a duality (i.e., an equivalence) between this view and an understanding in which God allows only a specific set of quantum branches at each decision point in an Everett universe, rather than allowing all quantum branches as in a standard Everett universe, wherein anything that can happen does happen.[13]

This proposed dualism between God's interaction with and within a multiverse provides a specific example of the non-interventionist objective divine action proposed by Robert Russell.[14] Limiting the specific set of allowed universes existing within a multiverse is a form of divine interaction with creation that makes objective differences in the course of nature without violating or suspending natural processes. Then from within a particular universe, it becomes essentially impossible to identify

---

12. Willem B. Drees, *Beyond the Big Bang* (La Salle, IL: Open Court, 1990).

13. In 1955 the physicist Hugh Everett III proposed the "many-worlds" interpretation of quantum mechanics, which he termed his "relative state" formulation. This has since been applied to multiverse theory. See for example, Peter Byrne, "The Many Worlds of Hugh Everett," *Scientific American* 297.6 (Dec 2007) 98–105.

14. Robert J. Russell, *Cosmology: From Alpha to Omega* (Minneapolis: Fortress, 2008).

any specific act of God. Nevertheless, by placing constraints on the set of possible quantum outcomes, one may say that God metaphorically issues a "seal of approval," distinguishing that multiverse from another that would contain a complete set of universes that realize all possible quantum outcomes.[15]

Multiverse Classifications

In the cosmological context, a multiverse is defined as a hypothetical set of possible universes, either finite or infinite in number, (including our own observable universe) that together comprise the entirety of space-time, matter, and energy, as well as an underlying set of physical metalaws (or equivalently, mathematical equations). Each universe existing within the multiverse may be subject to a distinct set of *local* physical laws, with each local set corresponding to a particular solution to the multiverse equations. This is especially true when there are numerous (perhaps infinite) distinct solutions to the underlying set of physical equations, as in string/M-theory, with its estimated 10,500 solutions.[16]

Alternately, two or more universes within a theoretical multiverse may have similar sets of physical laws, but different physical constants. Others may have both matching physical laws and physical constants, but different histories. Or others may have matching physical laws and physical constants and matching histories up to some point, and differing histories thereafter. Still others may be exact copies of one another, have matching physics laws, physical constants, and histories. Thus, between any two particular parallel universes, the local laws of physics may vary greatly, vary only slightly, or match exactly—likewise with regard to physical constants and/or histories. In most multiverse proposals, greater variation between universes is much more probable than slight variation, which itself is much more probable than exact matches.[17]

The structure of a multiverse, the nature of each universe within it, and the relationships between constituent universes, depend on the specific multiverse hypothesis considered. Means of classifying the hypothetical multiverses according

---

15. Don N. Page, "Does God So Love the Multiverse?" at arXiv:0801.0246v5 [physics.gen-ph].

16. An excellent introduction to string/M-theory is at superstringtheory.com.

17. With regard to comparison of physical laws and physical constants, matching universes would likely need to be defined modulo the limits of observable precision (including Planck scale uncertainty). At some limiting scale of precision, all physical parameters can be effectively understood as quantized, rather than continuous. Consider for example, two universes known by God to have all respective physical constants matching to thirty significant digits, but differing thereafter. These parameters might, however, be measurable to just twenty significant digits by the sentient life forms therein. Phenomenologically speaking, the two universes would be perceived by the sentient life forms as physically equivalent, even though the universes are physically distinct to higher precision.

to their structures and properties have been developed. In his 2003 paper "Parallel Universes," University of Chicago cosmologist Max Tegmark proposed a four-level taxonomy for multiverses that is somewhat analogous to the taxonomic ranks for biological classification.[18] Each of Tegmark's levels defines a different category of multiverse.[19] Higher level multiverses contain lower level multiverses: A Level 1 multiverse is a collection (likely infinite in number) of connected Hubble volumes with the same set of physical laws. It is a single vast universe. An infinite Level 1 multiverse is the simplest cosmological model (known as the cosmological concordance model) consistently to contain our visible universe, unless space-time has closed (periodic) boundary conditions. This model agrees with all current observational evidence and is used as the basis for most cosmology calculations and simulations.[20]

A Level 2 multiverse is defined by a set of metalaw mathematical equations (e.g., string theory) which has more than one set of physical laws as solutions. Each Level 2 multiverse contains a (finite or infinite) set of Level 1 multiverses, each of which is governed by its own set of distinct physical laws. A Level 3 multiverse, also referred to as an Everett multiverse, is defined to contain universes that branch apart each time choices are made. A Level 4 multiverse is defined to contain the entire set of Level 1 through 3 multiverses that are all based on a particular mathematical structure. Hypothetically, Level 2 through Level 4 multiverses contain, at any particular instant in a "global time" either a finite number of universes, an infinite but countable number of universes (referred to as an aleph-null set, which is analogous to the set of integers) or an infinite and uncountable number of universes (referred to as an aleph-one set, which is analogous to the set of real numbers).[21]

---

18. Max Tegmark, "Parallel Universes" in *Science and Ultimate Reality: Quantum Theory, Cosmology, and Complexity*, edited by John D. Barrow, Paul C. W. Davies, and Charles L. Harper, Jr. (Cambridge: Cambridge University Press, 2004) 459–91; A. Jones, "What are the Types of Parallel Universes?" http://physics.about.com/od/astronomy/f/ParallelUniverseTypes.htm.

19. A modified taxonomy appears in Brian Greene, *The Hidden Reality: Parallel Universes and the Deep Laws of the Cosmos* (New York: Vintage, 2011) and is reviewed in Andrew Zimmerman Jones, *String Theory for Dummies* (Hoboken, NJ: Wiley, 2010).

20. Brian Clegg, *Before the Big Bang: The Prehistory of Our Universg* (New York: St. Martin's, 2008).

21. In set theory the aleph notation devised by George Cantor (1845–1918) is a sequence of conceptual numbers used to represent the *size* of infinite sets. In mathematics these are referred to as *cardinalities*.

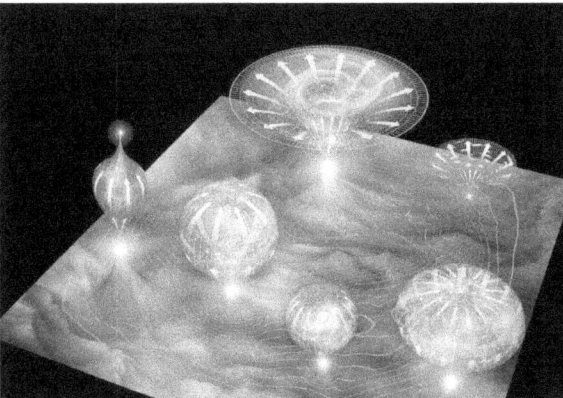

Figure 1. Representation of a Level 2 multiverse. A vast, perhaps infinite, collection of Level 1 multiverses embedded within a Level 2 multiverse[22]

Level 1 multiverses independently inflate within an unstable background space-time false vacuum of a Level 2 multiverse. The set of physical laws in each Level 1 multiverse may vary, but each set is a solution to the fundamental physical equations (a.k.a. metalaws) defining the nature of the Level 2 multiverse.

Multiverse Controversy

The possibility that our universe is but one of many in a vast multiverse is a speculative concept indeed. Nevertheless, in efforts to answer fundamental questions about the origin of the universe and about its properties, many cosmologists, theoretical physicists, and philosophers have converged on the idea of a multiverse of one form or another. While a proposed multiverse can take different forms, the idea that a vast collection of universes exists beyond the limits of our observable universe is common to all of them. However, even if a multiverse does exist, it is essentially unobservable to us (and likely always will be) beyond our own Hubble volume. Thus, both opponents and advocates of the multiverse proposal are limited by the same observable universe horizon. Hence, the multiverse hypothesis remains controversial within the scientific and philosophical communities. There is disagreement not just about whether the multiverse exists, but even if it does, also about whether the multiverse is a proper subject of scientific inquiry. Some argue that the concept belongs more in the realm of philosophy than science.

Given the known properties of our universe, a key question is whether the existence of a multiverse (in any form) is more probable than its non-existence. Multiverse proponents ask which hypothesis seems more plausible: that all that exists is

---

22. Art by Moonrunner Design. Copied from http://news.nationalgeographic.com/news/2014/03/140318-multiverse-inflation-big-bang-science-space/

precisely just that which we can observe or detect, with observation and detectability limited by the speed of light and the accelerating expansion of space, or that there likely exists physical reality beyond the observational and detectable limits of sentient species within our observable universe. They argue to conclude ours is likely the sole universe essentially requires: (1) a positivist/empiricist stance that nothing exists except what has been physically proven to exist, and/or (2) the belief that the origin of our universe cannot be described in scientific language. Philosophers often point out that an element of faith is, in fact, required to either defend or reject the multiverse hypothesis. An example of condition two is belief that creation of a universe is only possible by a direct act of God superseding or modifying the physical laws within our physical reality. For theologians an associated aspect is whether it is more likely the will of God that exactly one universe exists or a multiverse exists. In the latter case there are also significant theological distinctions between a multiverse containing a finite collection of universes, a multiverse containing an infinite, but countable (aleph-null) set of universes, and a multiverse containing an infinite, uncountable (aleph-one) set of universes.

Multiverse—A Good Scientific Theory?

For most of the last century, a good scientific hypothesis or theory has been defined as something that is testable, meaning that it is possible to disprove. That is, it must be *falsifiable*. Because multiverses are (predominantly) undetectable beyond our observable universe component, multiverse proposals are viewed by opponents as being untestable and unfalsifiable, blurring the line between science and speculation. Therefore, opponents of the multiverse concept frequently claim that it is not good science. This is a primary reason multiverse is a controversial topic within the scientific community. Predominant support of the existence of a multiverse of some type is among theoretical physicists and cosmologists.

Predominant opposition is found among experimentalists, such as Burton Richter, who believes,

> what passes for the most advanced theory in particle physics these days is not really science.... [The multiverse proposal] looks to be more theological speculation, the development of models with no testable consequences, than it is the development of practical knowledge, the development of models with testable and falsifiable consequences (Karl Popper's definition of science).[23]

---

23. Burton Richter, "Theory in Particle Physics: Theological Speculation versus Practical Knowledge," *Physics Today* 59 (2006) 8–9, at 8.

Some theorists have also sided with Richter. Cosmologist Paul Steinhardt calls the multiverse a dangerous idea that he is unwilling to contemplate. In a 2003 *New York Times* opinion piece, "A Brief History of the Multiverse," Paul Davies opines that multiverse theories are non-scientific:

> How is the existence of the other universes to be tested? To be sure, all cosmologists accept that there are some regions of the universe that lie beyond the reach of our telescopes, but somewhere on the slippery slope between that and the idea that there are an infinite number of universes, credibility reaches a limit. As one slips down that slope, more and more must be accepted on faith, and less and less is open to scientific verification. Extreme multiverse explanations are therefore reminiscent of theological discussions. Indeed, invoking an infinity of unseen universes to explain the unusual features of the one we do see is just as ad hoc as invoking an unseen Creator. The multiverse theory may be dressed up in scientific language, but in essence it requires the same leap of faith.[24]

Tegmark and Page adamantly disagree with claims that the multiverse proposal is untestable and unfalsifiable. They believe that unobservable aspects of a theory do not inherently make that theory untestable.[25] For Tegmark the key question is not whether parallel universes in a multiverse exist, but rather how many levels a multiverse has. Tegmark and Page have separately shown that each of the four levels of multiverses have different sets of supporting arguments and evidence. Proofs have been developed that each level and type of multiverse can be tested and falsified *statistically* if the multiverse proposal can predict what its ensemble of universes is and also specify a probability distribution (a *measure*) over its collection of universes. (Though significantly less of an issue for Level 1 multiverses, Tegmark acknowledges that construction of a measure for Level 2 and 3 multiverses can be a much more serious difficulty. Constructing a measure for a Level 4 multiverse is completely unresolved and, indeed, may not be possible.)

Nobel laureate Frank Wilczek recognizes the value of the idea that physical reality is vastly larger than human perception of it and that the perceived part may not be representative of the whole. He emphasizes that this belief exists at many levels and has a long history. Wilczek points out that thought experiments are not difficult to design to show scientists have often formed an inadequate perception of the extent of physical reality. For him the laws we use successfully to describe the observable universe are most naturally formulated in a larger framework that includes

---

24. Paul Davies, "A Brief History of the Multiverse," *New York Times*, 12 April 2003. See http://www.nytimes.com/2003/04/12/opinion/a-brief-history-of-the-multiverse.html.

25. Tegmark, "Parallel Universes"; Don N. Page, "Predictions and Tests of Multiverse Theories," in *Universe or Multiverse*? ed. Bernard Carr (Cambridge: Cambridge University Press, 2007) 411–30.

unobservable parts. Wilczek argues positivist views are themselves not scientific but need to be identified as a "philosophical moral exhortation." Such positivist views should therefore bow to more scientific arguments for or against a multiverse.[26]

In his analysis of the multiverse, George Ellis offers a middle ground between the proponents and opponents. Ellis is concerned not only with the science but also with the scientific philosophy by which multiverse theories are generally substantiated. He, like most cosmologists, accepts Tegmark's Level I regions, even though they lie far outside our Hubble volume. Ellis also believes the multiverse of cosmic inflation exists very far away. However, he acknowledges that it would be so distant that it is extremely unlikely any evidence of an early interaction of our observable universe with any other part of the multiverse will be found. Ellis understands that for many theorists, the lack of empirical testability or falsifiability of a multiverse *is not* a major concern: "Many physicists who talk about the multiverse, especially advocates of the string landscape, do not care much about parallel universes per se. For them, objections to the multiverse as a concept are unimportant. Their theories live or die based on internal consistency and, one hopes, eventual (laboratory) testing."[27]

Although Ellis believes there is little hope that physical tests for existence of a multiverse will ever be possible, he grants that the theories on which the speculation is based are not without scientific merit. Ellis concludes that multiverse theory is a productive research program and urges:

> the contemplation of the multiverse is an excellent opportunity to reflect on the nature of science and on the ultimate nature of existence: Why we are here? In looking at this concept, we need an open mind, though not too open. It is a delicate path to tread. Parallel universes may or may not exist; the case is unproved. We are going to have to live with that uncertainty. Nothing is wrong with scientifically based philosophical speculation, which is what multiverse proposals are. But we should name it for what it is.[28]

Theological Implications of a Multiverse

Under the assumption that our universe does exist within an encompassing multiverse, this study now focuses on what a multiverse of universes in general suggests regarding God's interactions with creation. I will examine some implications of specific categories of multiverses. A general theme is the freedom inherently granted

---

26. Frank Wilczek, "Multiversality," Accessed: arXiv:1307.7376.
27. George Ellis, "Multiverses: Descriptions, Uniqueness and Testing," in *Universe or Multiverse?* ed. Bernard Carr (Cambridge: Cambridge University Press, 2007) 387–410; George F. L. Ellis, "Does the Multiverse Really Exist?" *Scientific American* 305.2 (Aug. 2011) 38–43.
28. Ellis, "Does the Multiverse Really Exist?" 38.

to creation through a multiverse. I will show how the indeterminacy endemic to a multiverse reveals much regarding the nature of God: that it is evidence of God's indeterminacy in action.

Consider that the entire universe, composed of both the observable region and the unobservable region outside of our Hubble volume, is very possibly at least a Level 1 multiverse of some sort or other as implied by the variety of extensions of BBI theory, such as chaotic inflation, string/M theory, blackhole propagation hypothesis, etc. The human understanding of the cosmos has grown from a single land mass, to a single planet, to a system of planets circling the sun, to a galaxy of stars, to a universe with galaxies counting into the trillions. The vastness of this reality is just cause for theists to pause and appreciate the creative nature of the Creator. For many scientists of theistic faith the search for an even more abundant creation continues. Those who believe in a God of the "omni" attributes (omniscience, omnipotence, omnipresence) should indeed be expecting something more in creation than just our observable universe. Several Christians in science and philosophy, such as Stephen Barr,[29] Don Page,[30] Robin Collins,[31] Klaas Kraay,[32] John Leslie[33] and the present author[34] have long suggested that for the infinite mind of God, our universe with a finite lifetime and a finite number of inhabitants is far too small, far too limited, and far too finite to be the totality of physical creation.

To be theologically consistent, creation should be vaster than we have yet ever understood. A multiverse of universes, perhaps as many as 10,500 or more at a time, with an infinite recycling of new and different universes seems far more in tune with the creative nature of a God of the infinities. The actuality of a multiverse would

---

29. Stephen M. Barr, *Modern Physics and Ancient Faith*, (Notre Dame, IN: University of Notre Dame Press, 2003).

30. Page, "Predictions and Tests of Multiverse Theories"; and his "Return of the Boltzmann Brains," *Physical Review D* 78 (2006) 063536.

31. Robin Collins, "Design and the Many-Worlds Hypothesis," in *Philosophy of Religion: A Reader and Guide*, ed. William Lane Craig, ed. (New Brunswick, NJ: Rutgers University Press, 2002) 130–48; "Design and the Designer: New Concepts, New Challenges," in *Spiritual Information: 100 Perspectives on Science and Religion*, ed. Charles S. Harper, Jr. (West Conshohocken, PA: Templeton Foundation, 2005) 161–7; "The Multiverse Hypothesis: a Theistic Perspective," in *Universe or Multiverse?* ed. Bernard Carr (Cambridge: Cambridge University Press, 2007) 459–80.

32. Klaas Kraay, "Theism and the Multiverse" and "Theism and Modal Collapse." See http://www.ryerson.ca/~kraay.

33. John Leslie, *Universes* (New York: Routledge, 1989); and *Infinite Minds* (Oxford: Clarendon, 2001).

34. Gerald Cleaver, "String/M-Theory Cosmology: God's Blueprint for the Universe," paper presented at the American Scientific Affiliation 2003 conference, Lakewood, CO; "Before the Big Bang," paper presented at Metanexus 2006 conference, Phoenix, AZ; "String Multiverse, Cosmological Anthropic Principle, and Anselm's Ontological Argument," paper presented at the American Scientific Affiliation 2009 conference, Waco, TX.

force us to let go of our often finite, limited vision of God, to break God out of the box we have envisioned God in for far too long.

Relatedly, multiverse theories have become embroiled in theological debate. At the heart of much of this is the multiverse's challenge to both humanity's uniqueness and its central place in creation, a challenge that also appeared with each prior paradigm shift. Indeed, the multiverse concept forces humanity to revise its understanding of the manner and means in which God, as Creator, interacts with his creation.

Some have feared the multiverse proposals will join evolution as another battleground in the claimed culture wars.[35] To some degree it has. For example, in a 2005 *New York Times* op-ed, Christoph Cardinal Schönborn, the archbishop of Vienna, accused scientists of concocting the idea of a multiverse "to avoid the overwhelming evidence for purpose and design found in modern science" and that it is "an abdication of human intelligence." A handful of prominent Christian thinkers have also argued that multiverse theory is motivated by a refusal to accept evidence of God's handiwork in the cosmos. In his article "The Multiverse Problem," Nathan Schneider points out that William Lane Craig has called the idea of a multiverse an act of "desperation on the part of atheist scientists," and that Canadian journalist Denyse O'Leary, an ally of the Intelligent Design movement, asserts "religious or anti-religious motives dominate the discussion among scientists developing multiverse models."[36]

For these multiverse critics, cosmology was once a source of theological promise, providing evidence that the universe is designed for life. As an example, cosmologists have shown that if space were expanding at a slightly higher speed, or if the strong nuclear force were just a little off, our universe would be a hydrogen mush incapable of supporting life. The chances that in a single universe the cosmic conditions needed for even a single living cell would come about are astonishingly low. O'Leary argues that "the most obvious explanation for fine-tuning is that fine-tuning is real, that we live in a designed universe."[37]

If, however, we live in a vast and varying multiverse, there could be on the order of 10,500 different universes in all (or depending on the particular type of multiverse, of another unimaginably large number, perhaps infinite) making the chance of a universe with our life-yielding properties occurring within the multiverse comfortably higher. Thus, multiverse theory eliminates the fine-tuning argument at the universe level for the existence of God.

---

35. N. Schneider, *The Multiverse Problem*, http://seedmagazine.com/content/article/the_multiverse_problem/ (March 30, 2009).

36. Ibid.

37. Ibid.

In "Does God So Love the Multiverse?" Don Page sees a parallel between the reason many Christians oppose evolution and the reason they oppose a multiverse. As evolution removed *one particular design argument* for the existence of God, multiverse removes *one particular fine-tuning argument* for the existence of God. Evolution taught us that "the marvelously many different species of living things on earth had not been separately and independently designed by God." Similarly, Christians who "take the marvels of the fine-tuning of the constants of physics as evidence of theism and often of separate and individual design of these constants by God" may be fearful of a multiverse that removes this particular evidence.[38]

In truth, the growing credibility of multiverse theory has failed to create the opposition between religion and the multiverse that Schönborn and his cohorts expected. O'Leary's accusation that multiverse proposals have been developed for antireligious purposes is demonstrably false, as evidenced by the multiverse debates within the scientific community and the associated range of pro and con arguments raised in that community. Rather than to avoid evidence of design in the cosmos, multiverse models arose within the physics community from key questions in particle physics, cosmic inflation, and string theory.

Nevertheless, one must acknowledge that a few voices within the "new atheist" movement have sought to use the multiverse to "disprove God," just as they have tried to use evolution. Examples include Carlos Calle's, *The Universe: Order Without Design*[39] and Steven Hawking and Leonard Mlodinow's, *The Grand Design*.[40] The common claim of both books is essentially that since string/M-theory implies a multiverse, which implies quantum gravity, which implies inflation of a vast number of vacuum bubbles, which probabilistically implies conditions for life should exist in some such bubbles, God is not needed.

Hawking believes that the existence of quantum gravity eliminates the need for God. The "new atheist" movement seeks to develop a false dichotomy of "either God or gravity." The logical fallacy is similar to that of old "either God or evolution" claim—just the scale is different. Calle himself draws the analogy between the purpose of his book and that of Richard Dawkins's writings, claiming that "biology can be explained through natural selection. The universe can be explained with the laws of nature."[41]

This is a false dichotomy, for no scientific theory or proposal can "prove" or "disprove" God. The existence of God can never be argued away by growth in human

---

38. Page, "Does God So Love the Multiverse?"
39. C. Calle, *The Universe: Order Without Design* (Amherst, NY: Prometheus, 2009).
40. S. Hawking and L. Mlodinow, (New York: Bantam, 2010).
41. Calle, *The Universe*, 20.

understanding of the physical laws of a universe or of a multiverse. Rather, gains in human understanding of nature can expand our understanding of the creative methods of God. Don Page reminds us "evolution did not disprove the existence of God or of some *overall design*."[42] The vast majority of leading theologians and theistic scientists, including Francis Collins, accept evolution as God's chosen method of generating life.

Similarly, Page urges Christians to develop a similar understanding for a multiverse. Just as evolution suggests a grand design for life through a non-interventionist objective divine action process, a multiverse

> can reveal an even more grand design of the universe, since the physical process that generates the multiverse would have to [possess] suitable basic laws and initial conditions to produce life at all, no matter what the constants of physics are, since often they seem to be fine-tuned for several different reasons. The laws and initial conditions [of a multiverse] would apparently have to be even more special to produce not just life, but life like ours observing the order we actually see around us.[43]

Intervention at a multiverse scale provides a non-interventionist objective divine action interaction that could make objective differences at the scales of each individual universe, without violating or suspending the natural processes *within* a given universe. Interaction at the multiverse scale would appear transcendent relative to the collection of space-times of component universes.

As Page emphasizes, evolution forced humankind to re-evaluate what being made in the image of God means. It taught us that humankind is related to all life on earth—that we were not separately created by an individual act, but arose within the whole of earth's biosphere. A multiverse with an even more diverse, perhaps, infinite range in life, would require us to further re-evaluate ourselves. We would need to reconsider the range of life flourishing throughout the vastness of creation.

Jeffrey Zweerink, an astrophysicist and member of Reasons to Believe ministry, has set out to make the multiverse a tool for evangelizing. In *Who's Afraid of the Multiverse?* Zweerink seeks to convince fellow Christians that a multiverse only replaces one design problem with another, but on a much vaster scale, strengthening the evidence of God. He concludes, "any multiverse model which can explain our observable universe requires a beginning and still exhibits design."[44] Zweerink devotes a monthly blog post on reasons.org to the theological advantages of multiverse

---

42. Page, "Does God So Love the Multiverse?"

43. Ibid.

44. J. Zweerink, *Who's Afraid of the Multiverse?* (Reasons to Believe, Glendora, 2008). The quotation is taken from Schneider, *The Multiverse Problem*.

theory. Even Andre Linde, avowed atheist, acknowledges that "expanding this area of positive knowledge does not remove the question of God . . . . It just pushes it further away."[45] A multiverse leaves unresolved the very question of its own origin. The BVG theorem, developed by cosmologists Borde, Vilenkin, and Guth in 2003, argues that any universe or multiverse that on average is expanding must have had in its finite past either a beginning or undergone a change of phase into its present state.[46]

Many scientists and theologians believe a multiverse actually expands the job description for God. Several believe this is necessary and implied by the nature of God: If our observable universe is the only universe, and if it does not go through Big Crunch/Big Bang cycles eternally forward,[47] then the theological implications are severe. That would imply God chooses to bring into existence only a finite number of sentient beings for whom to offer an eternal existence following physical death. This would imply that an eternal, infinite God is satisfied to create only a finite number of sentient beings with whom to interact eternally. This does not seem consistent with the nature of a God of the infinite and God's "omni" characteristics.

In Rom 1:20 Paul writes that "creation manifests the eternal attributes of God—God's eternal and infinite power." If God is truly eternal, infinite, and self-consistent, we should expect God to create eternally and infinitely, or not at all. We should expect an infinitely creative being to create far more than one finite universe—in fact (infinitely) many and maybe more kinds of realities. This equates to a Level 1 or higher multiverse or something equivalent.

This is consistent with an extension of Anselm of Canterbury's (1033–1109) ontological argument for the existence of God in his *Proslogian*.[48] The ontological argument is based on a priori proof using intuition and reason. Anselm made the distinction between necessary things—things that cannot not exist—and contingent beings—things that may exist but whose existence is not needed. God is the only necessary thing; all else is contingent. At the beginning of Anselm's ontological argument is his definition of God, or equivalently a necessary assumption about God's nature: God is "something that than which nothing greater can be conceived." If it

---

45. A. Linde, "The Inflationary Universe," in *Universe or Multiverse*, ed. Bernard Carr (Cambridge: Cambridge University Press, 2007) 127–50, at 145.

46. The authors of the BVG theorem have published a series of papers since 2003 strengthening the robustness of their conclusion. One exception the authors acknowledge is an oscillating universe or multiverse with a finite minimum volume at discrete points in time. In this case, the authors believe two separate arrows of time exist, each pointing temporally outward from minima volume positions, implying two expanding universes not one cycling.

47. An eternally cyclic universe is a Level 1 multiverse.

48. *Anselm's Proslogian*, trans. M. J. Charlesworth (Oxford: Clarendon, 1965).

is the nature of God to create and to interact with sentient life, but creation (and therefore self-aware life) is finite in space-time volume, then there will always be a greater version of God whose creation of space-time volume is more vast, containing more self-aware creatures with whom God can interact for eternity (assuming the sentient beings transform after physical death into existence in a heavenly realm). Anything less than some form of space-time creation with an infinite spatial volume or infinite temporal length producing an infinite set of sentient beings implies God as "that than which something greater *can* be conceived." Thus, a multiverse of a "dizzying variety, unending moments of new creation, and . . . infinite scope makes perfect sense as the work of a 'God of the infinitudes, who creates eternally.'"[49]

If we can imagine God creating on this scale, the extension of Anselm's ontological argument implies that creation should be *at least as grand as a multiverse*, if it is the nature of God to create. This was the nature of God and of creation as envisioned by C. S. Lewis in his Chronicles of Narnia. In *The Magician's Nephew* the children of earth find themselves in a realm in which they can journey to an infinite number of universes stretching into the distance. As the children look on, Aslan tells them that in these different realms he goes by many names but is Lord of all of them.[50]

God's immanence within the multiverse requires further theological contemplation, including the nature of the second person of the Trinity. Robin Collins, philosopher at Messiah College, is another who believes that multiverse models are consistent with God's creative capacities. He believes "if you start thinking about God as infinitely creative, it would be totally unexpected for God to just create us."[51] Collins imagines how the triune nature of God would be expressed in a multiverse. He asks, "What if God communicates with his sentient creatures in each universe through the advent of the second person of the Trinity in the physical form of the respective local sentient creatures?"[52] He is intrigued by the possibility of a Messiah with a multitude of faces that are universe and planet dependent.[53]

Collins is not the first to contemplate this; such theological considerations are also not unique to the multiverse. Rather, the possibility of life within other universes in a multiverse and related theological implications are essentially many orders-of-magnitude extensions of the possibility of extra-terrestrial life within this universe and its theological implications. The Catholic Church has addressed the latter for

---

49. T. Persuad, "Christ of the Klingons," *Christianity Today* (Dec. 2010) 46–47.
50. C. S. Lewis, *The Magician's Nephew* (London: Bodley Head, 1955).
51. Persuad, "Christ of the Klingons," 46–47, summarizing his interviews with Collins and Cleaver.
52. Ibid.
53. Ibid.

centuries. In the 1300s it was declared a heresy to state that other worlds like earth could not exist elsewhere in the universe.

By the 1600s some Catholic priests proposed life elsewhere in the universe and contemplated the implications. Dominican Friar Giordano Bruno (1548–1600) speculated that our sun was but one among an infinite number of stars circled by life-supporting planets, within an infinite universe.[54] A few years ago Pope Emeritus Benedict XVI held an international conference at the Vatican for leading scientists and theologians to study issues and implications of extra-terrestrial life. Vatican Observatory Director, Brother Guy Consolmagno (MS at M.I.T., PhD at University of Arizona in planetary science) reminds us, "if extraterrestrial life were to be discovered, it would not mean everything we believe [theologically] is wrong. Rather, we would discover that everything is truer in ways we could not ever have imagined."[55]

Collins emphasizes that the theology of God's Christ appearing on other planets is not heretical. Since the Council of Chalcedon in AD 451, "orthodox Christian theology has drawn a distinction between the divine nature and the human nature in the single person of Jesus." Christ's divine nature could unite with other incarnational forms elsewhere within a single universe or throughout a multiverse. Collins imagines far-flung civilizations in the multiverse in need of salvation and a multiplicity of Christs to meet each universe's redemptive needs. "If you had Klingons somewhere (a very fallen race as we know from Star Trek) God takes up their nature, and there is a Klingon version of the Son."[56]

Duality of God's Multiverse Activity

God's transcendence to the multiverse is consistent with God as creator and sustainer of the multiverse as a whole. What might a multiverse imply about other possible manifestations of God's connection with creation? What about God evolving by interacting with creation from within? This would be a multiverse process theology. The definition of process theology varies, but some general aspects seem common: First, because God interacts with the changing universe, God is perceived by process theologians to be changeable over the course of time. God is affected by the actions that take place in our space-time universe. Thus, God is considered to evolve through interaction with creation. Simultaneously, the abstract elements of God (goodness, wisdom, etc.) are deemed to remain eternal. Some versions of

---

54. Giordano Bruno, *Cause, Principle, and Unity*, Fifth Dialogue, trans. J. Lindsay (New York: International, 1962, originally published in 1588).

55. As quoted by Carol Glatz, "Do Space Aliens Have Souls? Inquiring Minds Can Check Jesuit's Book," Catholic Online, http://www.catholic.org/featured/headline.php?ID=5532.

56. As quoted by Persuad, "Christ of the Klingons," 46–47.

process theology suggest that God needs to be within creation, because the universe provides a physical framework for God's existence. Dipolar theism is the idea that God has both a changing aspect (God's existence as a living God) and an unchanging aspect (God's eternal essence).

Second, the universe is characterized by change carried out by agents of free will within creation. Self-determination characterizes everything in the universe, not just human beings. God cannot totally control any series of events or any individual, but God influences the creaturely exercise of free will by offering possibilities. For many process theologians God is believed to have a will in everything, but not everything that occurs is God's will. In our present, God does not know the future fully but predicts it based on current knowledge.

A multiverse is problematic regarding evolution and the changeability of God. Each universe within a Level 1 multiverse is causally (i.e., temporally) independent of all others. There is no frame of reference for a common "now" between different universes. This would seem to imply that the changing aspects of God reacting to events within a given universe become independent/divided/separated from the changing aspects of God in other universes within that multiverse. Even in a single universe, the God of process theology becomes consistently describable relativistically only in the rest frame of that universe. The rest frame of one universe cannot be correlated to the rest frame of another universe within a multiverse. Instead, the combination of process theology and multiverse seems to imply not just panentheism but pantheism, with God as Creator of the entire multiverse being separated into an infinite set of unique Gods with different evolving knowledge per universe. Each God within a specific universe would be affected uniquely by the events within that universe. Dipolar theism transforms into "multipolar" theism.[57] This apparent inconsistency between a multiverse and a process theology based God develops further when God is assumed to exist and evolve independently within each of the independent Level 1 multiverses embedded within a Level 2 multiverse.

The historic Christian understanding of transcendence is that God, as Creator/first person of the Trinity, is separate from his creation. St. Augustine described God as being transcendent to this universe such that all space-time events appear simultaneously in an interconnected four-dimensional picture, a "block universe."[58] Let us extend this picture for a multiverse: To understand multiverse transcendence, imagine a global multiverse time. Each universe results from its own individual BBI

---

57. This is not with reference to distinct realizations of the second person of the Trinity in each universe, but to the distinct divisions of the process theology first person of the Trinity within each universe.

58. St. Augustine's four-dimensional block universe concept is reviewed in section 3 of "The Eternalist View in Eternity," *Stanford Encyclopedia of Religion*. See plato.stanford. edu/entries/eternity/.

and defines its own time as measured within, uncorrelated to the respective times measured within all other universes. However, an overall global time frame should be possible to define within a multiverse and should specify the specific times and locations for the set of BBI's generating the universes.

A transcendent God of a multiverse is transcendent to the space-time of each universe within the multiverse. Demanding one infinite, almighty, eternal, Creator God of the multiverse suggests an extension of Augustine's block universe to which God transcends the bulk multiverse itself. The histories of all space-times of all causally independent universes would likewise appear as a moment to God.

The equivalence between the entire collections of universes in Level 1 and in Level 3 multiverses offers an intriguing and impactful *duality* (indistinguishable equivalence) between a view of God as transcendent, who interacts with creation only (or primarily) through the creation and sustaining of the multiverse as a whole, and a view of God as an interventionist, who interacts directly with creation via micromanaging specific events within each given universe. Consider a Level 3 multiverse with a given universe branching into a set (finite or infinite) of universes at each quantum mechanical decision point. Imagine universe A splitting into universes U and D, where in U a flipped coin lands "heads up" and in D it lands "heads down." In the deist picture, if it is divine will that the coin lands heads up, then God does not need to modify universe D by interacting with the coin flip for the coin to land heads up rather than down. That would make two copies of the same universe. Instead, God could act at the most deistic level and simply forbid the universe D from coming into existence from A. Instead, at the multiverse level, God wills only U into existence from A and not D. Sentient beings in A would see no sign of God's interaction; for them the natural outcome was U, as a result of a collapse of their wave function.

In the case that U is realized and D is forbidden, there was never any sentient being to identify D changing into U. The consistent theological and scientific assumption for sentient beings to assume is that their universe naturally flowed from A to U, without God needing to interfere in their universe for that path to be taken. Otherwise, for God independently to alter path A-D into A-U has the implication of both God changing his mind and then creating a pair of identical universes. This would imply that the creator God evolves and exists within some frame of time, even if God's time transcends space-time.

The effect of God's action would not be observed at the universe scale, but only at the multiverse scale by observation of the non-existence of universe D within the multiverse, when its existence is predicted by prior probability in a global multiverse frame. Thus, we understand how the net result could be obtained by God either acting at a mostly deistic level either allowing or not allowing a universe with a certain characteristic to come into existence as a whole or to interact within a universe at the quantum mechanical level to alter the outcome to enforce divine will. Sentient creatures within these universes could in no way determine which interaction process God uses. God would not by viewed as acting.

Nevertheless, it seems more consistent with God's infinite/omni nature for God to exercise divine will at the whole multiverse level by allowing an entire universe in an Everett multiverse to either exist or not to exist, rather than micromanaging local events within a specific universe by altering its probability outcomes. The former seems more in keeping with a multiverse-creating, self-consistent God of infinite and omni-properties.

Multiverse Divine Seal of Approval

Robert Mann and others express concern about the "everything is possible" aspect of multiverses.[59] They argue that such a multiverse really does not explain "anything" because it allows "everything." This gets to what is predicable within a multiverse as a whole versus the probability of certain events occurring within a particular universe.

Mann's theological concern is that a multiverse allowing "everything" physically consistent may imply a drastic increase in both the occurrence rate of natural evil and of sentient evil, the latter defined as evil caused by the actions of one sentient being to another (especially sentient) life form. One resolution posited is God may set some quantitative limit to the amount of evil (natural and/or sentient) that occurs in a universe physically realized by God. That is, a potential universe with too much evil is not realized into existence by God.

God preventing a particular event such as a coin landing heads down within any universe would alter a multiverse significantly, but not a particular universe noticeably. Someone examining the totality of creation from the bulk multiverse stage could distinguish between the multiverse without divine will enforced and the multiverse with divine will enforced. The multiverse without heads down flips would possess God's clearly observable seal of approval. God's intervention in a multiverse would be identified by a shift in some expectation values of events, from an unbiased probability to a biased probability.

The coin-flipping event is trivial, but more significant events with a constrained set of quantum outcomes can be imagined. Consider a divine will for a Level 3 multiverse, whereby God does not allow universe branching to be realized that allows

---

59. Robert Mann, "Inconstant Multiverse," *Perspectives on Science and Christian Faith* 57 (2005) 302–310; and "The Puzzle of Existence," *Perspectives on Science and Christian Faith* 61 (2009) 139–50.

evil dictators to kill more than some specific number of people. A fundamental list of constraint equations could be applied by God to the basic framework of the multiverse and the universes it contains. This might resolve the concerns about a generic multiverse expressed by some Christian cosmologists such as Ellis and Mann. On the other hand, specifically imagine that God forbids any universe from existence wherein an evil dictator would kill more than 50,000,000 people. Then Anselm's Ontological Argument might suggest a greater God would not allow universes to exist wherein an evil dictator kills more than 49,999,999 people.

Don Page proposes an alternative version of God's seal of approval. He reminds us, "God seems loath to violate elegant laws of physics that He chooses to adopt within His creations, . . . even if their violation could greatly reduce human suffering (e.g., from falls)."[60]

Page suggests a multiverse *seal of approval* results from God imposing *no* constraints. Page's argument is a particular interpretation of Anselm's ontological argument. Page poses a simple hypothesis about the world (defined as the entirety of all that exists): *The actual world is the best possible world.* This is indeed consistent with an extension of Anselm's ontology arguments. Otherwise there could be a better God that creates a better world. By this Page means the value of the world is maximized, which he takes to be the intrinsic value of conscious or sentient experiences. He does not assume that entities with consciousness have only intrinsic value. Page recognizes that humans can be highly instrumental in leading to intrinsic value in the happiness of the conscious experience of others, including God.

Page defines the total goodness of the world as an intrinsic value defined by pleasure minus suffering, happiness minus unhappiness, joy minus agony, of all conscious experiences that occur. He assumes that in our actual world this total goodness is the greatest that is logically possible. Nevertheless, Page recognizes that while our universe does have considerable positive intrinsic value, there is also much suffering and unhappiness. So he concludes that it does not seem very plausible that the intrinsic happiness within the universe alone is the maximum logically possible, and that is of key importance.

However, Page emphasizes that our universe has a very high degree of mathematical elegance and beauty, which humans can at least partially appreciate. He believes elegance may increase the intrinsic value of the universe. Yet, clearly most of us would be happier if disasters, diseases, and human evil were eliminated from the universe by constraints imposed by God at the multiverse level of allowed universes, even at the cost of less mathematical elegance and beauty for the laws of physics. Page

---

60. Don N. Page, "A Theological Argument for an Everett Multiverse," arXiv:1212.5608 [phys.gen-ph].

suggests that this might be outweighed by God's appreciation for the mathematical elegance of the universe. Page proposes that the actual world is the best possible world. This leads to his *optimal argument for the existence of God*, as such a being outside the universe or multiverse who creates and experiences tremendous value in having much greater knowledge and appreciation for the mathematical elegance of the universe than we creatures within the universe can acquire.

Cancer and earthquakes may be logical consequences of our laws of physics. While Page argues that although God may grieve over the evils that are consequences, the laws of physics must give him even greater joy. So this inevitable trade-off may be a necessity. Page suggests that if God had chosen to eliminate the evil in this universe, then the laws of physics that he would have picked would have differed significantly compared to what they actually are. Page believes these laws would have had to be less elegant and beautiful to God than the actual laws God chooses. Less orderly laws may have made God much less joyful, so that the total value of the world could well have been reduced significantly.

Concluding Multiverse Thoughts

From the latter half of the twentieth century, the cosmic multiverse concept has earned growing recognition as a scientific, philosophical, and theological concept. The multiverse is now a realm of cutting-edge science, simultaneously raising profound philosophical and theological questions. The coming of age of the multiverse is the result of a long chain of paradigm advancements in humankind's perception of reality. With each advancing step, our understanding of the physical environment around us has grown larger, grander, more complex, yet simultaneously more unified and ordered. Over a period of several thousand years, we have moved from regionocentric paradigms, to geocentric, heliocentric, and to the present univercentric paradigm, and the paradigm shift beyond univercentric is in process.

Unanswered puzzles about our universe and its properties have led many scientists to join philosophers and theologians to ponder and propose the existence of a vast collection of additional universes. For many a multiverse of one form or another offers resolutions to many of the underlying science questions. For others a multiverse raises more questions than answers. Nevertheless, the overall momentum grows for acceptance of the existence of physical reality beyond our observable universe.

That space-time continues beyond the limit of our observable universe is a mainstay of the Standard Model of Cosmology. In that sense the transformation from a univercentric to a multivercentric paradigm is indeed far along. Whether humanity will ever determine, at least theoretically, what exists beyond the veils of our finite Hubble volume remains an underlying as yet unanswered question.

With growing understanding of the likelihood of a multiverse, the human perception of physical reality is expanding by previously unimaginable orders of magnitude. If a quantum gravity theory is proven correct, we have begun the next step in understanding the beauty, splendor, complexity, and vastness of God's creation. A paradigm shift to a multivercentric reality would be vastly more comprehensive than all of the preceding shifts. The emerging story has profound implications for theological views of God, including the manner and methods by which God interacts with creation. The existence of a multiverse was shown consistent with belief in a God of infinite and "omni" traits.

Two alternative views were presented regarding what it may mean for God to place his *seal of approval* on a multiverse. Both cases provide a duality in the perception of how God acts, either from a (predominantly) deist view of God working at the multiverse stage to realize or prohibit specific universes or from a (predominantly) interventionist view of God interacting directly within universes at specific (quantum) decision branch points in Everett universes, altering the path that a universe would have otherwise taken. The proposed dualism between God interacting with a multiverse as a whole and God acting within the particular universes contained within the multiverse provides a particular realization of the non-interventionist objective divine action proposed by Robert Russell: Limiting the specific set of allowed universes existing within a multiverse is a form of divine interaction that makes objective differences in the course of nature without violating or suspending natural processes. Although God's actions may directly limit the realities that exist within a multiverse, from inside any particular universe such actions are essentially impossible to identify beyond the underlying local laws of physics. Via a multiverse God may simultaneously realize a deistic non-interventionist objective divine action approach that offers a means of interaction with the inhabitants of the plethora of embedded universes. The freedom this grants to the creation is perhaps God's greatest gift.

MADE AS MIRRORS: BIBLICAL AND NEUROSCIENTIFIC REFLECTIONS ON IMAGING GOD

Joshua M. Moritz

"And all of us, with unveiled faces, seeing the glory of the Lord as though reflected in a mirror, are being transformed into the same image from one degree of glory to another; for this comes from the Lord, the Spirit."

—2 Corinthians 3:18

We live in a culture immersed in images. We watch movies on Netflix, post photos of our key life moments on Instagram, share selfies on Snapchat, construct and manicure our social self-image on Facebook, and so on. We expend great effort to convey the right image of ourselves. Many of us would never dream of leaving home to go to work or school without first looking in the mirror. The Bible is full of images too: portraits of love and reconciliation, warnings about the dangers of graven images, and teachings about the true meaning of the image that matters most to God—namely, *God's own image in us*. At the thematic center of Scripture is the affirmation that human beings are made as mirrors to image their Creator. Though tarnished by sin and broken by death, the embodied human reflection of God is cleansed and healed by the incarnate Jesus Christ, who—as the final Adam and *true human*—is the renewed and perfect image of God. Created and destined to be reflections of God, humans are called to imitate Christ, even as Jesus reflects his Father in Heaven. Mirroring Christ we become mirrors of God.

While the Bible affirms through *faith* that humans are made as mirrors, the natural sciences have discovered the "human mirror" as an *empirical* reality. "Human beings are the most imitative creatures on the planet,"[1] and the social neurosciences have revealed that the capacity to "mirror" the minds of others through mental simulation is a key dimension of what it means to be human. Investigating how mirror-

---

1. Wolfgang Prinz and Andrew Meltzoff, "An Introduction to the Imitative Mind and Brain," in *The Imitative Mind: Development, Evolution, and Brain Bases*, ed. Andrew Meltzoff and Wolfgang Prinz (Cambridge: Cambridge University Press, 2002) 1–18, at 1.

ing systems and simulation systems in the brain play a central role in the evolution and development of interrelationality, researchers have proposed that such systems are the neurological basis for many of the distinctive characteristics that make us human, such as the capacities for self-awareness, empathy, theory of mind, language, sophisticated tool use, imitation learning, culture, and even morality.

How, then, does the human capacity to simulate and mirror the minds of others relate to the biblical meaning of humans as the image and likeness of God (or *imago Dei*)? Is the image of God in human beings *essentially* our human neurological capacity to image, imitate, and/or simulate others' minds? Since our capacity for mirroring and mental simulation may serve as the biological basis of many other key characteristics that comprise human distinctiveness—such as interpersonal relatedness—some scientists and theologians have been compelled to make this connection.[2] Others, however, including myself, have contended that the *imago Dei* is a *functional* designation that is not concerned with the material origins of human beings or founded upon the possession of particular biological or behavioral capacities. This latter group of scholars have maintained that the *imago Dei* should not be equated with any of the presumably unique features that scientifically define what it means to be human.

While the first group approaches the imago Dei as a *substantive* question that can be settled through an empirical investigation of the basis of human uniqueness, the second group tends to treat scientific questions regarding human uniqueness as entirely distinct from the scriptural understandings of humans as the created beings who have been *functionally* designated as God's image and likeness. The substantive interpretation of the imago Dei sees the theological issue as one that can be ultimately resolved and decided through the findings of the natural sciences, while the functional interpretation sees the scientific search for human uniqueness as having little or no bearing on the scriptural question of the meaning of the imago Dei. A number of key unresolved issues remain at the interface of these two perspectives. The act of functionally designating humans as the imago Dei *presupposes* that there is such an entity that can be identified as a human being in the first place. In other words one needs substantively to know what a human *is* before one can talk about the *function* that humans are called to serve. Is the Hebrew term 'ādām in Gen 1:26 equivalent to the biological category *Homo sapiens*? If there is an unbroken evolutionary continuity between humans and other animals, how and where does one draw the line? Moreover, how do nonhuman hominins fit into the biblical picture?

---

2. See Malcolm Jeeves, "Neuroscience, Evolutionary Psychology, and the Image of God," *Perspectives on Science and Christian Faith* 57 (2005) 170–186; and Anne Runehov, "*Imago Dei* and *Simulatio* or *Imitatio Dei*: A Philosophical Essay on Empathy," *Theology and Science*, 10 (2012) 411–30.

In this article I would like to approach such questions by offering a *via media* that explores the oft-overlooked middle ground lying between the functional and substantive alternatives. Viewing the *imago Dei* as an act of God's historical election whereby the human lineage is functionally designated as priests of creation, I propose that the neurobiological capacities for mirroring and mental simulation—if and when such capacities are clearly shown to exist within humans—can be viewed as key substantive *preconditions* that are required for any beings who would be called and elected to fulfill the vocation of the imago Dei. In this way the capacity for mirroring and neuro-simulation would be *necessary* requirements for election as the imago Dei but not *sufficient* in and of themselves to establish their possessor *as* the imago Dei. It is God's election alone that establishes human beings as God's living reflections and imitators, but without certain *capacities* (such as the ability to mirror and/or simulate the minds of others) the calling of the imago Dei could not be fulfilled.

Made as Mental Mirrors

Among all known species of animals, human beings are the foremost as emulators, simulators, and imitators. "Mental simulation, both intrapersonal and interpersonal, is a robust phenomenon of the human mind."[3] One type of mental simulation is *mirroring*. Mirroring involves a type of *unmediated* neurological resonance where the perception of another person's emotional expression or motor activity *directly* (subconsciously) triggers the activation of the same neural substrate in the observer as in the person displaying the emotions or actions in question. Mirroring is the sharing of a given mental state by two individuals. While mirroring involves a full or complete mental simulation in the observer's brain of that which is being observed, many types of mental simulation involve only *partial* mirroring (or incomplete resonance). *Simulation theory* holds that through "a partial simulation of those states within the person doing the judging"[4] an observer is able to judge accurately the mental states of others. It is important to note that "simulation and mirroring are not equivalent; mirroring is just one species of simulation."[5]

---

3. Alvin I. Goldman, *Simulating Minds: The Philosophy, Psychology, and Neuroscience of Mindreading* (Oxford: Oxford University Press, 2006) 50.

4. Michael Spezio, "Narrative in Holistic Healing: Empathy, Sympathy, & Simulation Theory," in *Spiritual Transformation and Healing: Anthropological, Theological, Neuroscientific, and Clinical Perspectives*, edited by Joan D. Koss-Chioino and Philip Hefner (Lanham, MD: Rowman Altamira, 2006) 206–22, at 214.

5. Alvin I. Goldman, "Mirroring, Mindreading, and Simulation," in *Mirror Neuron System: The Role of Mirroring Processes in Social Cognition*, edited by J. A. Pineda (New York: Humana, 2009) 311–30, at 324. Nor is it the case that all instances of mental mirroring necessarily constitute mental

Key support for simulation theory comes from "evidence of broadly overlapping neural tissue involved in both the sensation and in the judgment of emotion."[6] Simulation theory has likewise gained significant empirical backing from the discovery of *mirror neurons* in macaque monkeys. Mirror neurons are "are a class of neuron that modulate their activity both when an individual executes a specific motor act and when they observe the same or similar act performed by another individual."[7] These neurons are activated in *both* the performance of specific actions *and* in the observation of the same types of actions by others, as if the neurons in the observer's brain are *mirroring* the neurons in the brain of the acting agent. A network of these neurons is called a mirror neuron system. Mirror neurons were first discovered when researchers noticed that certain neurons which fired in association with a particular action (such as grasping an object) also fired when a monkey passively observed a similar action performed by another agent (such as when it passively observed an object being grasped by the hand of the experimenter).[8] Mirror neurons would become active when the monkey would see an interaction between an agent and an object—and not just in response to an object without an agent interacting with it.[9] Researchers have identified many different types of mirroring systems including audiovisual, communicative, tool-responding, peripersonal, and extrapersonal mirroring systems.[10]

Soon after mirror neuron systems were discovered in macaque monkeys, researchers began to search for similar types of mirroring mechanisms in the human brain. Moreover, many scientists believed that mirroring mechanisms in the human brain would be much more extensive than those found in monkeys. Whether, and to what degree, mirror neurons exist in the human brain remains a matter of debate.[11]

---

simulation. "Mirroring does not necessarily constitute mental simulation as specified by the simulation theory of mindreading." Mitchell Herschbach, "Mirroring versus Simulation: On the Representational Function of Simulation," *Synthese* 189 (2012) 483–513, at 483.

6. Spezio, "Narrative in Holistic Healing," 215.

7. J. M. Kilner and R. N. Lemon, "What We Know Currently about Mirror Neurons," *Current Biology* 23.23 (December 2013) R1057–62, R1057.

8. G. di Pellegrino, et al., "Understanding motor events: a neurophysiological study," *Experimental Brain Research* 91 (1992) 176–80.

9. Giacomo Rizzolatti and Vittorio Gallese, "Mirror Neurons," *Encyclopedia of Cognitive Science* (New York: Nature, 2003) 41.

10. Christian Keysers, et al., "Audiovisual Mirror Neurons and Action Recognition," *Experimental Brain Research* 153 (2003) 628–36; P. F. Ferrari, S. Rozzi, and L. Fogassi, "Mirror Neuron Responding to Observation of Actions Made with Tools in Monkey Ventral Premotor Cortex," *Journal of Cognitive Neuroscience* 17 (2005) 212–26; V. Caggiano, et al., "Mirror Neurons Differentially Encode the Peripersonal and Extrapersonal Space of Monkeys," *Science* 324 (2009) 403–6.

11. For recent evidence see Roy Mukamel, et al., "Single-Neuron Responses in Humans during Execution and Observation of Actions," *Current Biology* 20 (2010) 750–6. For a critique of evidence for mirror neurons in humans see Gregory Hickok, *The Myth of Mirror Neurons: The Real Neuroscience of*

Evidence that mirror neuron systems exist in humans comes from electroencephalography, magnetoencephalography, transcranial magnetic stimulation, and brain imaging studies.[12] According to neuroscientists Giacomo Rizzolatti and Vittorio Gallese "these results indicate that when individuals observe an action, a replica of that action is automatically generated in their cortex, recruiting the same circuits that are active when the observed action is internally generated by the observer."[13] In addition to mirror neuron systems, which involve the mirroring of intentional actions, there also appear to be mirroring systems involving emotion where "seeing the emotions of others also recruits regions involved in experiencing similar emotions."[14] Recent evidence likewise points to mirroring systems involved in sensory processing. These findings "suggest mechanisms that encode seen touch in similar terms as felt touch, much as a mirror-neuron mechanism translates observed actions to potentially executed ones."[15]

Mirroring Systems and Action Understanding

If mirroring systems do exist in the human brain, it would go a long way towards helping researchers address a number of central questions in the scientific study of cognition. One area on which mirror neuron research has shed light is the question of how we can understand actions made by other individuals (known as "action understanding"). For instance, how do we know that a person sitting in front of us is eating an orange or writing with a pen? Giacomo Rizollatti and Corrado Sinigaglia have proposed that the direct matching processes of the mirror neuron systems in the observer leads to an immediate understanding of the actions of the actor.[16] Because the same neurons fire both when *doing* an action and when *observing* the same action performed by another person, the observer is "performing a

---

Communication and Cognition (New York: W.W. Norton, 2014).

12. Giacomo Rizzolatti, "The Mirror Neuron System and Imitation," in *Perspectives on Imitation: From Neuroscience to Social Science. Volume 1: Mechanisms of Imitation and Imitation in Animals*, ed. S. Hurley and N. Chater (Cambridge, MA: MIT, 2005) 55–76.

13. Rizzolatti and Gallese, "Mirror Neurons," 41.

14. Jojanneke Bastiaansen, Marc Thioux, and Christian Keysers, "Evidence for Mirror Systems in Emotions," *Philosophical Transactions of the Royal Society B: Biological Sciences* 364.1528 (2009) 2391–404, at 2391.

15. India Morrison, et. al., "Vicarious Responses to Social Touch in Posterior Insular Cortex Are Tuned to Pleasant Caressing Speeds," *Journal of Neuroscience* 31 (2011) 9554–62, at 9561.

16. Giacomo Rizzolatti and Corrado Sinigaglia, "The Functional Role of the Parieto-frontal Mirror Circuit: Interpretations and Misinterpretations," *Nature Reviews Neuroscience* 11 (April 2010) 264–74. For a critique of their proposal see Alina Steinhorst and Joachim Funke, "Mirror Neuron Activity Is No Proof for Action Understanding," *Frontiers in Human Neuroscience* 8 (2014) 1–4.

mental simulation of the agent's observed movements."[17] Whenever an individual observes an action, his or her understanding of that action is mediated by the same population of neurons that also control his or her own execution of that action. In this way the relevant action is effectively reenacted within the observer's own brain.[18] Through this simulation process, "the activity of mirror neurons is seen as enabling the observer to recognize the agent's action."[19] As Rizzolatti explains, "An action is understood when its observation causes the motor system of the observer to resonate."[20] The observer does not simply perceive an action or an emotion *passively*, but he or she *actively* internalizes representations of the physical and neural states associated with it. Thus, when an observer sees the hand of the person sitting next to her writing with a pen, "the same population of neurons that control the execution of grasping movements becomes active in the observer's motor areas. By this approach the motor knowledge of the observer is used to understand the observed action."[21] Rizzolatti and Sinigaglia argue that the action understanding mediated by the mirror neuron mechanism is *direct* in the sense that it can be achieved without needing "inferential processing" or other "high-level mental processes."[22] Through a type of "embodied cognition" the mirror matching mechanism gives the premotor cortex of the observer "the sensation of actually performing the actions in a first person perspective."[23]

In addition to providing a neurological mechanism for action understanding, the direct matching of neurons in the observer's brain with those in the acting agent's brain also provides a way for the passive observer to understand directly the *goals* and *intentions* of the acting agent. During social cognition, "mirror neurons cause the visual information we receive to be integrated into our own experiences so that we directly experience our observation as 'first-person' and not as 'third-person.'"[24] Encoding observed actions in terms of our own motor possibilities, mirroring systems in the brain "allow us to understand the actions of others 'from the inside.'"[25]

17. Pierre Jacob, "What Do Mirror Neurons Contribute to Human Social Cognition?" *Mind and Language* 23 (April 2008) 190–223, at 191.

18. Rizzolatti and Sinigaglia, "The Functional Role of the Parieto-frontal Mirror Circuit," 265.

19. Jacob, "What Do Mirror Neurons Contribute to Human Social Cognition?" 191.

20. Giacomo Rizzolatti, Leonardo Fogassi, and Vittorio Gallese, "Neurophysiological Mechanisms Underlying the Understanding and Imitation of Action," *Nature Reviews Neuroscience* 2 (September 2001) 661–70, at 661.

21. Ibid., 661.

22. Rizzolatti and Sinigaglia, "The Functional Role of the Parieto-frontal Mirror Circuit," 268.

23. Grace S. Ki, "Mirror Neuron System and Social Cognition: Understanding Others by Embodiment," *Western Undergraduate Psychology Journal* 1 (2013) article 15, 1–12, at 4.

24. Ibid., 15.

25. Corrado Sinigaglia and Giacomo Rizzolatti, "Through the Looking Glass: Self and Others,"

According to Sinigaglia and Rizzolatti, "What the mirror mechanism tells us is that the self and the others are so strictly intertwined that, at least at the basic level, they are intimately rooted in a common motor ground."[26] In this way mirror neuron systems directly bridge the gap between self and other to enable interpersonal understanding without employing higher-order reasoning.[27]

From the first moment after birth human beings imitate others in social interactions. Many researchers have argued that mirroring systems in the brain facilitate this initial human ability to embody rapidly the actions of others.[28] In infancy and early childhood the process of mirroring through imitation might likewise function as a foundation for communication and understanding others.[29] Psychologist Andrew Meltzoff has found that even newborns are capable of imitation and that prelinguistic children are able to understand others' minds and the intentions lying behind the goal-directed actions of others. By eighteen months, says Meltzoff, "Infants are already beginning to adopt an 'intentional stance' toward their fellow human beings. They make an important differentiation between the acts of humans and the movements of inanimate devices." For these prelinguistic infants, "human acts are not interpreted as mere movements in space, the transformations of an automaton with no deeper meaning. When they see an action they 'read beyond' what was literally done, and infer the goal or intention that lies behind it."[30] Meltzoff argues that both newborn infants and prelinguistic children cognitively map the similarities and differences between the self and the other through mirroring, simulation, and imitation of the other's goal-directed behavior.[31]

Mirroring Systems, Self-Awareness, and Mindreading

If mirroring systems are present in the human brain, this would also help to address a central research question in social cognition and philosophy of mind known as the

---

Consciousness and Cognition 20 (2011) 64–74.

26. Ibid., 69.

27. Ibid., 66: "The similarity between these two activations allows the observer to understand directly others' actions without the necessity of any inferential processing."

28. Andrew N. Meltzoff, "'Like Me': A Foundation for Social Cognition," *Developmental Science* 10 (2007) 126–34.

29. Andrew N. Meltzoff and Rebecca A. Williamson, "The Importance of Imitation for Theories of Social-Cognitive Development" in *The Wiley-Blackwell Handbook of Infant Development, Volume 1: Basic Research*, eds. J. Gavin Bremner and Theodore D. Wachs (Chichester, West Sussex: Wiley-Blackwell, 2010).

30. Andrew N. Meltzoff, "Born to Learn: What Infants Learn from Watching Us" in *The Role of Early Experience in Infant Development*, edited by Nathan Fox, Lewis Leavitt, and John Warhol (Skillman, NJ: Pediatric Institute, 1999) 7.

31. Ibid.

"problem of mindreading" or "theory of mind"—namely, what kinds of experience or reasoning allow us indirectly to know what is going on in the minds of people around us and what are the cognitive processes that enable people to understand each other? Meltzoff has argued that the intention reading that is present in prelinguistic infants "is an essential baby step toward the development of a theory of mind, the idea that other humans do not just behave but have internal thoughts, emotions, and desires."[32] Seeing actions in others that are also performed by the self (and vice versa) the infant employs mirroring systems to represent the other as "like me." In this way the newborn is not a "social isolate" but is provided with a mental bridge connecting self and other. From the beginning of infancy the mirroring or imitation of bodily movements is a mechanism for making a basic connection between self and other. Imitation provides an initial toehold in self-other mapping, but it also supplies a means for elaborating it. In this way the same cognitive mechanisms that enable infants to imitate allows them to recognize when the social other is imitating them.[33]

Neural mirroring is a particularly effortless and direct nonverbal kind of simulation where people understand others by putting themselves in their place and running their own mental states to generate similar experiences and behaviors.[34] Mirror neurons "provide a prereflective, automatic mechanism of mirroring what is going on in the brains of other people that seems more compatible with our ability to understand others effortlessly and with our tendency to imitate others automatically."[35] Performing a mental simulation of an agent's observed movements, the activity of mirror neurons and other types of mirroring systems in an observer's brain would enable the observer to recognize and understand the observed agent's action, to represent his or her intentions (or goals) to internalize observed emotions, and to embody observed sensations. Since the internal mental representation of an external agent's intentions and emotions is a central component of third-person mindreading, it would seem that the mirroring systems, whose fundamental function is to create such internal representations, would also provide a crucial foundation to such mindreading.[36] Because mirroring systems give us a window that allows us effort-

32. Ibid.
33. Ibid.
34. Goldman, *Simulating Minds*; and his "Mirroring, Mindreading, and Simulation."
35. Marco Iacoboni, "Imitation, Empathy, and Mirror Neurons," *Annual Review of Psychology* 60 (2009) 653–70, at 666.
36. Pierre Jacob, "What Do Mirror Neurons Contribute to Human Social Cognition?" 191. Though not the only component that is necessary—contrary to the suggestion of V. Gallese, C. Keysers, and R. Rizzolatti, ("A Unifying View of the Basis of Social Cognition," *Trends in Cognitive Sciences*, 8, [2004] 396–403) mirror neurons do not provide a novel, stand-alone alternative theory of mindreading but rather a useful supplement to simulation accounts. For a discussion see Paul Thagard, "I Feel Your

lessly to access, experience, and understand the actions, emotions, and sensations of others, neural mirroring would make intersubjectivity possible and thus provide a critical insight into solving the problem of other minds.[37]

Many researchers have suggested that in addition to providing an empirical foundation to the phenomenon of mindreading, mirroring systems might also be pivotally involved in how we form the distinction between our sense of *self* and our sense of *others*. Neural mechanisms for mirroring allow the sharing of mental states between individuals. Because the functional properties of mirror mechanisms lead to a direct neural matching between the observer and the actor, the attribution of "self" and "other" are mutually interrelated in this process. According to Sinigaglia and Rizzolatti this type of shared "motor representation of action is the prerequisite of the self (and other) attribution."[38] The shared representational network of mirroring systems gives humans an innate capacity to imitate the actions of others, and this ability to imitate others "holds the key to our understanding what it is for others to be like us and for us to be like them."[39] Some researchers have suggested that "self-awareness may result from mirror-like systems capable of creating an internal simulation of your own self from the point of view of others." Self-awareness emerges when the mirror mechanisms that originally evolved to help the observer adopt another's point of view are turned inward to facilitate an awareness of self.[40]

In the same way that that the mirroring mechanisms involved in infant imitation would provide a foundation for a theory of mind that understands that others are "like me," Andrew Meltzoff and Jean Decety suggest that these mechanisms may also underlie the development of empathy for others.[41] Empathy is an "analogical

---

Pain: Mirror Neurons, Empathy, and Moral Motivation," *Journal of Cognitive Science* 8 (2007) 109-36.

37. Marco Iacoboni says it "solves the problem of the other minds." See his "Imitation, Empathy, and Mirror Neurons," 653; See also his "The Problem of Other Minds Is Not a Problem: Mirror Neurons and Intersubjectivity," in *Mirror Neuron System: The Role of Mirroring Processes in Social Cognition*, ed. J.A. Pineda (Totowa, NJ: Humana, 2008). However, others say that it only provides a key piece of the puzzle. G. Rizzolatti and L. Fogassi suggest that we can grasp the minds of others through a combination of direct simulation using mirror neurons and conceptional reasoning. See their "Mirror Neurons and Social Cognition," in *The Oxford Handbook of Evolutionary Psychology*, edited by R. I. M. Dunbar and L. Barrett (Oxford: Oxford University Press, 2007) 179-195. See also R. Krznaric, *Empathy: A Handbook for Revolution* (London: Ebury, 2014) 21-22.

38. Sinigaglia and Rizzolatti, "Through the Looking Glass," 69.

39. Andrew N. Meltzoff and Jean Decety, "What Imitation Tells Us about Social Cognition: A Rapprochement between Developmental Psychology and Cognitive Neuroscience," *Philosophical Transactions of The Royal Society B Biological Sciences*; 358:1431 (March 29, 2003) 491-500.

40. Lindsay M. Oberman and V. S. Ramachandran, "Reflections on the Mirror Neuron System: Their Evolutionary Functions Beyond Motor Representation," in *Mirror Neuron Systems: The Role of Mirroring Processes in Social Cognition*, edited by J. A. Pineda (Totowa, NJ: Humana, 2008) 39-59, at 49.

41. Meltzoff and Decety, "What Imitation Tells Us about Social Cognition."

mapping between someone else's situation and your own."[42] It is the capacity to feel what someone else feels. Employing mirroring systems in the brain, "through imitation and mimicry, we are able to feel what other people feel. By being able to feel what other people feel, we are also able to respond compassionately to other people's emotional states."[43] According to Frans DeWaal, "Perception of the emotional state of another automatically activates shared representations causing a matching emotional state in the observer. With increasing cognition, state-matching evolved into more complex forms, including concern for the other and perspective-taking. Empathy-induced altruism derives its strength from the emotional stake it offers the self in the other's welfare."[44]

Research on mirror neurons, emotional mirroring, imitation, and empathy suggests that rather than being the outcome of higher level cognitive processes involving introspection, our ability to empathize "has been built 'bottom up' from relatively simple mechanisms of action production and perception."[45] In contrast to the popular notion that our biology is essentially expressed in self-serving individualism, the recent work on the relationships between mirroring systems, imitation, and empathy suggests "that the evolutionary process made us wired for empathy."[46]

Mirroring Systems and Morality

The empathic ability to imagine oneself in someone else's situation and place oneself in their emotional state is crucial for understanding other people and for making moral decisions about them. Our ability to empathize is thus "a building block of our sociality and morality."[47] By allowing two or more persons to directly share the same mental and emotional state without employing verbal communication, mirroring systems in the brain provide a mechanism which allows for an instantaneous and immediate form of empathy. According to Meltzoff the developmental progression from mirroring to empathy starts with "seeing a person as someone who behaves as

---

42. Paul Thagard, *The Brain and the Meaning of Life* (Princeton: Princeton University Press, 2012) 190.

43. Iacoboni, "Imitation, Empathy, and Mirror Neurons," 659; for an in depth discussion see Jean Decety, *The Social Neuroscience of Empathy* (Cambridge, MA: MIT, 2011).

44. Frans B. M. DeWaal, "Putting the Altruism Back into Altruism: The Evolution of Empathy," *Annual Review of Psychology* 59 (2008) 279–300; DeWaal says "Evidence is accumulating that this mechanism is phylogenetically ancient, probably as old as mammals and birds," 279.

45. Iacoboni, "Imitation, Empathy, and Mirror Neurons," 667.

46. Marco Iacoboni, "Imitation, Empathy, and Mirror Neurons," 666. For a discussion of the role of early learning experiences, culture, and socialization in the development of empathy, see Claus Lamm, et al. "The Role of Shared Neural Activations, Mirror Neurons, and Morality in Empathy—A Critical Comment," *Neuroscience Research* 90 (2015) 15–24.

47. Marco Iacoboni, "Imitation, Empathy, and Mirror Neurons," 667.

they do," progresses "to seeing a person as someone who shares deeper equivalences (such as goals, desires, and intentions)—and further along the developmental pathway—as someone deserving empathy and moral rights equivalent to one's own."[48]

Recent research in the foundations of moral psychology has highlighted the central role of emotional processing in moral judgment.[49] This research has shown that "we judge actions to be right or wrong, and the people who carry them out to be good or bad, based on emotion, inference, automatic and reflective processing, and a host of processes that have evolved to subserve reciprocity, fairness, loyalty, respect, and other behavioral dispositions."[50] Mirroring systems in the brain provide a fundamental motivation to not harm others by virtue of their giving us a direct understanding of what it is for another to be harmed. Because of mirroring systems "people not only observe the pain and disgust of others, they experience their own versions of that pain and disgust, as shown by the mirroring activity in cortical regions such as the insula and anterior cingulate."[51]

If mirroring mechanisms underlie morality, cognitively normal developing children do not need to reason abstractly about why harm is bad for other people or to be taught or indoctrinated with abstract moral rules because they can actually *feel* that harm is bad.[52] According to cognitive neuroscientist Jeffrey Zacks, "Witnessing a violent event is intrinsically aversive. . . . When you see someone get hurt . . . you are also experiencing a 'virtual' pain response as your brain mirrors the person in pain."[53] One of the things that stops persons from acting on their violent impulses is that when they start to do so, they experience this aversive response. However, if seeing people getting hurt becomes a regular and habitual part of one's existence, these aversive responses get dampened down and one's emotional aversion to violence gets desensitized. Exposure to violence (whether dramatized or real) desensitizes our emotional response to violence, makes us less compassionate, and makes us more aggressive. Through the influence of culture children can become desensitized and override their natural aversion to pain in others. When the empathic mirroring response is dampened down, a major force for moral motivation is gone.

48. Meltzoff, "Born to Learn," 9.

49. Jonathan Haidt, "The Emotional Dog and its Rational Tail: A Social Intuitionist Approach to Moral Judgment," *Psychological Review* 108 (2001) 814–34.

50. R. Adolphs, "The Social Brain: Neural Basis of Social Knowledge," *Annual Review of Psychology* 60 (2009) 693–716, at 698.

51. Thagard, *The Brain and the Meaning of Life*, 193.

52. According to Thagard there is evidence "that psychopaths' deficits in emotional learning, attributed to disrupted functioning of the amygdala, are partly due to mirror neuron malfunctioning." Thagard, *The Brain and the Meaning of Life*, 194. See also James Blair, Derek Mitchell, and Karina Blair, *The Psychopath: Emotion and the Brain* (Blackwell, 2005).

53. Jeffrey Zacks, *Flicker: Your Brain on Movies* (Oxford University Press, 2014) 119–20.

Owing to the activity of neural mirroring systems, the capacity to feel the pain of others and thus to seek to avoid harming others is biologically part of what it means to be human. Many cognitive and social additions in the form of moral rules and expectations can be built on top of the foundation provided by mirroring, but without mirroring morality becomes a disembodied exercise in philosophical or theological abstraction.[54]

Mirroring Systems and Language

The use of symbolic language has long been put forth as a key distinguishing characteristic of humans, and many have even argued that "the faculty of language is unique to the human species."[55] Research on mirroring systems in the brain has offered insights on how language may have first evolved in humans. Investigators of mirror neurons have argued that the premotor mirror neuron system in humans is located in close proximity to speech production regions, thus "suggesting a role for mirror neurons in language and specifically speech perception."[56] Giacomo Rizzolatti and Michael Arbib have hypothesized that mirror neurons may have facilitated the emergence of language in the human brain by providing the neurophysiological basis from which language developed as an extension of gestural communication.[57] The suggested link between mirror neuron systems and the evolution of language received important empirical backing when researchers discovered that mirror neurons can also work with auditory-motor representations. In 2002 the research team of Evelyne Kohler "found neurons in [the] monkey premotor cortex that discharge when the animal performs a specific action and when it hears the related sound."[58] In 2003 a series of neuromagnetic and neuroimaging studies provided empirical support to the hypothesis that the mirror neuron system is involved in speech perception.[59] More recently, "FMRI studies have also shown specific activation of speech

---

54. Philippe Rochat and Claudia Passos-Ferreira argue that imitation and mirroring processes are necessary but not sufficient conditions for children to develop human sociality. See their "From Imitation to Reciprocation and Mutual Recognition," in *Mirror Neuron Systems: The Role of Mirroring Processes in Social Cognition*, edited by Jaime A. Pineda (Totowa, NJ: Humana, 2008) 191–212.

55. Mohinish Shukla, "Language from a Biological Perspective," *Journal of Biosciences* 30 (2005) 119.

56. Oberman and Ramachandran, "Reflections on the Mirror Neuron System," 45.

57. Giacomo Rizzolatti, and M. A. Arbib, "Language within Our Grasp," *Trends in Neurosciences* 21(1998) 188–194; M. A. Arbib, "From Monkey-like Action Recognition to Human Language: An Evolutionary Framework for Neurolinguistics," *Behavioral Brain Sciences*, 28 (2005) 105–67; M. A. Arbib "From Grasp to Language: Embodied Concepts and the Challenge of Abstraction" *Journal of Physiology-Paris* 102 (2008) 4–20.

58. Cited in Thagard, *The Brain and the Meaning of Life*, 189.

59. K. E. Watkins, A. P. Strafella, and T. Paus, "Seeing and Hearing Speech Excites the Motor

production areas during the listening of speech sounds."[60] This evidence demonstrating mirror neuron responses to auditory stimuli strongly suggests that mirror neurons may be important neural elements in language evolution.[61]

Mirroring Systems and Human Uniqueness

The presumed human capacity to mirror has been held up by neuroscientists as a key component of what it means to be distinctively human. Prominent neuroscientist V. S. Ramachandran writes that human beings are "something unique, something unprecedented, something transcendent. We are something truly new under the sun, with uncharted and perhaps limitless potential."[62] Michael Gazzaniga, a key founder of the field of cognitive neuroscience, agrees and says "that something like a phase shift has occurred in becoming human."[63] Ramachandran asks, "How can we account for all of those mysterious faculties that are so quintessentially human, such as art, language, metaphor, creativity, self-awareness, and even religious sensibilities?"[64] His answer is that all of these defining human capacities have mirror neurons and mirroring systems in the brain as their essential biological foundation. Mirroring systems, explains Gazzaniga, may be the key to understanding "how new abilities, exclusively human in nature, arose during cortical evolution."[65]

Mirroring Systems and the Imago Dei as a Unique Capacity for Personal Relatedness

In Gen 1:26–27 we read that humans were created as the image and likeness of God. The Bible affirms that at the deep core of human nature is our capacity to reflect or mirror. Human beings are *created as* reflections of God and their intended destiny (or telos) is *to become* reflections of God. Many contemporary theologians understand the *imago Dei* in *interrelational* terms which mirror the Christian conception

---

System Involved in Speech Production," *Neuropsychologia* 41 (2003) 989–94. For a general discussion of the significance of this evidence see Oberman and Ramachandran, "Reflections on the Mirror Neuron System."

60. Stephen Wilson, et al., "Listening to Speech Activates Motor Areas Involved in Speech Production," *Nature Neuroscience* 7 (July 2004) 701–2.

61. See Iacoboni, "Imitation, Empathy, and Mirror Neurons."

62. V. S. Ramachandran, *The Tell-Tale Brain: A Neuroscientist's Quest for What Makes Us Human* (W. W. Norton, 2011) 16.

63. Michael Gazzaniga, *Human: The Science Behind What Makes Us Unique*, (New York: HarperCollins, 2008) 3.

64. Ramachandran, *Tell-Tale Brain*; R. Adolphs says, "Human social cognition is special." Adolphs, "The Social Brain," 697.

65. Gazzaniga, *Human*, 32.

of God's own Trinitarian interrelationality.[66] In the modern era Karl Barth was foremost in realizing the importance of the Christian confession that God is a Trinitarian being who is fundamentality characterized by interpersonal mutuality and love.[67] Barth rejects any substantive understanding which locates the image of God within an anthropological "description of the being of man, its structure, disposition, capacities, etc."[68] It is a mistake, argues Barth, to look for the image of God among the capacities and characteristics of solitary individual human beings. Turning from anthropology to Scripture as his source, Barth points to Gen 1:27 as the text which most clearly describes the nature of the *imago Dei*: "So God created man in his own image, in the image of God he created him; male and female he created them."[69] Reflecting upon the meaning of this verse Barth explains, "Could anything be more obvious than to conclude from this clear indication that the image and likeness of the being created by God signifies existence in confrontation, i.e., in this confrontation, and conjunction of man and man which is that of male and female?"[70] In the confrontational I and Thou relationship of man and woman described in Gen 2:7, Barth discerns a mirror unto God's own Trinitarian nature.[71] For Barth, then, the image of God consists first and foremost not within the human *capacity* for relationship but in the *very relationship* of the Divine-human encounter.[72]

The human relationship to God is the primary meaning of the *imago Dei*. From the Genesis passage, says Barth, we can detect a second meaning as well—that in the relationship between man and woman we discover "a copy of the relationship within the triune God, which then serves as a prototype for all human-human relationships."[73] For Barth the image of God is not anything humans *are* or anything humans *do*, but rather it is a type of relationship—our relationship with God and our relationship with our neighbors.

---

66. Claus Westermann is one prominent biblical scholar who argues for a relational understanding. See Claus Westermann, *Genesis 1–11: A Continental Commentary*, translated by John J. Scullion (Minneapolis: Augsburg, 1984) 153.

67. While it was Dietrich Bonhoeffer who introduced this understanding of the *analogia relationis* between humans and God, Karl Barth must be credited with popularizing the concept. See Stanley J. Grenz, *The Social God and the Relational Self: A Trinitarian Theology of the Imago Dei* (Louisville: Westminster John Knox, 2001) 295–97.

68. Karl Barth, *Church Dogmatics* III/1, The Doctrine of Creation, translated by H. Knight, et al. (Edinburgh: T & T Clark, 1958) 195.

69. Ibid.

70. Ibid.

71. Karl Barth, *Church Dogmatics*, III/2, The Doctrine of Creation, Part II, translated by H. Knight, et al. (Edinburgh: T & T Clark, 1960) 185.

72. Ibid., 203.

73. Noreen L. Herzfeld, *In Our Image: Artificial Intelligence and the Human Spirit* (Minneapolis: Fortress, 2002) 26.

Spearheaded by Barth, the "relational model of the *imago Dei* became the dominant approach among systematic theologians in the mid to late twentieth century."[74] The relational understanding of the *imago Dei* has been taken up and developed by scholars from a variety of theological traditions—including Dietrich Bonhoeffer, Wolfhart Pannenberg, Emil Brunner, Karl Rahner, Jürgen Moltmann, Gerrit Berkhouwer, Hans Küng, Robert Jensen, Colin Gunton, John Zizioulas, Miroslav Volf, and many others. These theologians all agree that "to be a *person* is to be made in the image of God . . . it is in our relatedness to others that our being human consists."[75]

While none of the theologians cited above would speak of this human-divine relationship in *biological* terms, others have pointed out that the human capacity for relationship is fundamentally grounded within our human biology. Recognizing that "the contemporary focus of theological thinking is to see the *imago Dei* as evidenced in our capacity for relatedness," psychologist Malcolm Jeeves points out that "the capacity for relatedness is not some capacity free-floating above the head or out there in space."[76] Jeeves explains that "the evidence from neuroscience and evolutionary psychology both point to the beginnings of an understanding of the neural substrates required to be functioning normally for the possession of a full capacity for personal interrelatedness."[77] In a similar way systematic theologian Wentzel van Huyssteen recognizes that the interrelational human person is "a being that has emerged biologically as a center of embodied self-awareness, identity, and moral responsibility."[78] If theologians are to take science "seriously on the issue of human uniqueness" and human interrelatedness, says van Huyssteen, then our notion of the *imago Dei* needs to be "strikingly revisioned as emerging from nature itself."[79] Jeeves specifically highlights the role that mirroring systems play in human interrelationality. For Jeeves "the mirror neuron story makes it clear that our capacity for personal relatedness to a degree depends upon the intactness of our neural substrates."[80] If the capacity for interpersonal relatedness "is to be seen as the key to

---

74. Ibid., 29.

75. Colin Gunton, *The Promise of Trinitarian Theology* (London: T. & T. Clark, 2003) 113.

76. Malcolm Jeeves, "Brains, Minds, Souls, and People: A Scientific Perspective on Complex Human Personhood," *The Depth of the Human Person: A Multidisciplinary Approach*, edited by in Michael Welker (Grand Rapids: Eerdmans, 2014) 93–108, at 106.

77. Jeeves, "Neuroscience, Evolutionary Psychology, and the Image of God," 181.

78. J. Wentzel van Huyssteen, *Alone In the World? Human Uniqueness in Science and Theology* (Grand Rapids: Eerdmans, 2006) 215.

79. J. Wentzel van Huyssteen, "Human Origins and Religious Awareness," *Studia Theologica Nordic Journal of Theology* 59 (2005) 104-28, at 124; Van Huyssteen, *Alone in the World*, xviii.

80. Jeeves, "Neuroscience, Evolutionary Psychology, and the Image of God," 181.

understanding the *imago Dei*" then, says Jeeves, this capacity is an embodied reality that emerges as a function of mirror neurons and other mirroring systems.[81]

The Imago Dei as an Elected Reflection of God

A decade ago I proposed that the *imago Dei* is the functional designation of *election*, as opposed to being a substance-based distinction which is based on the possession of certain biological and behavioral capacities. I suggested:

> As Abraham was chosen by God from among the nations, so humans are chosen by God from among the multiplicity of life-forms to serve as priests of the cosmic temple, and to represent God's purposes and will to their fellow organic co-heirs of God's kingdom. Humans are the image of God, not by biological nature or right, but through *election* from among the animals by divine grace. As human animals by form and nature, we are biological priests by vocation, and as such are called and anointed to be agents in the renewal of God's whole creation—from Adam to Noah, and from Abraham to Christ."[82]

A number of scriptural and scientific considerations have led me to continue to make this case.[83] The first is that a close examination of the "image and likeness of God" passages in Scripture reveals that the *imago Dei* is never defined according to one characteristic or a specific collection of qualities that set humans apart from other creatures.[84] In the Bible the "image and likeness of God" is never said to be

---

81. Ibid., 181; See also Runehov, "*Imago Dei* and *Simulatio* or *Imitatio Dei*."

82. Joshua Moritz, "Natures, Human Nature, Genes and Souls," *Dialog* 46 (2007) 263–80. As I have been continuing to make this case, I was recently encouraged to see that John Walton and N. T. Wright have independently come to similar conclusions. Walton says, "As with Abram, who was given a significant role as the ancestor of Israel (though not the first ancestor of Israel) Adam and Eve would be viewed as established as significant by their election. This would be true whether or not other people were around. Their election is to a priestly role, the first to be placed in sacred space." See his *The Lost World of Adam and Eve: Genesis 2–3 and the Human Origins Debate* (Downers Grove, IL: IVP Academic, 2015) 112. In the same volume Wright has an article entitled "Including an Excursus on Paul's Use of Adam," 169–180 and at 177 says, "And it leads me to my proposal: that just as God chose Israel from the rest of humankind for a special, strange, demanding vocation, so perhaps what Genesis is telling us is that *God chose one pair from the rest of early hominids for a special, strange, demanding vocation.*"

83. For a more in depth discussion see Joshua M. Moritz, *Human Uniqueness and the Image of God: Bridging Evolutionary Biology and Theological Anthropology through Biblical Election* (Kitchener, ON: Pandora, forthcoming 2017); Joshua M. Moritz "Evolutionary Biology and Theological Anthropology," in *The Routledge Companion to Theological Anthropology,* eds. Charles Taliaferro and Joshua Farris (Aldershot: Ashgate, 2015); 65–96; Joshua M. Moritz, "Human Uniqueness, The Other Hominids, and 'Anthropocentrism of the Gaps' in the Religion and Science Dialogue," *Zygon* (2012) 307–39; Joshua M. Moritz "Evolution, the End of Human Uniqueness, and the Election of the *Imago Dei*," *Theology and Science* (2011); and "Animals and the Image of God in the Bible and Beyond," *Dialog* (Summer 2009) 134–46.

84. For example Hebrew scholar Phyllis Bird points out that the scriptural context of the phrase

about exceptional capacities or traits that humans alone have which *automatically qualify them* (and disqualify other creatures) for inclusion in the *imago Dei* category. Assertions of human uniqueness based on certain characteristics and "claims for a 'special creation' of humanity in comparison with animals and the material world conflict with the strong assertion in Gen 2 that, physically (organically) Adam does not differ from the 'beasts of the field.'"[85] As Old Testament scholar Iain Provan points out, the scriptural "emphasis lies on the commonality that exists between the humans and the rest of the animal creation."[86] The theological language of anthropology in Gen 1 and 2 "underscores Adam's linkage with the animal creation, not his difference from it."[87]

There is no reason, explains Hebrew scholar James Barr, to believe that the author of Gen 1 "had in his mind any definite idea about the content or location of the image of God."[88] The terms "'image' and 'likeness' . . . make no statements about the *nature* of human beings."[89] When we read of "the creation of human beings in God's image (Gen 1:26) . . . the biblical narrative remains silent . . . about *any qualities* of human nature that might account for their special standing."[90] Nor does the Bible ever equate the image of God in humans with an immaterial soul that *Homo sapiens* possess and other creatures do not.[91] Scripture, when read in the original languages, clearly describes both humans and animals as possessing "the breath of life" and refers to both equally as "souls." In this way the Bible makes no substantial distinctions between humans and nonhuman animals. If we are to understand properly the

---

"image and likeness of God" makes it plain that "its theological significance is in the place it gives to humans within the created order, not in any physical or moral attribute of the species, in either its present or 'original' state." Phyllis A. Bird, "Theological Anthropology in the Hebrew Bible," in *The Blackwell Companion to the Hebrew Bible*, edited by Leo G. Perdue (Malden, MA: Blackwell, 2001) 258–75, at 262.

85. Lawson G. Stone, "The Soul: Possession, Part, or Person? The Genesis of Human Nature in Genesis 2:7" in *What About the Soul? Neuroscience and Christian Anthropology*, edited by Joel B. Green (Nashville: Abingdon, 2004) 47–61, at 50.

86. Iain Provan, "The Land Is Mine and You Are Only Tenants (Leviticus 25:23): Earth-keeping and People-keeping in the Old Testament," *Crux* 42 (2006) 3–16, at 5.

87. Stone, "The Soul," 57.

88. James Barr, "The Image of God in the Book of Genesis: A Study of Terminology," *Bulletin of the John Rylands Library* 51 (1968–69) 11–26, at 13.

89. Horst Dietrich Preuss, *Old Testament Theology*, vol 2, translated by Leo G. Perdue (Edinburgh: T & T Clark, 1996) 115

90. Kathryn Tanner, "The Difference Theological Anthropology Makes," *Theology Today* 50 (1994) 567–80, at 573.

91. For example, Gordon Wenham explains that in Gen 2:7, which describes the human being as a *nephesh*, "It is not man's possession of the 'breath of life' or his status as a 'living creature' that differentiates him from the animals—animals are described in exactly the same terms." Gordon Wenham, *Genesis 1–15; Word Biblical Commentary* (Waco: Word, 1987) 61.

meaning of the *imago Dei* texts, says Claus Westermann, we must confidently resist "the tendency to see the image and likeness of God as a something, a quality."[92]

The second consideration that led me to first propose the *imago Dei* as election is that it has proven extremely difficult to establish or explicate human uniqueness in any scientifically meaningful or consistent way. For instance, many modern accounts of human uniqueness center on claims regarding the distinctiveness of the human brain in comparison with that of other animals. However, the human brain in general is not anatomically unique,[93] humans do not have the largest brain in absolute terms,[94] humans do not have the largest brain relative to body size,[95] and humans do not have the largest cerebral cortex or prefrontal cortex.[96] While it is often claimed that human beings uniquely possess certain speech centers in the brain, according to behavioral physiologist and developmental neurobiologist Gerhard Roth, "It is to date unclear whether these speech centers are true evolutionary novelties. All mammals studied so far have a center for intraspecific communication within the temporal lobe (mostly left side) which may be homologous to the Wernicke center for semantics." Moreover, says Roth, studies in animals have shown that "destruction of these areas leads to deficits in intraspecific vocal communication."[97]

Neither are neural mirroring systems unique to humans (if they exist within the human brain at all). Sinigaglia explains that "the mirror mechanism is present in many cortical areas and brain centers of birds, monkeys, and humans."[98] Recent studies have shown "that nonhuman primates can actually reason about other minds, even to the extent of using the intentional structure of behavior to distinguish identical actions," and this evidence is consistent with "a 'predictive' rather than 'imita-

---

92. Claus Westermann, *Creation*, trans. John H. Scullion (Philadelphia: Fortress, 1974) 57–58.

93. Gerhard Roth, "All tetrapod vertebrates (amphibians, reptiles, birds, mammals) have brains that—despite enormous differences in outer appearance, overall size and relative size of major parts of the brain—are very similar in their general organization and even in many details." Gerhard Roth, "Is the Human Brain Unique?" in *Mirror Neurons and the Evolution of Brain and Language*, edited by Maksim Stamenov and Vittorio Gallese (Amsterdam: John Benjamins, 2002) 63–76, at 63.

94. Roth says, "The largest mammalian brains (and of all animals) are found in elephants (up to 5.7 kg) and whales (up to 10 kg)." Roth, "Is the Human Brain Unique?" 65.

95. Roth explains, "While the human brain occupies about 2 percent of bodymass, in very small rodents relative brain size goes up to 10 percent. . . . Humans have a much larger brain than expected among primates, but even in this respect their brain is by no means unique, as the example of dolphins shows." Roth, "Is the Human Brain Unique?" 69.

96. Roth says, "Assuming that the number of cortical neurons is 2/3 the value found in primates, elephants should have at least as many cortical neurons and cortical synapses as humans." On the same page he adds, "Cetaceans as well as elephants have prefrontal cortices which are much larger in absolute terms than the human PFC, but what they do with this massive "highest" brain center, remains a mystery so far." Roth, "Is the Human Brain Unique?" 71.

97. Ibid., 73.

98. C. Sinigaglia, "Through the Looking Glass," 67.

tive' function for mirror neurons" in these animals.[99] Mirror-like neurons in birds "are involved in song learning," and it has been shown that these neurons "respond to particular songs both when the bird sings them and when it hears them." In these birds the function of mirroring systems "reflects a general mechanism by which songbirds learn vocal communication."[100] Mirroring systems also undergird imitation in nonhuman primates, birds, and dolphins.[101] Thus, says UCLA neuroscientist Marco Iacoboni, "Imitative behavior appears to be the product of *convergent evolution*," rather than a behavior that is unique to mirroring systems in human beings.[102] In light of such evidence, Roth concludes, "We have not yet found anything in brain anatomy that would explain the factual or alleged uniqueness of the human brain and of humans regarding cognition and consciousness."[103]

Another problem with the quest for a normative definition of humanity by which we may demarcate human uniqueness concerns the question Who among currently living humans will be excluded by this classification? Can we really speak of biological traits, such as fully functioning mirror neurons, or behavioral capacities, such as complex language, that all human beings share without exception? Many human beings, such as those with Rett Syndrome or severe autism, do not have the capacity for speech or even the genetic potential. Some recent theories propose that one of the causes of autism is a malfunction of the mirror neuron matching system.[104] If human nature and uniqueness are defined by key characteristics such as possession of fully functioning mirror neurons, language, and higher-order rationality, then are individuals who lack advanced metacognition (due to autism) or those who lack a developed capacity for language (due to Rett syndrome) considered fully human? Developmental psychologist Justin Barrett has recently suggested that one gender may on average have a more advanced degree of metacognition than the other. If further research establishes this claim, does that mean that the other gender

---

99. Jaime A. Pineda, "Preface," *Mirror Neuron Systems: The Role of Mirroring Processes in Social Cognition* (New York: Humana, 2009) v–viii, at vi.

100. Leonie Welberg, "Mirror Neurons: Singing in the Brain," *Nature Reviews Neuroscience* 9 (2008) 163.

101. C. K. Akins, E. D. Klein, T. R. Zentall, "Imitative Learning in Japanese Quail (*Coturnix japonica*) Using the Bidirectional Control Procedure," *Animal Learning and Behavior* 30 (2002) 275–81; L. M. Herman, "Body and Self in Dolphins," *Consciousness and Cognition* 21 (2012) 526–45.

102. Marco Iacoboni, "Imitation, Empathy, and Mirror Neurons," *Annual Review of Psychology* 60 (2009) 653–70, at 656 (emphasis mine).

103. Roth, "Is the Human Brain Unique?" 71–72.

104. Raphael Bernier and Geraldine Dawson, "The Role of Mirror Neuron Dysfunction in Autism," in *Mirror Neuron Systems: The Role of Mirroring Processes in Social Cognition*, edited by J. A. Pineda (New York: Humana, 2009) 261–86.

is less than fully human?[105] Should children be considered less human than adults since children possess certain capacities to a lesser degree? Scientifically speaking, Marc Ereshefsky concludes, "There is no essential feature that all and only humans must have to be part of *Homo sapiens*. Humans are not *essentially* rational beings or social animals or ethical agents. An organism can be born without any of these features and still be a human. From a biological perspective, being part of the lineage *Homo sapiens* is both necessary and sufficient for being a human."[106]

In light of these scriptural and scientific considerations I have advocated viewing the "image and likeness of God" as God's historical *choosing* or *election* of human beings *from among the animals* and setting them apart for the sake and fulfillment of God's purposes.[107] When perceived in light of the original linguistic, historical, and cultural context of the Hebrew theological framework of *historical* (or *biblical*) *election*, the image and likeness of God in humans is not recognized by reference to any mirror neurons, skills, behaviors, or souls that *Homo sapiens* might possess in distinction from animals or other nonhuman creatures. Rather, the *imago Dei* emerges as a designation given through the *free historical action of God* in God's own choosing of *Homo sapiens* and his calling them out from among the multiplicity of life-forms that God also created "from the dust" to serve as his representatives to creation and to uphold his justice and orient the creation towards fellowship with him.

The early Jewish and early Christian concepts of *historical* or *biblical election*, through which I have suggested that one view the *imago Dei*, is to be clearly distinguished from the *classical theological concept of election,* which was developed by Augustine and various Protestant Reformers as a way to understand the *eschatological* destiny of *individual* human beings in light of a *timeless* act of God's "unconditional election." Unlike the classical theological understanding of election, *biblical* or *historical election* is always conceived as "a concrete *historical* act on God's part that forms the starting point and basis of the salvation history of God with his *people*."[108] Election in the biblical understanding relates to *a whole people* (and often a person who is the beginning of a *lineage*) whom God has chosen *in the midst of history* for a special *purpose* within the wider context of God's design. This purpose of his-

---

105. Justin Barrett, "The Evolution of Religious Brains," Lecture, The Faraday Institute for Science and Religion, Cambridge (4 July 2009). Others have made similar claims with regard to gender differences in rationality and empathy. See Simon Baron-Cohen, *The Essential Difference: Male and Female Brains and the Truth about Autism* (New York: Basic, 2004).

106. Marc Ereshefsky, "Species," in *The Stanford Encyclopedia of Philosophy*, edited by Edward N. Zalta (2010) http://plato.stanford.edu/entries/species/.

107. Joshua M. Moritz, "Evolution, the End of Human Uniqueness."

108. Wolfhart Pannenberg, *Systematic Theology*, vol. 3, translated by Geoffrey Bromiley (Grand Rapids: Eerdmans, 1998) 442.

torical election is furthermore defined *not* in terms of *privilege* (or even individual salvation) but rather for the sake of *service*. For example, the elected Israelite king and his lineage are called to be "the guardians of the humble and the needy, the weak and the helpless" and the mission of the divinely elected king is to establish righteousness and justice throughout the land.[109] Thus, in exercising dominion the king and his line of successors are to "watch carefully over the rights of his subjects, and so ensure, in particular, that the weaker members of society may enjoy his protection and thus have justice done to them according to their need."[110]

In the Hebrew Scriptures the service of the chosen or elect ones is rendered through their *obedience* to God's commandment. By obeying God's commandments, the elected live in community or fellowship with both God and their neighbor. Likewise, the mission of the elected is to represent God to "the many" in terms of God's sacredness, authority, and dominion. For instance, with regard to Abraham, "the many" are "all the families of the earth" (Gen 12:3) who will be blessed through his election; for Israel, "the many" are the gentile nations to whom Israel—as God's elect—is to bear God's light and justice. Chosenness in this way serves a larger purpose in that "the chosen people does not withdraw from the human family, but exercises a special office within it, an office defined by the particular character and will of their universal God."[111]

Within this ancient Jewish context the non-elect are to be blessed in and through their relationship with the elect. In this way, explains Hebrew scholar Joel Kaminsky, "The concept of election was never assumed to be only for the benefit of the elect, but it was always about God's plan for the whole world, the elect and the non-elect alike."[112] Rather than election being a matter of *exclusivism* and *particularity*, then—as in the classical view—the historical concept of election has an *inclusive* and *universalistic* tendency. In fact, with regard to election "*the horizon of particularism is universal.*"[113] One clearly sees this universalistic trend in the election traditions of Noah, Abraham, and Israel. Here "the particularism of the love of God for the elected one is to be related to the more comprehensive horizon of God's love for all."[114] In this way the chosen one "is assigned a function for that wider context.

---

109. Aubrey R. Johnson, *Sacral Kingship in Ancient Israel* (Eugene, OR: Wipf & Stock, 2006; originally published by University of Wales Press, 1955) 10.

110. Ibid., 7; see Ps 72:12–14.

111. Jon D. Levenson, "The Universal Horizon of Biblical Particularism" in *Ethnicity and the Bible*, ed. Mark G. Brett (Leiden: Brill, 2002) 143–70, at 155.

112. Joel S. Kaminsky, *Yet I Loved Jacob: Reclaiming the Concept of Biblical Election* (Nashville: Abingdon, 2007) 25–26.

113. Levenson, "The Universal Horizon of Biblical Particularism," 155.

114. Ibid.

He is elected in order to serve as God's agent in relation to a more comprehensive object of God's love."[115] To this end the prophet Isaiah speaks of the people of Israel as elected "to act as God's servant among the nations to the effect that 'he will bring forth justice to the nations' (Isa 42:1)."[116] The aim of the election of Israel was that it should live out and "proclaim the righteous will of God to the nations. On this view the election of Israel is not an end in itself. It serves the will of God *on behalf of* the human race as a whole."[117]

The historical concept of election, as the central interpretive framework in biblical Hebrew thought, illuminates the meaning of how humans are designated and created as the image and likeness of God. As is well known, the concept of the "image" as used in Genesis "has a deep ancient Near Eastern background."[118] Beyond this, each of the structural elements describing historical election within the Hebrew textual tradition—including divine *blessing*, the *multiplication of progeny*, the giving of *commandments* and the promise of the *land*—are also present in the early chapters of Genesis as they describe the first humans who are created as the image and likeness of God (Gen 1:28 and Gen 2:15–16). Structurally the election narratives of Abraham and Israel link their calling and vocation to that of Adam. In his election, "Abraham is to restore what Adam has done" and thus reaffirm the true meaning and purpose of humanity.[119] As Abraham and Sarah together with their future lineage are elected by God to be a *nation* (ethnicity or race) of priests and a light to the other *nations* (ethnicities or races) so Adam and Eve and their lineage are chosen and called to be a race (or species) of priests to the *nonhuman creatures*. In this very *calling* to the vocation of *Homo sanctus* ("humans as priests set apart") the human species was simultaneously *created* and *designated* as the image of God. "In the day when God *created* humanity, God *ordained* (*ʿāśāh*) them in the likeness of God" (Gen 5:1).

The Capacity for Reflection as a Prerequisite for Election

The biblical or historical concept of election as described above focuses on the notion of lineages as new genealogies or lines of descent that are constituted through God's

---

115. Wolfhart Pannenberg, *Human Nature, Election, and History* (Philadelphia, Westminster, 1977) 49.

116. Ibid.

117. Wolfhart Pannenberg, *Systematic Theology*, 2.322.

118. W. Randall Garr, "The Nouns דמות and צלם," in *In His Own Image and Likeness: Humanity, Divinity, and Monotheism* (Leiden: Brill, 2003) 136.

119. N. T. Wright, *The New Testament and the People of God*. Vol. 1: Christian Origins and the Question of God (Minneapolis: Fortress, 1992) 266.

"selection of one out of many."[120] Given this framework for both human evolution and biblical election, one can envision the evolutionary selection or founding event that initiated the phylogenetic break between humans and the preceding hominin lineage to be synonymous with the theological and historical event of God's electing human beings as his divine image. Presupposing that the God of Scripture is objectively real and that this God really acts within the historical process of events, I have suggested that one may think of God as calling out the first generation (or generations) of those who would become humans—the small founding population of individuals who began the process of reproductive isolation—from among their ancestral hominid family.[121] As Abraham and his family were called out from the land of Ur to found a distinct people or ethnic group, the human species commenced as the first humans were called out from among the hominin species from which they came. In this very *calling* to the vocation of human priest, the human species was simultaneously *created* and *designated* as the image of God.

Exegetically the image and likeness of God is *genealogically* and *corporately* defined, and as such it belongs to the *entire human species* apart from the characteristics and capacities of particular individuals. The Hebrews were unique among Near Eastern cultures in broadening the understanding of "the image and likeness" of a god to include the whole human species. What we find in Gen 1, explains Richard Middleton, is "a genuine democratization of ancient Near Eastern royal ideology." In this way "humanity is dignified with a status and role vis-à-vis the nonhuman creation that is analogous to the status and role of kings in the ancient near East vis-à-vis their subjects." As the image and likeness of God, the whole human species "is called to be the representative and intermediary of God's power and blessing on earth."[122]

The *imago Dei* depends on the ancestral unity or common ancestry of the human race as this species has been freely chosen by God for the sake of his divine purposes and service. Within the framework of divine election there was thus no ontological or biological *necessity* for God to choose humans as God's image. Nevertheless, in order properly to carry out the commission given to the elected image of God, there were certain conditions and required capacities that the human species

---

120. Pannenberg, *Human Nature, Election*, 48.

121. For a discussion on the philosophical and scientific viability of affirming this kind of divine action see F. LeRon Shults, Nancey Murphy, and Robert J. Russell, *Philosophy, Science and Divine Action*. Vol 1. Philosophical Studies in Science and Religion (Leiden: Brill, 2009); See also *Neuroscience and the Person: Scientific Perspectives on Divine Action*, edited by Robert J. Russell, et al. (Vatican City State and Berkeley, CA: Vatican Observatory and CTNS, 1999).

122. J. Richard Middleton, *The Liberating Image: The Imago Dei in Genesis 1* (Grand Rapids: Brazos, 2005) 121.

as a whole—or any other species that God could have chosen—needed to possess. These *necessary prerequisites* relate directly to the *function* that the elected image of God serves and to the *vocational tasks* which the *imago Dei* is called to perform, namely representing God as his royal vice-regents and serving the Creator and the creation as a species of priests.[123]

Elected and created as priests, human beings' very origination is marked by a divine command: one tree of all the trees in the garden may not be eaten, on penalty of death. According to Phyllis Bird, God's initial commandment and "prohibition assumes the freedom to disobey and the capacity for moral discrimination—to know right from wrong and to weigh the consequences of actions."[124] *Free agency* and *moral discernment* are thus necessary conditions that must precede the capacity to obey. The giving of the divine command likewise presupposes a *capacity for communication* and/or a *language* ability that enables one to hear and understand God's commands. In a similar way the kingly and priestly vocations of God's image requires a capacity for *empathy* and *compassion*, along with a *sense of justice* that is necessary to discern injustices within the creation and to protect and care for the weaker subjects of creation. The possession of *rationality*, *culture*, and *technology* are also needed in order for human beings to carry out the task of dominion and the establishment of order and peace throughout the creation. The telos of the election of the *imago Dei* is love—to love God, to love our neighbors as ourselves, to love our enemies, and to embody love in our lives even as Jesus embodied love in his (Matt 22:38; 1 Tim 1:5).[125] For a species to have been elected as the divine image would thus require that this species can develop a *sense of self* and a *sense of others* in such a way that self and others can grow together into a deeply relational community characterized *by* intimacy, fellowship, and love.

As we have seen above, many, if not all, of these prerequisite capacities for election as the *imago Dei* flow from the deeper capacity of having the *ability to mirror* or to simulate the minds of others. In this way the first precondition for imaging God is that the chosen species must have a biological capacity to image. With the capacity to image in place as a necessary neurological foundation, the other required capacities—such as self-awareness, other-awareness, empathy, culture, technology,

---

123. Middleton, *The Liberating Image,* also provides a discussion of the royal representative function and associated tasks of human beings as the *imago Dei*.

124. Phyllis A. Bird, "Theological Anthropology in the Hebrew Bible," 260–61, 268.

125. As Wolfhart Pannenberg affirms, "Jesus is the prototype of true human perfection, and every individual human being approaches his human destiny to the extent that his life is transformed into the likeness of the love of God revealed in Jesus' deeds, in order in that way to become *truly human*." Wolfhart Pannenberg, *Faith and Reality*, translated by John Maxwell (Philadelphia: Westminster, 1977) 48–49. Emphasis mine.

morality, and language—can further develop within both individual human beings and within the human species as a whole. The first anatomically modern culture-bearing human beings possessed the capacity to image and satisfied all of the other preconditions for election. However, so did many nonhuman culture-bearing hominins who both preceded and were contemporaneous with humans.[126] Why then were humans called and chosen as the image of God and not Neanderthals, *Homo floresiensis*, *Homo Denisova*, or *Homo erectus*? My answer is that the prerequisites of election are *necessary but not sufficient conditions* for a species to be chosen. As in *all* cases of divine election, no ultimate reason is to be given for God's actions except that such acts of election are the consequence of God's free historical choosing. Those who are elected are not chosen because they are "the greatest" or inherently more worthy than others, but rather they are elected as a result of mysterious acts of divine love and grace. God did not select humans because they were the strongest among the hominins, the most numerous, the smartest, the most cultured or the best spoken.[127] Indeed, early humans were the physically weakest of the hominins and had smaller brains than Neanderthals.[128] It is of no theological consequence if

---

126. It has been recently argued that the faculty for complex language was possessed by several nonhuman hominins such as Neanderthals, the Denisovans, the Flores hominins, and at least one unknown African hominin that can be inferred from genetic admixture. Michael F. Hammer et al., "Genetic Evidence for Archaic Admixture in Africa" *Proceedings of the National Academy of Sciences* 108(37) (2011) 15123–8; The language related "mutations in FOXP2 ... may actually have occurred some 1.8 million years ago, when *Homo habilis* and *Homo ergaster* were appearing in the fossil record, and as the human brain began gradually to triple in size from the 450 cc of chimpanzee and australopithecine brains to the 1,350 cc of modern human brains." Karl C. Diller and Rebecca L. Cann, "Evidence against a Genetic-based Revolution in Language 50,000 years ago," in *The Cradle of Language*, edited by Rudolf Botha and Chris Knight (New York: Oxford University Press, 2009) 135–49, at 136. Moreover, Neanderthals share with modern humans the key language-related changes or genetic mutations in FOXP2—results which indicate that such changes "predate the common ancestor (which existed about 300,000–400,000 years ago) of modern human and Neandertal populations." J. Krause, et al., "The Derived *FOXP2* Variant of Modern Humans Was Shared with Neanderthals," *Current Biology* 17 (2007) 1908–12.

127. Recent studies point to the presence of symbolic art in nonhuman hominins, and investigators have shown that nonhuman hominins were even as technologically innovative as their human counterparts. For instance, studies on the development of specialized bone tools among Neanderthals (such as lissoirs or burnishers) indicate that a number of such advanced tool types found among Neanderthals predate the arrival of *Homo sapiens*. This shows that Neanderthals developed such tools independently of humans. Joao Zilhao, "The Emergence of Ornaments and Art: An Archaeological Perspective on the Origins of 'Behavioral Modernity,'" *Journal of Archaeological Research* 15 (2007) 1–54. Marie Soressi, et al. "Neandertals Made the First Specialized Bone Tools in Europe," *Proceedings of the National Academy of Sciences* 110.35 (2013) 14186–90.

128. Christopher Stringer and Robin McKie, *African Exodus: The Origins of Modern Humanity* (New York: Henry Holt: 1997) 97; As paleoanthropologist Ian Tattersall comments, "Neanderthals who inhabited Europe toward the end of the Ice Age had brains that were, on average, even larger than ours are today. Classic Neanderthal brains averaged about 1500 ml in volume, while the current worldwide average is less than 1400 ml." See Ian Tattersall, *The Last Neanderthal: The Rise, Success, and Mysterious Extinction of Our Closest Human Relatives* (Boulder, CO: Westview, 1999) 11.

the other hominins exceeded humans in some of the above capacities or even if they were superior to humans in all of them. The election of humans is not a testimony to the superiority of *Homo sapiens* but rather a witness to God's sovereign grace and love. God may have even chosen humans as the weakest of the hominins in order to make God's strength known (2 Cor 12:9).

On a similar note, because the image of God in humans is based on God's sovereign *choosing* and not on particular *capacities* that humans possess, the human species is not in danger of losing the image of God as a result of the discovery of other creatures who display comparable characteristics. There are animals today—such as dolphins, corvids, and chimpanzees—that bear all of the necessary prerequisites for election to some degree. If after the next million years of evolution the culture and technology of crows or chimpanzees comes to rival or supersede that of humans, it will make no difference with regard to the status of the election of the human species as the image of God. In the same way, the discovery of advanced extra-terrestrial intelligent life will in no way nullify the election of humans as the *imago Dei*. Indeed, this is even clear from the immediate scriptural context of the *imago Dei* designation itself. In the first chapters of Genesis we find a description of a *nonhuman animal* who possesses intelligence, rationality, language, moral discernment, and death-awareness. The serpent, who is described as a clever "wild animal" in the Genesis story, is depicted as the intellectual equal of the human pair, has an understanding of God's commandments, and knows the consequences of breaking them. Nevertheless, the serpent's possession of all these qualities does not allow him to be automatically designated as the image of God.[129]

Conclusion

Reflecting on the meaning of the *imago Dei*, N. T. Wright explains that, "the notion of the 'image' doesn't refer to a particular spiritual endowment, a secret 'property' that humans possess somewhere in their genetic makeup, something that might be found by a scientific observation of humans as opposed to chimps. The image is a *vocation,* a calling. It is the call to be *an angled mirror,* reflecting God's wise order into the world and reflecting the praises of all creation back to the Creator."[130] In this way, says Middleton, "the human vocation as *imago Dei* in God's world . . .

---

129. I suggest that to understand the original meaning of this Gen 3 text, one should resist reading into the text the deutero-canonical *Wisdom of Solomon*'s interpretation of the serpent as Satan. It is clear the Genesis author considered the serpent to be a clever representative from the animal world and not a fallen angel. However, this does not necessarily rule out the possibility of spiritual influences working through the serpent.

130. N. T. Wright, "Including an Excursus," 175.

corresponds in important respects to Israel's vocation as a 'royal priesthood' among the nations (Exod 19:6)."[131] The framework of historical election assumes that there are entities such as individuals, ethnicities, and species from which God may choose for the sake of God's own purposes. These entities are not defined according to salient characteristics, however, but rather are demarcated according to their ancestral lineage or genealogy. In the same way, evolutionary biology defines the units called species in terms of their genealogy. Both theologically and biologically, the human *species* is understood *as such* only in light of its particular ancestry and not because of certain exclusive physical traits or unique behavioral characteristics. Both election-theological anthropology and evolutionary biology view *Homo sapiens*, non-sapien hominins, and other animals as equivalents who together share the breath of life, the land, and the resources of the earth. In election-theological anthropology the only difference between humans and nonhumans is that humans alone are chosen as the royal priesthood of creation and commissioned with the task to serve other creatures and lead them to God. This *fact* that humans have been chosen for this royal and priestly task is the core meaning of our creation as the "image and likeness of God." In the discussion above I described how a key prerequisite to fulfill this task and vocation is the biological capacity to image which presumably emerges from the abilities to mirror mentally and to simulate. Yet, even while there are certain substantially necessary prerequisites for election as the *imago Dei* these characteristics in and of themselves are not *sufficient* to establish any given being who possesses them as the image of God. In this way the *imago Dei* is, and always will remain, a radical expression of God's grace and love as God continually enters into the dynamics of creation to heal all those who are perishing and restore all those who are lost (Luke 19:10).

---

131. Middleton, *The Liberating Image*, 90.

RESPONSE TO MORITZ

Tyler Johnson

I would like to thank Joshua Moritz for his paper. It is illuminating, and I find much in it worthy of commendation. Through his election model of the *imago Dei* Moritz does indeed plot a fine *via media* that takes the scientific data seriously, without losing sight of the theology that is truly at the center of the text, or of reducing that theology to a science by making it fully testable. There is much to say for his approach in this paper.

I want to focus my response on two implications that arise from the priestly-election model of the *imago Dei* that Moritz offers. The first has to do with the theological framework in which we understand creation. The second has to do with what it means that, from the very beginning, our human nature had a priestly function to it. I will discuss both of these implications through the question: What is the *telos* of the priesthood?

Moritz offers an answer to this question when he posits that, "The ultimate telos of the election to the *imago Dei* is to love God and to love other as ourselves (Matt 22:38)." I believe this assertion is too narrow in its teleological scope. This I hope to show by considering both the horizontal and vertical dynamics of the *imago Dei*. The horizontal question of the *imago Dei* lies in the distinction between the human and the nonhuman creature. This is the secondary question according to Colin Gunton. The primary question of the *imago Dei*, Gunton offers, is the vertical question—the distinction between humanity and God.[1] Moritz's paper focuses primarily on the horizontal question of the *imago Dei*. I wish to argue that it is in the vertical dynamic that we find the true *telos* of the priesthood.

First consider the implications of the priesthood with regard to the horizontal question, the relationship between the human and the nonhuman creation. Primarily we find in the priestly-election model of the *imago Dei* the impetus to reject an Augustinian paradigm of creation for one more in line with the teachings of the church father Irenaeus. Augustine's basic framework for creation is probably one with which we are quite familiar. It is that of paradise and paradise lost. For

---

1. Colin Gunton, *The Triune Creator* (Grand Rapids: Eerdmans, 1998) 193. Gunton's theology of creation has informed this response in numerous places.

Augustine, Eden was paradise. It was perfect and complete in itself, but with the sin of Adam and Eve that paradise was lost. Through the work of Christ the primordial paradise will eventually be regained.

Irenaeus wrote in the late second century, roughly two-hundred years before Augustine, and offers a different framework in which we can understand God's original creation as a project. For Irenaeus, Eden was never the final and complete intention that God had for creation. God created a dynamic world, a project that would one day be completed. For Irenaeus, creation was teleological from the beginning. It was always anticipating its consummation.

The evolutionary history of life that science offers us is far more commensurate with Irenaeus's model of creation as a project than with Augustine's initial perfection. This is not simply due to the vast spans of time required by evolution to produce life of hominin-level complexity and characteristics. The larger issue has to do with the wastefulness and inefficiency of the evolutionary process, including the mass amounts of suffering and death that have made possible the complex life that could then be elected by God and created into humans in the image of God.[2] From an evolutionary perspective the creation has been "groaning in labor pains"[3] for billions of years.

This evolutionary history of suffering and death gives credence to an election model of the *imago Dei*, where humans are called to a priestly function in creation, for priests in the Bible play a mediating and atoning role. Priests mediate the relationship between a holy God and his creation and through that mediation come elements of atonement and redemption. If the first humans had a priestly role, it stands to reason that the creation was not perfect and complete at the time of their election and that mediating and atoning functions were already necessary between creation and Creator. C. S. Lewis considered this idea in *The Problem of Pain*, where he wondered if humans from the beginning might have a "redemptive function to perform" that might include the restoration of "peace to the animal world."[4] If from the beginning humans had a priestly role, what then was the purpose, the *telos*, of the priesthood?

This question brings us to considerations of the vertical dynamic of the *imago Dei*, that being the relationship between the human in God's image and the Triune God. The answer to this question it would seem, must lie in Christology, and

---

2. See Christopher Southgate, *The Groaning of Creation: God, Evolution, and the Problem of Evil* (Louisville: Westminster John Knox, 2008) and Ronald E. Osborn, *Death Before the Fall: Biblical Literalism and the Problem of Animal Suffering* (Downers Grove: InterVarsity, 2014).

3. Rom 8:22.

4. C. S. Lewis, "The Problem of Pain," in *The Complete C. S. Lewis Signature Classics* (San Francisco: HarperCollins, 2002) 632–33.

following from that also in eschatology. It is in Christ, the God-man, both fully God and fully human, that we see what it means to be fully made in the image of God. Christ is the perfect mirror in which we see God's image in a human. "Anyone who has seen me," Christ said, "has seen the Father."[5]

If our identity as humans lies in the *imago Dei*, and thus our election as a "species of priests," then we can agree with Gunton that, "one cannot understand the image of God apart from the person of Christ."[6] It is Christ who becomes the final high priest, having "no need to offer sacrifices day after day" because "this he did once for all when he offered himself."[7] Christ is the mediator of a new covenant, the final covenant. Christ is the *telos* of the priesthood because Christ becomes the absolute and eternal mediator between creation and Creator. It is through Christ that God reconciles all things to himself.[8]

So if the first humans were elected to function in a priestly role, preserving sacred space and mediating the relationship between creation and Creator, then the *imago Dei* is most fully fleshed out in Christ, who is the *telos* of the priesthood. We can thus say that we are made in the image and likeness of Christ, and to be fully human means to be mirrors of Christ.[9] We are like God inasmuch as we are like Christ. With Christ as the *telos* of the priesthood, the first humans were called to begin the work of Christ in their election as a species of priests, proleptically anticipating his incarnation.

Both the horizontal and vertical considerations suggest that a model of the *imago Dei* as election to a species of priests set us within a paradigm of creation in line with Irenaeus. Creation is a project. From the very beginning God intended to bring his creation to its final consummation. This suggests an eschatological dimension to the creation of the world and to the election of humanity as a species of priests. While the biblical texts make it clear that Christ's work has not obviated humanity's priestly election in the current era,[10] the question remains as to the final, eschatological, *telos* of the priesthood.

To this question the answer seems relatively clear in the Scriptural texts. In John's vision of the new creation he sees a holy city coming from heaven to earth.

---

5. John 14:9.
6. Gunton, *Triune Creator*, 200.
7. Heb 7:27.
8. Col 1:20.
9. Cf. Rom 8:29, "For those whom he foreknew he also predestined to be conformed to the image of his Son, in order that he might be the firstborn within a large family" (NRSV). Moritz notes in his first paragraph that "mirroring Christ we become mirrors of God," but this theme is never developed in his paper.
10. E.g., 1 Pet 2:9; Rev 1:6.

Within this city John says, "I saw no temple . . . for its temple is the Lord God the Almighty and the Lamb."[11] The temple is no longer necessary because God's presence suffuses the new creation, and there is no longer any need for mediation aside from the presence of the Lamb. In this new creation all things are subjected to God the Father, who is all in all.[12] The eschatological *telos* of the human election to priesthood is for that function to be fully taken up by Christ. We find our true humanity in the person of Jesus Christ.

Now we come to my primary critique to Moritz's paper. Without a robust consideration of the vertical dimension of the *imago Dei*, we find ourselves in a line of circular reasoning when it comes to the horizontal dimension. Without the person and work of Jesus Christ as the *telos* of the *imago Dei*, we must define the criteria, characteristics, and capacities necessary for the *imago Dei* by our own damaged self-reflection. We see in a mirror dimly. However, if we place Christ as the proper *telos* of the *imago Dei*, we find in his person and his work the criteria, characteristics, and capacities necessary to the species which bears the image of God. I would suggest that God's election to a species of priests must have primarily considered the capacities of that species to perform the atoning and redemptive work of Jesus Christ. Most likely these capacities have great continuity with what Moritz outlined in his paper, but without Christ as the primary motivation for these capacities, we lack a firm rubric outside of ourselves by which to evaluate our choices for what is essential to the *imago Dei*.

To conclude, I greatly appreciate Moritz's paper and his work on the horizontal dynamics of the *imago Dei*. However, I think his overall argument can be strengthened with more considerations of the vertical dynamics of the *imago Dei*, with Christ as the *telos* of humanity's election to a priestly species.

---

11. Rev 21:22.

12. 1 Cor 15:28.

FORMING IDENTITIES IN GRACE: *IMITATIO* AND HABITUS AS CONTEMPORARY CATEGORIES FOR THE SCIENCES OF MINDFULNESS AND VIRTUE[1]

Michael Spezio

Mindfulness is a theme that currently spans theology, religious studies, education, health, psychology, and neuroscience.[2] Popular authors, journalists, and scholars have worked hard in the last two to three decades to clear space for mindfulness and contemplative practices in the secular and religiously affiliated academies. This intense effort gives mindfulness many dimensions, some of which are widely accepted

---

1. I gratefully acknowledge comments generously provided by Kirk Wegter-McNelly, John Makransky, and Rabbi Or Rose on initial drafts. I am also grateful for helpful discussions with Father Thomas Keating, Sister Anita Maroun, Robert Sackel, Robert Roberts, Andrea Hollingsworth, Vanessa Kettering, Andrew Olendzki, Stephen Pope, Frank Rogers, Rabbi Or Rose, Michael Warren, Wesley Wildman, Kevin Reimer, Warren Brown, and Mark Yaconelli. Additionally, I am grateful to St. Benedict's Monastery in Snowmass, CO, and The Mind and Life Summer Research Institute for opportunities to present earlier versions of this work. Funding supporting this work was generously provided by the Fetzer Institute, the Mind and Life Institute; the Science and Transcendence Advanced Research Series of the Center for Theology and the Natural Sciences in Berkeley, CA; the John Templeton Foundation; the Center of Theological Inquiry in Princeton, NJ; the Self, Motivation, and Virtue Project; and the Templeton Religion Trust.

2. Ruth A. Baer, "Measuring Mindfulness," *Contemporary Buddhism* 12 (2011) 241–61; Scott R. Bishop et al., "Mindfulness: A Proposed Operational Definition," *Clinical Psychology: Science and Practice* 11 (2006) 230–41; Dusana Dorjee, "Kinds and Dimensions of Mindfulness: Why It Is Important to Distinguish Them," *Mindfulness* 1 (2010) 152–60; Nicole Geschwind et al., "Mindfulness Training Increases Momentary Positive Emotions and Reward Experience in Adults Vulnerable to Depression: A Randomized Controlled Trial," *Journal of Consulting and Clinical Psychology* 79 (2011) 618–28; Paul Grossman and Nicholas T. Van Dam, "Mindfulness, by Any Other Name . . .: Trials and Tribulations of Sati in Western Psychology and Science," *Contemporary Buddhism* 12 (2011) 219–39; J. Kabat-Zinn, L. Lipworth, and R. Burney," The Clinical Use of Mindfulness Meditation for the Self-Regulation of Chronic Pain," *Journal of Behavioral Medicine* 8 (1985) 163–90; J. Kabat-Zinn et al., "Effectiveness of a Meditation-Based Stress Reduction Program in the Treatment of Anxiety Disorders," *American Journal of Psychiatry* 149 (1992) 936–43; Sharon Salzberg, "Mindfulness and Loving-Kindness," *Contemporary Buddhism* 12 (2011) 177–82; Shauna Shapiro, "The Integration of Mindfulness and Psychology," *Journal of Clinical Psychology* 65 (2009) 555–60; Y. Y. Tang and M. I. Posner, "Special Issue on Mindfulness Neuroscience," *Social Cognitive and Affective Neuroscience* 8 (2013) 1–3; David R. Vago and David A. Silbersweig, "Self-Awareness, Self-Regulation, and Self-Transcendence (S-Art): A Framework for Understanding the Neurobiological Mechanisms of Mindfulness," *Frontiers in Human Neuroscience* 6 (2012) Accessed: https://doi.org/10.3389/fnhum.2012.00296; Baldwin M. Way et al., "Dispositional Mindfulness and Depressive Symptomatology: Correlations with Limbic and Self-Referential Neural Activity During Rest," *Emotion* 10 (2010) 12–24.

and some of which are hotly debated or even discarded.[3] Most accounts identify some version of three core elements: 1) attention *and* its regulation; 2) emotional regulation (not emotion itself but its regulation) generally taken to mean *down* regulation or suppression of some emotions (e.g., sadness, grief, anger) and *up* regulation of others; and 3) meta-awareness, or becoming aware of what is in one's awareness. Recent efforts have also begun to identify notions of "wholesomeness" or other ethical and/or spiritual categories[4] as important for mindfulness, as John Makransky has long held is the case for Buddhist thought.[5] Though most discussions about mindfulness emerge from Dharmic (i.e., Buddhist, Yogic, and Hindu) traditions or secularized versions of their practices, some draw from the work of scholars and practitioners of Christian contemplative traditions.[6] With rare exceptions[7] most discussions that seek models of mindfulness based in Christian tradition and experience fall back on the three core aspects so prevalent in secular theories of mindfulness. These exceptions are notable because they come from extensive interpersonal encounter between Christian and Buddhist contemplative practitioner-scholars, encounters which sometimes lasted several days. One record of such a meeting between Christian and Buddhist contemplatives, partially recorded in *The Gethsemani Encounter*, is particularly important and will influence some of the discussion below. However, despite an overt claim to be driven by empirical concerns and evidence, most contemporary psychological work that engages Christian tradition

---

3. Nicholas T. Van Dam, Mitch Earleywine, and Ashley Borders, "Measuring Mindfulness? An Item Response Theory Analysis of the Mindful Attention Awareness Scale," *Personality and Individual Differences* 49 (2010) 805–10; Andrew Olendzki, "The Construction of Mindfulness," *Contemporary Buddhism* 12 (2011) 55–70; Ulrich S. Tran, Tobias M. Glück, and Ingo W. Nader, "Investigating the Five Facet Mindfulness Questionnaire (Ffmq): Construction of a Short Form and Evidence of a Two-Factor Higher Order Structure of Mindfulness," *Journal of Clinical Psychology* 69 (2013) 951–65.

4. Aloysius Pieris, "Spirituality as Mindfulness: Biblical and Buddhist Approaches," *Spiritus: A Journal of Christian Spirituality* 10 (2010) 38–51. Regina Chow Trammel, "Mindfulness as Enhancing Ethical Decision-Making and the Christian Integration of Mindful Practice," *Social Work Christianity* 43 (2015) 165–77.

5. John Makransky, *Buddhahood Embodied: Sources of Controversy in India and Tibet*, ed. Matthew Kaptstein; Suny Series in Buddhist Studies (Albany, NY: State University of New York, 1997); *Awakening through Love: Unveiling Your Deepest Goodness* (Somerville, MA: Wisdom, 2007).

6. Jesse Fox et al., "A Phenomenological Investigation of Centering Prayer Using Conventional Content Analysis," *Pastoral Psychology* 64 (2015) 803–25; Daniel Gutierrez, Jesse Fox, and Andrew W. Wood, "Center, Light, and Sound: The Psychological Benefits of Three Distinct Meditative Practices," *Counseling and Values* 60 (2015) 234–47; P. Gregg Blanton, "The Other Mindful Practice: Centering Prayer & Psychotherapy," *Pastoral Psychology* 60 (2010) 133–47; C. G. Zaleski, "Attention as a Key to Buddhist-Christian Dialogue," *Buddhist-Christian Studies* 14 (1994) 89–110, at 89.

7. Donald W. Mitchell and James A. Wiseman, eds., *The Gethsemani Encounter: A Dialogue on the Spiritual Life by Buddhist and Christian Monastics* (New York: Continuum, 1999); Nathaniel Miles-Yepez, ed. *The Common Heart: An Experience of Interreligious Dialogue* (New York: Lantern, 2006).

marginalizes these rich textual records in order to privilege accounts of mindfulness that tend to prevent recognition of its Christian forms.

For example, a prominent model of Christian mindfulness developed for pastoral counseling by Melissa and Scott Symington begins its account of mindfulness with work done in the 1970s by Jon Kabat-Zinn and others.[8] In their defense of this view, they state that Christianity can "extract and employ" aspects of other traditions that carry "truth" and are compatible with Christian teaching, implying that Christianity has no mindfulness practices of its own. Yet this approach does not consider the rich historical traditions of biblically based, contemplative Christianity. Joshua Knabb follows this approach very closely, resulting in his claims that mindfulness is separate from centering prayer in the Christian tradition.[9] Other failures to recognize historically Christian forms of mindfulness shape the recent work of Jesse Fox and colleagues. They define the practice of centering prayer and the participatory belonging to and the indwelling of divine mind as clearly distinct from "mindfulness" practice.[10] Yet, within a Christian or even Abrahamic standpoint, what could be more "mindful" than opening oneself to having one's own mind, heart, thought, and love conformed to the mind and love of God? In their papers Fox and his colleagues repeat almost verbatim the rich accounts of centering prayer detailed by Father Thomas Keating, Father Basil Pennington, and others, and cover familiar ground of tracing these accounts to the *Cloud of Unknowing*, John of the Cross, and older sources.[11] Yet time and again, they deny any connection between the transformation of mind and self, on the one hand, with mindfulness, on the other, even though there are clear precedents in Christian spiritual studies for making just these connections.[12]

A failure to connect mindfulness with the rich history of participation in and mystical communion with God in Christian tradition is doubtless due to an unhelpful prioritization on the part of some scholars of concepts within secular mindfulness theory, along with a deference to concepts of concentrative, selective control

---

8. Scott H. Symington and Melissa F. Symington, "A Christian Model of Mindfulness: Using Mindfulness Principles to Support Psychological Well-Being, Value-Based Behavior, and the Christian Spiritual Journey," *Journal of Psychology and Christianity* 31 (2012) 71–77.

9. Joshua J. Knabb, "Centering Prayer as an Alternative to Mindfulness-Based Cognitive Therapy for Depression Relapse Prevention," *Journal of Religion and Health* 51 (2012) 908–24.

10. Fox et al.; "A Phenomenological Investigation of Centering Prayer"; Gutierrez, Fox, and Wood, "Center, Light, and Sound."

11. Thomas Keating, *Invitation to Love: The Way of Christian Contemplation* (New York: Continuum, 2004); M. Basil Pennington, Thomas Keating, and Thomas E. Clarke, *Finding Grace at the Center: The Beginning of Centering Prayer* (Woodstock, VT: Skylight Paths, 2007).

12. Pieris, "Spirituality as Mindfulness"; Bernard McGinn, "Love, Knowledge, and Mystical Union in Western Christianity: Twelfth to Sixteenth Centuries," *Church History* 56 (1987) 7–24.

that so strongly shape cognitive psychological and cognitive science theory in the West. As Christian communities and scholars move forward for greater theological, scriptural, ecumenical, and scientific engagement with mindfulness theory and practice in the twenty-first century, we require greater interdisciplinary partnerships that recover concepts of mind, heart, intention, and action in Christian spirituality and contemplative traditions. Above all, we should not privilege concepts of mindfulness that have developed without, and primarily via exclusion of, a close examination of what is meant by mind and its fullness in Christian spirituality and contemplative tradition. Indeed, it is highly likely that, just as Buddhist and other Dharmic contributions continue to shape scientific concepts of mind and mindfulness, Christian and other Abrahamic views will as well.

Mindfulness as Enactive Remembrance of the Love of God

Aloysius Pieris wrote a very perceptive paper linking spirituality, mindfulness, and the transformation of self and identity in the Ignatian tradition.[13] For Ignatius and in Jesuit tradition, teachings about mindfulness identify "spirituality as mindfulness," where the "spirituality" that forms the heart of spiritual formation and transformation is the ongoing practice of the presence of God. This "practice of the presence" does not mean simply acknowledging that God is present as some additional element in all daily activity. Rather, it means that one is transformed into a "'discerning person' (*anthrōpos diakritikos*) . . . someone perpetually mindful or watchful of God working in all things and at all times."[14] Such a person is ever conscious of God's love. Mindfulness in this view develops capacities for the self and identity, but not simply of specific mental processes like attention and emotional regulation and meta-awareness. Also, according to Pieris's view, mindfulness is grounded in knowledge of the ultimate reality of God's love, but it is not an individually directed, epistemological endeavor whose object is true knowledge of the mind or of ultimate reality. Rather, mindfulness is enactive and enacted contemplation with and for others.[15] Mind and act are integrated in the inbreaking vision and intentionality of God

13. Pieris, "Spirituality as Mindfulness."

14. Ibid., 39.

15. It should be noted that a view of mindfulness being grounded in love "with and for others" is not present in absolutely all forms of historically Christian contemplative practices, especially in those strongly influenced by neoplatonism via the works of Proclus of Athens and Pseudo-Dionysius the Areopagite. The latter's works had significant influence in Christian mysticism and contemplative communities for centuries, in part because their author was believed to be the Dionysius the Areopagite whom the apostle Paul converted to Christianity in the first century CE (Acts 17:34). Still, even in the strongly neoplatonist Christian mysticism of Meister Eckhart, we find participation in the love of God central, as made clear in the commentaries of Bernard McGinn, Ursula Fleming, and Richard J. Woods. See Bernard McGinn and Ursula Fleming, *Meister Eckhart: The Man from Whom God Hid*

in which the mindful self participates. Other-regard and action in solidarity with and for others are constitutive of mindfulness. Since mindfulness is enactive and enacted, it cannot be conceptually focused, but "is commensurate with its *experiential* character."[16] Openness to the experience of being conscious of God's love connects spirituality with the metaphor of heartfulness, such that "Ignatius of Loyola lamented that the study of scholastic theology had dried up his heart."[17]

Pieris names this heartful mindfulness *remembrance*, or *anamnesis*. The word *anamnesis* is Greek and means to recall or remember and is from the Greek word for memory, *mneme*. In Pieris's conception of mindfulness, the remembrance that is "mindfulness of God" does not mean a mindfulness in which "God" is an object or static reality that must be "kept in mind." On the contrary, the "mindfulness of God" that Pieris develops is the active encounter with others and the world "from God's own perspective." Mindfulness practice so understood leads to "growing familiarity with God, which I acquire mainly by my constant remembrance of God's deeds in the past." My remembrance of the love of God makes "it easy to recognize Her voice and Her activity in my life at the present moment and respond to it promptly and with joy."[18] Rather than interrupting daily activity and action, spirituality as a mindful resighting, a construal of all things in the divine, is not akin to a practice that is only done while sitting silently. It is not a time-out from life but is an "attitude or an incessantly loving mindfulness of God that accompanies action."[19] Pieris takes pains to insist that this practice of the "loving mindfulness of God" in action is the ground for other, more traditional prayer and practices of sitting silently, such as infused mystical prayer and formal imaginative "anamnesis by which past events become our here and now."[20]

Imitatio as Enactive Remembrance of the Loving Heart and Mind of God

This section presents a view that heartful mindfulness is connected to traditions of *imitatio* in Christianity. Such "loving mindfulness of God" in action engages with and for others from the perspective of, and out of, the infusion of divine love. These

---

Nothing (New York: Collins, 1988); Richard J. Woods, *Meister Eckhart: Master of Mystics* (New York: Bloomsbury Academic, 2011).

16. Pieris, "Spirituality as Mindfulness," 38.
17. Ibid.
18. Ibid., 44.
19. Ibid., 42.
20. Ibid., 41.

traditions are present within the Abrahamic traditions of Islam and Judaism as well, though this paper will only touch on Christianity.[21]

The *imitatio Christi*, or "imitation of Christ," found in Thomas à Kempis and other Christian traditions means moving beyond cold or distant "imitation" to actual "participation in" the life and mind that are the source of divine love. As Gilchrist Lavigne put it at the 1996 Gethsemani encounter, the experiences of "deeper self-knowledge, mindfulness, modesty, simplicity of life, and concern for what benefits the neighbor," come from "the context of love and a following of Christ that is not just an imitation of the life of Jesus, but a real participation in his life. In the words of St. Paul, it is a 'putting on Christ,' a becoming Christ so that Christ is the reference point of all one is and lives."[22] This echoes Pieris and again grounds particular practices in remembrance of divine love, in putting on and participating in divine love, the divine heart, via *imitatio*. An exploration of *imitatio* by interdisciplinary teams of theologians, biblical scholars, and scientists will allow a greater inclusion and engagement with Christian mindfulness, and likely with Islamic and Jewish perspectives as well.

A prominent source in Christian contemplative tradition that links theological interpretation of Scripture to the grace-grounded formation of the self via enactive love comes from the twelfth-century monastic and abbot William of Saint-Thierry. William expressed this across the breadth of his writings, from one of his earliest books, *The Nature and Dignity of Love*, to his last, *The Golden Epistle*. William was a contemporary and friend of Bernard of Clairvaux, a member of "the original Cistercian School" of contemplative monastic practice, and his writings were until recently thought to be by the more famous Bernard.[23] As such, they were highly influential and widely used for guidance in the formation of monks for Christian mindfulness. Not surprisingly, William's guidance focused on the cultivation of love through and in community and in contemplative prayer and practice.

William's treatise on the nature and dignity of love invokes perhaps the most well-known summary of Christian ethical teaching, the double love command in

---

21. See the following: Nancy Roberts, "Imitatio Christi, Imitatio Muhammadi, Imitatio Dei," *Journal of Ecumenical Studies* 47 (2012) 227–48; Menachem Kellner, "Gersonides on Imitatio Dei and the Dissemination of Scientific Knowledge," *The Jewish Quarterly Review* 85 (1995) 275–96; Howard Kreisel, "Imitatio Dei in Maimonides' Guide of the Perplexed," *Association for Jewish Studies Review* 19 (1994) 169–212. To be clear, accounts and experiences of *imitatio* will differ depending on the differing kinds of encounter envisioned. As Pieris ("Spirituality as Mindfulness," 49) himself says in "Spirituality as Mindfulness," with regard to remembrance, opening to a living presence in one's experience and action is different from opening to memory about a departed teacher. This distinction seems even sharper, especially if memories about a teacher are only semantic and not episodic.

22. Mitchell and Wiseman, *The Gethsemani Encounter*, 91–92.

23. William of St. Thierry, *The Golden Epistle: A Letter to the Brethren at Mont Dieu*, translated by Theodore Berkeley; Cistercian Fathers Series (Collegeville, MN: Cistercian, 1971) xv.

Luke 10:27, and one of the clearest guides to *imitatio* as enactive mindful love of the other. The original summary of the law and prophets derives from the Hebrew Scriptures, including the command to "love the one near you as yourself" (Lev 19:18). Part of this summary is the focus on *neighbor*, which is a suboptimal English translation of the original Greek word *plēsion*, or the Latin *proximos*, meaning the one who is proximal to you, "the one who is near." *Plēsion* is also the word used to translate the original Hebrew in the Septuagint. In the original Hebrew the term in Leviticus also means much more than the English word "neighbor" and instead refers to one's fellow companion.[24] William's quotation from Luke is immediately followed by the parable generally known as the Good Samaritan, but which might just as well be called the Samaritan Pair because of the relationship between near ones at its heart. The parable results from an epistemological inquiry, a clarification that one could interpret as a concern about one's own individual, accurate perception of ultimate reality: "And who is my neighbor?" The story tells of an outsider, a Samaritan, providing care for a suffering man who had been physically beaten. Upon seeing the man's suffering, as Luke tells it, the Samaritan was moved by compassion. The Greek word in Luke usually translated as "compassion" declares a movement of the gut or a visceral encounter that is highly affective, which moves the Samaritan to caring action. At the end of the story the point is not that the Samaritan showed a greater insight into who his "neighbor" really was or saw more deeply into the reality of who his neighbor was. Rather, the point of the story is that the epistemological question seeking an accurate perception of ultimate reality was an unhelpful response to being asked to love the neighbor, the one who is near. Luke notably does not have Jesus ask who had insightfully *seen* or even *felt with* the neighbor. Instead, he asked who had compassionately *been* the neighbor. The answer, of course, was the Samaritan, and Luke closes with this command of *imitatio*: "Go and do likewise." Being the neighbor, being the one who is near to others in their need, active love rather than active gaze, was the point of the story and is the definition of *caritas* for William.

How does *imitatio* help the formation of love or *caritas* for William? He traces the stages of love's development, ultimately culminating in *caritas*, the Latin word used most often to translate the Greek *agapē*. William explicitly grounds love in memory, since memory allows one to recall "the goodness of the Creator": "Memory possesses and contains that to which it must strive."[25] To develop the memory and so

---

24. See also Jacob Milgrom, *Leviticus: A Book of Ritual and Ethics*, Continental Commentaries (Minneapolis, MN: Augsburg Fortress, 2004) 231–36. As Milgrom also makes clear, love in this sense is enactive. He asks, "How can love be commanded? The answer is simply that the verb 'love' signifies not only an emotion or attitude but also deeds."

25. William of St. Thierry, *The Nature and Dignity of Love*, translated by Thomas X. Davis; Cistercian Fathers Series (Kalamazoo, MI: Cistercian, 1981) 54.

to move past the youthful stage of love, William says, means to engage in *imitatio* of divine love through the example of an exemplary other. One's recollected judgment is that of the exemplary teacher, opening one's heart to take on the mind of that teacher "until long and patient experience gives [one] an understanding concerning the things . . . heard."[26] Through active, effortful encounter and *imitatio* in relationship with a teacher and the community as teacher, a monk begins to transform inwardly. The actions and the relations come first, the inward transformation after. William puts it this way: "For we work with our hands first, then we rub our eye with our hand. For this reason it is said: 'By your commandments I have understood.'"[27]

Encounters with an exemplar and with the community as teacher require effort, especially in initial and intermediary stages, and they draw upon the natural attachment to one's origins, one's parents, and those persons in one's childhood development. Following this, William describes stages in which one's actions gradually free one from loving only those whom one perceives as similar, with whom one already has a tangible mutuality of perspective and commitment. This liberation includes freedom from an exclusive love of one's own community. Instead, the third stage of love is benevolence, the "natural love which naturally loves every man because of the likeness of nature itself and companionship, without any hope of recompense . . . so that it permits nothing human to be foreign to itself."[28] After benevolence comes the love of enemies, which "is said to be truly spiritual in that it promotes likeness to the Son of God and the dignity of the sons of God,"[29] and so depends on a greater degree of *imitatio* on behalf of others who have caused one harm. At the fifth stage there is the fullness of divine love, *caritas*, "when we love the Lord our God with our whole heart and with our whole soul and with all our strength, and our neighbor as ourselves."[30]

For *caritas* to be created, in William's view, however, requires the integrated cooperation of both love and reason, "because one of them—reason—cannot see God except in what he is not, but love cannot bring itself to rest except in what he is."[31] At this point it is only because one has the *caritas* that is of the divine and identified with the divine that one willingly stays embedded in solidarity with and for communities of living persons. As William describes the actions of the apostle Paul, "To be with Christ, here in contemplation and there in the actual state of blessed-

26. Ibid., 60.
27. Ibid., 69.
28. Ibid., 74.
29. Ibid., 75.
30. Ibid., 76.
31. Ibid., 77.

ness—what a blessed and glorious happiness for Paul! Therefore the *caritas* of God lifted him on high, but *caritas* for neighbor pressed him down like a weight hanging from his neck. So he goes on to say: But to abide still in the flesh is necessary for your sakes."[32] Such desire to act for others at the height of Christian heartful mindfulness is, for William, the culmination of *imitatio*, of the contemplative now participating fully and being taken over by divine love: "The *affectus* of *caritas* adheres indissolubly to God and gathers all judgments according to the light of His countenance, so that she may act or perform exteriorly what the good and pleasing will of God speaks inwardly to her. . . . For already the Spirit of knowledge openly teaches the saintly soul what to do and how to do it."[33]

Much more of great value could be found in William's work, especially for recognizing the rich historical tradition of Christian mindfulness. For now, a brief look at his final book will help clarify that he means the progression of love to be the life of constant prayer, similar to what Pieris described. In *The Golden Epistle*'s chapter on prayer, William is again clear on the central role of the practice of *imitatio* as relational remembrance via action, not just *imitatio* of Christ but of the great exemplars whose lives and teachings are seen as manifestations of Christ's *caritas*:

> The best and safest reading matter and subject for meditation for the animal man, newly come to Christ, to train him in the interior life, is the outward actions of our Redeemer. In them he should find an example of humility, a stimulant to *caritas* and to sentiments of piety. . . . He should also be given the lives of the saints and the accounts of their martyrdoms. He should not trouble himself with historical details but should always find something to stir his novice's mind to love God and despise himself.[34]

Further, William explicitly differentiates "prayer" from "petition" and "supplication." Prayer is not asking for anything, nor is it "turning to God during one's spiritual exercises, in which to add fresh knowledge."[35] Prayer for William is affective contemplation, it is "familiar and devout conversation, a state in which the enlightened mind enjoys God as long as it is permitted."[36] The "enjoyment" of God is simultaneously an attestation and a resting in the grace of God, the grace that makes possible the transformation of mind.

Thanksgiving follows from this prayer, "an unwearying and undistracted attention of the good will to God in understanding and knowledge of God's grace. . . .

---

32. Ibid., 79–80.
33. Ibid., 80.
34. William, *The Golden Epistle: A Letter to the Brethren at Mont Dieu*, 68.
35. Ibid., 71.
36. Ibid., 70–71.

[Thanksgiving is] a certain resemblance to the goodness of . . . God, on the part of God's sons . . . sharing its neighbor's pains or joys."[37] The sage, says William, through prayer and thanksgiving finds that "eventually love arrives at some likeness of that love which made God like to man by accepting the humiliation of our human lot in order that man might be made like to God . . . to make his own the mind which is in Christ Jesus our Lord."[38] By now this sounds familiar and William the Cistercian and Pieris the Jesuit both ground the contemplative life in the participation in divine love, in *caritas*, via *imitatio*.

If scholars, and especially cognitive scientists, engage the practices of *imitatio* from perspectives of partnering and respectful inquiry, new insights into human capability and new approaches in the sciences themselves will likely result. Rather than dividing between mindfulness on this side and the core of Christian tradition on the other side, there will be a recognition that Christianity—and indeed also Islam and Judaism—present versions of *imitatio* that can teach us about the human mind, human affectivity, human intention, and human action. If cognitive science is to approach better such heartful mindfulness as *imitatio*, are there resources it already has on which it could build?

A Model for Future Interdisciplinary Work

Imitatio occurs in relationship, both in real and imagined encounter, with concrete others and with "the lovingly intended exemplar" who "draws and invites, and we 'follow.'"[39] This way of understanding *imitatio* helps to shift the interdisciplinary study of loving encounter away from wholly internal, isolated processes and their stability or lack thereof toward a focus on the construal of relationships. Construals of relationships concern first of all the perception of self and of other in relationship. If encounter can be expressed and understood in this way, then remembrance of connection via traditions of virtue may be understood as perfection of the construal of relationship. Virtue is a way of construing relation, and its primary construal is love understood as *caritas*. Virtuous construals shape the seeing of the I and the You in relation. Such construals require certain perspectival and perceptual sensitivities and will likely entail a greater reliance on affective openness, a sensitivity to the situation, context, and the value of the other person.

---

37. Ibid., 71.

38. Ibid., 98.

39. Max Scheler, *Formalism in Ethics and Non-Formal Ethics of Values*, translated by Manfred S. Frings and Roger L. Funk (Evanston, IL: Northwestern University Press, 1973 repr. of 1916 edition) 580.

Recovering a sense that situated, embodied valuation is at the core of cognition, and resisting the subtraction of value and neutralization of cognitive processes, are emerging projects in twenty-first century cognitive science. By no means universally acclaimed, nevertheless such efforts are recognizable and active areas of cognitive science under terms such as embodied cognition,[40] enactive cognition,[41] neurophenomenology,[42] and second-person neuroscience.[43] For example, recent work in social neuroscience highlights evidence supporting the view of human skin as a "social organ"[44] and a theory of affective touch in which emotional significance shapes the earliest signals of touch in the human somatosensory cortex.[45] As a group, embodied, enactive, and second-person perspectives aim at enriching both theory and method in mind science to the point of more fully including a person's stance in the world. "Stance" is used in a way related to the historical origins of the word: one's standing or resting place, abode, and position(ing) *preparatory to and constitutive of action*. Stance implies an action in the process of becoming. Stance itself is enactive as the unique outlook, orientation, attitude, disposition, situation, and plans of the

---

40. Embodied cognition is the view that conceptual processing is based in or uses the same systems used for perceptual processing and motor action. See L. W. Barsalou, "Grounded Cognition," *Annual Review of Psychology* 59 (2008) 617–45; R. L. Goldstone and L. W. Barsalou, "Reuniting Perception and Conception," *Cognition* 65 (1998) 231–62.

41. Enactive cognition includes a spectrum of views that begin by holding that the mind's processes are constituted by the participatory, purposeful action of the organism in its situation. Francisco Varela, one of the neuroscientists who inspired the enactive turn in cognitive science, held this view. Extreme enactive cognition denies any representational function of the mind at all and simply views the mind/brain as a participant in an ongoing interaction of organism and embedded situation. See S. Gallagher et al., "The Brain as Part of an Enactive System," *Behavioral and Brain Sciences* 36 (2013) 421–22; Shaun Gallagher and Dan Zahavi, *The Phenomenological Mind: An Introduction to Philosophy of Mind and Cognitive Science* (New York: Routledge, 2008).

42. Neurophenomenology is a collection of views that grounds the science of mind in understanding the formation of stable conscious states. Though it originally rejected Husserl in favor of Merleau-Ponty, subsequent work privileges perspectives from Husserl and is beginning to see connections to the thought of Hans Jonas. See Evan Thompson, *Mind in Life: Biology, Phenomenology and the Sciences of Mind* (Cambridge, MA: Belknap, 2007); Evan Thompson and Francisco J. Varela, "Radical Embodiment: Neural Dynamics and Consciousness," *Trends in Cognitive Sciences* 5 (2001) 418–25; Francisco J. Varela, "Patterns of Life: Intertwining Identity and Cognition," *Brain and Cognition* 34 (1997) 72–87.

43. Second-person neuroscience is a collection of views that grounds the methodological study and theoretical understanding of social cognition and other cognitive processes in interactive dynamics between persons in dyads and small groups. For example, it denies that facial processing can be modeled or understood correctly outside of studying it within dynamical social interaction. See Leonhard Schilbach et al., "Toward a Second-Person Neuroscience," *Behavioral and Brain Sciences* 36 (2013) 393–414.

44. I. Morrison, L. Loeken, and H. Olausson, "The Skin as a Social Organ," *Experimental Brain Research* 204 (2010) 305–14.

45. Valeria Gazzola et al., "Primary Somatosensory Cortex Discriminates Affective Significance in Social Touch," *Proceedings of the National Academy of Sciences* 109 (2012) E1657–E66.

person, understood as emerging from a person's formative history and goals or ends. The extent of the ends depends on the vicinity of the view. A person's formational history is biological, morphological, developmental, close-relational, social, and cultural, of course, but in all of this what is most central is formation itself. Evolutionary and physiological accounts of biological organisms include a focus on formation in the language of homeostasis. That which actively and dynamically "stands still" in homeo*stasis* is generally labeled as the "milieu interieur" or set of "bodily states" enabling the organism's flourishing.[46] Homeostasis depends on corrective action whenever the range of states exceeds that required for flourishing. Yet the notion of homeostatic corrective action first requires the notion of dynamic stability whose core is purpose. The classic 1943 paper on negative feedback, "Behavior, Purpose, and Teleology," made this clear, as it argued for renewed "recognition of the importance of purpose."[47] This is not merely an instrumental purpose, but a formational one, a purpose whose coherence depends upon development in relation, upon growth intelligible only in light of the organism's flourishing.[48]

To see with another's eyes and to have the mind of another inhabit one's full self is possible only through deeply personal encounter reliant upon processes whose meanings are partially explored in, but perhaps ultimately beyond, concepts in social neuroscience and decision science. These concepts include simulation, imitation, perspective taking, joint attention, or other forms of other-knowing. These social cognitive categories are too often narrowly defined by philosophical and scientific accounts that emerged prior to embodied, enactive, second-person turns in cognitive science. For cognitive science to understand the formation that is authentic human becoming—the absorption into a way of being in the world that is loving without limit—requires exploring the practice of contemplative encounter that is *imitatio*.

Imitatio, as discussed throughout the paper, has only the barest of connections to prevailing concepts of mimesis and imitation. Michael Taussig, in his *Mimesis and Alterity*, notes this problem of accounting for *imitatio* via cold imitation. *Imitatio* is never possible apart from emotionally empathic resonance, a taking on the mind

46. S. J. Cooper, "From Claude Bernard to Walter Cannon. Emergence of the Concept of Homeostasis," *Appetite* 51 (2008) 419–27; Walter B. Cannon, *The Wisdom of the Body: How the Human Body Reacts to Disturbance and Danger and Maintains the Stability Essential to Life*, 2nd ed. (New York: W. W. Norton, 1939).

47. Arturo Rosenblueth, Norbert Wiener, and Julian Bigelow, "Behavior, Purpose and Teleology," *Philosophy of Science* 10 (1943) 18–24.

48. See Hans Jonas, *The Phenomenon of Life: Toward a Philosophical Biology* (Evanston, IL: Northwestern University Press, 1966). Jonas explicitly cites the 1943 paper on purpose and negative feedback but does not connect it to the biology of homeostasis or the work of Walter Cannon or Claude Bernard.

of the other in encounter. Indeed, in contrast to *imitatio*, mimesis and imitation, and even cognitive empathy and simulation, are not primarily about placing ourselves into the shoes and skins of others, but rather about placing *them* into our own for our own ends. How is it possible to take another person's perspective without the episodic memory formation, the experience of being and walking alongside that person? Cold perspective shifts are not the stuff of *imitatio*. Instead, *imitatio* is grounded in loving relation, in contact and encounter giving rise to a stance in which one is prepared to give way, to believe in the other, participate in the other, even become the other for the sake of the other and of one's authentic self that cannot be fully authentic without including the other. Taussig says that "to ponder mimesis is to become sooner or later caught . . . in sticky webs of copy and contact, image and bodily involvement of the perceiver in the image, a complexity we too easily elide as nonmysterious."[49]

Cognitive science, in its recent embodied, enactive, and second-person turns, contains new possibilities for meaningful dialogue about ascetical practices in terms of contemplative encounter, about *imitatio* at the core of Christian and, perhaps, Abrahamic mindfulness. A transformation of knowing must follow a transformation of becoming, so that what is known flows from who is knowing. Embodied, enactive, and second-personal frameworks, always bringing one back to emotionally empathic engagement, can appreciate and incorporate this relationally grounded dependence of mind on stance in ways that were previously thought irrelevant or impossible.

Cognitive scientific engagements in interdisciplinary explorations of *imitatio* need to move beyond models that depend on treating the practitioner as spectator. This movement entails new theoretical frameworks that leverage existing literatures in social learning, social modeling, social referencing, and social comparison. These frameworks also recognize that the mental processes in each of these emerge from encounter and are grounded in values. That is, encounters elicit value and affect that are constitutive of the subsequent perceptions in the encounter, the memories activated during the encounter, and the formation of new episodic memories following the encounter. Conceptual distancing from affect no longer makes theoretical sense once theory includes memory-dependent valuation.

---

49. Michael Taussig, *Mimesis and Alterity: A Particular History of the Senses* (New York: Routledge, 1993). Though Taussig does not cite him, Max Scheler expanded on the poverty of imitation to capture the relation to the exemplar or model person. See Scheler, *Formalism in Ethics*. Dietrich Bonhoeffer uses the last chapter of *Nachfolge* to elaborate on the difference between imitation, which is something done by one's "own deed and decision", and *imitatio*; see Dietrich Bonhoeffer, *Discipleship*, vol. 4 of Dietrich Bonhoeffer Works, English (Minneapolis: Fortress, 2001).

As an example, take the "dangerous driver" scenarios presented in the influential 2014 paper on secular mindfulness by Vago and colleagues.[50] When a dangerous driver "cuts in front of us" either through negligence or through intent, the emphasis in Vago's theory is on spectatorial perception, "without the automatic seasonings of judgment." Contrast this, however, with the enactive-exemplar-relational stress by Bernardo Olivera, who was Abbot-General of the Trappist order at the time of the 1996 summer conversations recorded in *The Gethsemani Encounter*.[51] He shared that he forgave entirely those who killed the monks of Atlas in Algeria, where he had been to collect the remains just weeks earlier.[52] Olivera's "automatic seasonings of judgment" were those of forgiveness, resulting from *imitatio* of divine love which he saw and felt in the person of Jesus. In *imitatio* there is no teaching of "losing" or "letting go" of evaluation. Instead, one begins to "judge" as God does, in love, in forgiveness, and in compassion and in the process gains discernment. What results automatically is love, forgiveness, solidarity, and affirmation of the full personhood of the one loved in the encounter. Father Thomas Keating also tells a story of a dangerous driver, but of one whose hostility was apparent. It is the story of a Christian practitioner of centering prayer who also engaged in "presencing practice" of the kind spoken of by Pieris and William of Saint Thierry. She took as her practice the silent, *imitatio* exercise of recreating the mind of Ps 133:1: "How very good and pleasant it is when sisters and brothers live together in unity!" One day after she had been practicing this text, she stopped her car at a traffic light, and her driver's side window was open. Another car pulled up on her left, and suddenly she felt a slightly warm, gelatinous mass on the side of her face. The light turned, and the other car sped away, with both people in it laughing. She realized that the passenger in the car had spit his mucous onto her face. She told Father Thomas that she did not hesitate, but again, and now with the two people in clear intention, said, "How very good and pleasant it is when sisters and brothers live together in unity!" Then she kept saying it in love, loving the two who had expressed such contempt for her, and she cleaned up and went about her day, holding the one who spit upon her and his companion in her practice via *imitatio* of divine love. The point of her reaction is that it did not even entail forgiveness, at least not immediately. The love for those specific people was present, and its enactive judgment was clear.

Father Thomas's story is an example of an intentional *imitatio*, where there is an intentional, communal practice of connection in memory with the memory of one's

---

50. Gaëlle Desbordes et al., "Moving Beyond Mindfulness: Defining Equanimity as an Outcome Measure in Meditation and Contemplative Research," *Mindfulness* 6 (2015) 356–72.

51. Mitchell and Wiseman, *The Gethsemani Encounter*, 231–33.

52. Bernardo Olivera, *How Far to Follow: The Martyrs of Atlas* (Kalamazoo, MI: Cistercian, 1997).

community and most central exemplars. The type of *imitation* and the variety of processes of social-relational embeddedness, engagement, and perception will likely depend on whether the exemplars are experienced as living, present, and relationally engaged or as imaginative and based in the community's narrative. In either case, loving encounter in the context of the community's narrative, experienced as grace, will generate affectively rich, episodic memory that can ground the remembrance of *imitatio* in one's ongoing practice.

For the purposes of developing approaches that may include cognitive science, there are at least two broad categories involved in *imitatio* as taking on or consenting to participate in the mind of another, whether that other is the community, a person directly given in encounter, or an exemplar.

The first approach may be called *symmnesis*, or a "remembrance with" another person or community of persons. From the perspective of cognitive science, *symmnesis* includes shared perspectives, shared valuations, and aims in action. *Symmnesis* is likely ubiquitous, prior to and the conduit of any influences of wider scope, say of family, peer group, or culture. Certainly, *symmnesis* and its lack could begin to explain why sharing a common language and culture is rarely a guarantee of shared perspective. Because *symmnesis* is a second-person agential perspective (see fig. B below) which includes the person seeking understanding of others in the interaction which grounds understanding, it is sharply different from a third-person process perspective, in which the person seeking understanding is a "spectator" outside of the interactive encounter (see fig. A).

Through formation in a community whose narratives include core exemplars and practices designed to develop *habitus*, and aided by encounters with teachers, stories, and contemplative practices, *symmnesis* takes on exemplar remembrance (see fig. C). *Symmnesis* supports symmnetic actions on the part of the one in formation via participation in the mind of the exemplar (e.g., participation in divine love). Finally, as exemplar remembrance shifts to increased participation in, and active indwelling of, the exemplar mind, one's own limited view, one's individualist self, falls away, giving rise to an expansive, holistic self. This more complete infusion of the exemplar mind is reflected in the "omnesis" of the term *synomnesis* (see fig. D). This is never a property intrinsic to the one infused, but inherent only through indwelling. In this state there is no separate or even differentiable perceiver, but the person achieves a flow entailed by nearly complete *imitatio*. The descriptive term *synomnesis* may serve as a translational concept for a theologically engaged contemplative study, one that includes second-person neuroscience and enactive cognition, so that it may approach interior dimensions and aspects of mental life that are implied in theologically salient terms such as *theosis*, *union*, and *caritas*. Both *symmnesis* and *synomnesis* depend entirely on the gift of relationality and of acceptance in that relation; consequently they are to be understood as forms of, and effects of, grace.

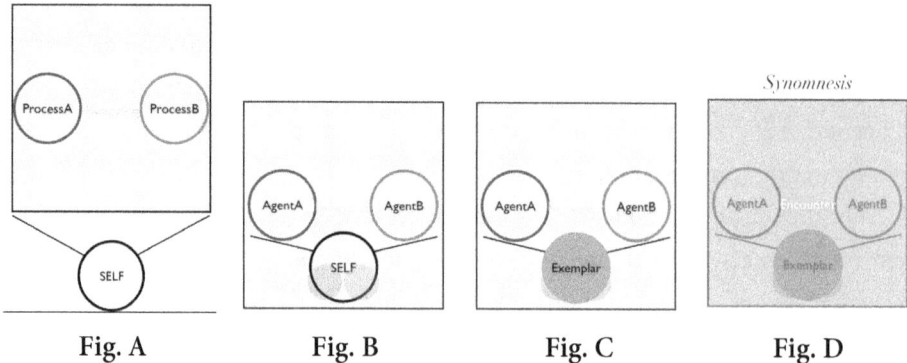

Fig. A   Fig. B   Fig. C   Fig. D

Figure A: a third-person processing perspective; Figure B: a second-person agential perspective, effortful *symmnesis*; Figure C: exemplar remembrance, transition away from *symmnesis* to *synomnesis*; Figure D: *synomnesis,* in which the exemplar remembrance infuses one's understanding and perspective of encounters that fully include others and oneself.

Scholars of biblical ethics and of moral theology often refer to the cultivation and formation of the person in terms of developing habits and of becoming habituated to and in a way of seeing, acting, and being. Integrative work requires such theological and philosophical sensitivity to the *how* of the processes that form the very core of the theories being advanced. Yet even a cursory review of the current science of learning and decision-making reveals that reigning accounts of habituation are not at all what Aristotle or Aquinas meant by *habitus* formation. Why does this matter? If one's goal is to present a virtue theory grounded in habituation and mimesis, then a clear view of cognitive science and brain function is necessary, for these two processes are central to the understanding of human psychology. There are enough situations where scientific approaches are of little help in clarifying terminology relevant to moral philosophy and theology, but this is not one of them. I have already provided some scientifically grounded, interdisciplinary accounts of *habitus* as complex, exemplar-focused learning.[53] Here, I will summarize the main points of these inquiries.

Habits in cognitive and psychological science are unlike *habitus*. They are not goal-directed behaviors. For an action to be goal-directed, there must be a learned association between an organism's response and the outcome of that response (i.e.,

---

53. See Joshua Mauldin and Robin W. Lovin, eds., *Theology as Interdisciplinary Inquiry* (Grand Rapids: Eerdmans, forthcoming 2017); and Gregory Peterson et al., eds., *Habits in Mind: Integrating Theology, Philosophy, and the Cognitive Science of Virtue, Emotion, and Character Formation* (Leiden: Brill, 2017).

"R-O control") and the expected outcome must align with motivation at the time of response. Habits have nothing to do with either of these basic conditions. Habits are behaviors that are completely independent of an outcome's *current* value and only depend on past, overlearned associations. Thus, habits are not sensitive to contextual changes, they are inflexible and are difficult to unlearn, and they are purely stimulus-response behaviors[54] where the "stimulus" can be a complex context. Another way to frame habits is provided by the social psychologists Wendy Wood and David T. Neal, who state the two key principles that characterize habits are: 1) "an outsourcing of behavioral control to context cues that were, in the past, contiguous with performance"; and 2) "performed without mediation of a goal to achieve a particular outcome or a goal to respond (i.e., a behavioral intention)."[55] They are, as the authors point out, "the residue of past goal pursuit," where the residue is free of any intention or sensitivity to context or sensitivity to outcome. These definitions are by no means outliers in the scientific field but are almost universally understood when cognitive scientists theorize about habit learning, otherwise known as habituation.

What is clear right away is that habits and habituation are not related to *habitus* or to the processes of virtue formation, since *imitatio* and the transformation of self via the reconstitution of self and other require exquisite sensitivity to context and the deep learning that goes beyond recitation of surface concepts. The processes of *symmnesis* and *synomnesis* require remembrance of the kind that lives in communities, their historical traditions, and the texts and practices that continue to be enacted in shared intention. Deep learning, requiring the entire mind—affectivity, knowledge, understanding, and wisdom—is a better description of *habitus* and is scientifically within the scope of interdisciplinary engagement. Habits and habituation, though these terms need not be discarded in theological interpretation of Scripture, should not be confused with scientific accounts of the same. Enactive, relational, exemplar-following learning is what is meant instead, and in this there is much fruitful interdisciplinary work to come.

---

54. Ray J. Dolan, and Peter Dayan. "Goals and Habits in the Brain," *Neuron* 80 (2013) 312–25.

55. Wendy Wood, and David T. Neal. "A New Look at Habits and the Habit-Goal Interface," *Psychological Review* 114 (2007) 843–63.

KNOWING IN PART: THE DEMANDS OF SCIENTIFIC AND RELIGIOUS KNOWLEDGE IN EVERYDAY DECISIONS

or

"SHE BLINDED ME WITH SCIENCE!" AND DECIDING WHETHER TO WEAR CHECKS WITH STRIPES

Johnny Wei-Bing Lin

It was spring in Chicago. Mere months remained before my third child entered our world, and the time had come to buy a minivan. As much as I wanted to keep my beloved Subaru Impreza, there is no way to fit three car seats into the back. So, my wife and I bought a subscription to *Consumer Reports* and pored over their new and old car ratings. We talked to our friends who have minivans and asked our trusted, long-time mechanic for his advice. We visited various dealerships, looked over the cars on the lot, opened and closed doors, checked seats and compartments, and test drove two of the vans. We thought and talked about our needs and wants: Did it have to have four-wheel drive? Was I okay with the layout of the instrument panel? How easily did the back seats fold down? What could we afford? Could I reach the gas pedal? We prayed about our decision, and in the end we were new owners of a Honda Odyssey.

In that decision and any of a number of small, medium, and large decisions we all make every day, what role did scientific and religious knowledge play? On the surface, it seems like neither science nor religion played much of a role in our decision. After all, does not everyone want to buy a car that best meets their practical needs and lasts the longest, all for the least amount of money? But what tells us that a car meets our practical needs? How do we know that one car will last but another will not? Are not both questions answered by science, through studies of the material properties of metals, plastics, and composites, the properties of various structural designs, the probability distribution of a car's reliability, the most efficient way to set up an assembly line, quality control mechanisms, etc.? What led us to believe that efficiency and productivity—getting the most "bang for the buck"—is the primary standard by which we should make our decision? Did (or should) religion have had a role in answering that question?

In the present work, I will investigate the roles scientific and religious knowledge (and other forms of knowledge) play in everyday decisions. I will not provide a comprehensive treatment of the topic, but I have two more modest goals: (1) to provide a framework of topics for questions to ask in understanding how scientific, religious, and other forms of knowledge relate to everyday decisions; and (2) to provide a few general conclusions regarding science and religion and everyday decisions as to how, as our title suggests, science and religion each provide partial input into such decisions. To help guide our inquiry, I adapt a taxonomy developed to help think through what goes into excellent creation care. That taxonomy is described in my book *The Nature of Environmental Stewardship: Understanding Creation Care Solutions to Environmental Problems* (Eugene, OR: Pickwick, 2016). In the present work I analyze everyday decisions in two phases. First, I ask what kinds of knowledge and knowing are available for the decision. Second, I ask what these ways of knowing tell us about the importance, goals, and practice of the decision, items that make up the "criteria" for the decision. The importance criterion describes how important achieving the goals of the decision stacks up against other goals that may be impacted by our choice. The goals of the decision are what we hope to achieve or be true because of the decision. The practice of the decision is what we actually do to implement the decision.

I begin with the question how we know anything at all and describe the strengths and weaknesses of each kind of knowing. (Throughout the present work I will often use "ways of knowing" and "knowledge" interchangeably, even though, properly speaking, the two are not the same. However, for our purposes, since how we know greatly affects what we know, in many cases the use of one term encompasses the other term.) Second, I investigate what kinds of knowing science and religion use and what science and religion are able to learn about the world through these ways of knowing. Third, I describe ways scientific and religious knowledge tells us about the importance, goals, and practice of everyday decisions. Fourth, I will apply this framework to some examples. Finally, I will draw out some pastoral implications of our analysis. While the focus of this paper is on how scientific and religious knowledge affect everyday decisions, there are, of course, other kinds of knowledge that will be important, and it will be clear through our discussion how to incorporate those other kinds of knowledge into our analytical framework.

How Do We Know

There are two general ways we know something: someone tells us or we figure it out ourselves. When someone tells us whether something is true, this is called revelation. When we figure it out, we use some sort of means of apprehending for ourselves whatever we claim to know. The three main means of apprehending truth are reason, intuition, and feelings. In this section I describe the strengths and weaknesses of these four ways of knowing.

While Christians generally use the term "revelation" to refer to knowledge given to us by God, more generally revelation is any knowledge given to us by some authority. God is the ultimate authority, but human beings can also be considered authorities. The source of that authority might be the "expert" who has special knowledge from detailed study. The source of the authority might be moral in nature, such as that possessed by a saint or other moral exemplar. Moral authority does not come from scholarly expertise but from the experience and credibility of a life well-lived. While revelation from a moral authority generally addresses moral subjects, this need not be the case. A third source of authority is political in nature. It is the authority related to the system of how we organize the structure of our common life and distribute power and responsibility. In a democracy authority is grounded on the consent of the governed. In a monarchy authority rests in the monarch and may be grounded on the personal *charism* of the monarch, tradition, the aristocracy, or divine mandate.

The quality of revealed knowledge as knowledge depends entirely on the quality of the authority behind the revelation. In the case of divine revelation, because an all-knowing, all-powerful, and all-loving God is the source of the knowledge, such revelation is the most authoritative knowing possible. (Of course, someone who does not believe that such knowledge is divinely revealed will not accept the knowledge as authoritative.) Revelation from human authorities, by necessity, is less authoritative than divine revelation, but in cases where we perceive the authority of our opinions is much lower than the opinions of another human authority, the revelation of that other human authority can be quite authoritative. For instance, a man who is injured in a car accident, when told by the emergency room doctor that he needs to undergo surgery immediately, will seldom question the authority of the knowledge the doctor is revealing to him. Even though the man, under normal circumstances, would argue he knows what is best for himself, in this circumstance the expert authority of the doctor gives her knowledge near-absolute authority. While in the case of the emergency room doctor's advice this authority almost certainly results in a particular decision (to undergo the surgery) the authority of knowledge does not, as a general rule, *necessarily* result in a particular decision. We will address this in more detail later when we consider how to translate knowledge into decisions.

Revelatory knowledge has the following strengths: potentially very high quality, efficient production, and as a source of new information. As I mentioned earlier, the quality of revelatory knowledge is entirely based on the authority producing the knowledge. If the authority is unimpeachable, the quality of the knowledge given by the authority is also very high. Additionally, because revelation comes from an authority, it takes relatively little work by the recipients to appropriate the knowledge for themselves, outside of determining the authority of the source. Finally, revelation has the potential of providing new knowledge previously unknown to the recipient, because the revelation originates outside of the recipient. Revelation transcends the personal limitations of the recipient and offers the possibility of "something that was not there before."

Revelatory knowledge has one main weakness: if the authority behind the knowledge is in error, the recipient will be led astray with incorrect knowledge, with correction difficult. In order to correct revelatory knowledge, the recipient needs to correct their understanding of the authority of the source. Perhaps the source does not have the expertise pertinent to the problem or the authority's moral authority does not apply in this particular case. Correcting one's understanding of authority, however, is time consuming, and efforts at correction have to work against feelings of loyalty associated with trust in an authority. Efforts at correction erase the efficiency benefits of revelatory knowledge.

When we engage in the second way of knowing—figuring it out ourselves—we generally use one or more of these three means: reason, intuition, and feelings. The first means, reason, operates by using the rules of logic to move from a set of premises to a set of conclusions. This process may be deductive (moving from general principles to specific instances) inductive (moving from specific instances to general principles) or retroductive (moving from specific instances to general principles and back to specific instances, etc.).[1] If the premises of a logical argument are true and the logic is valid, then the conclusions must be true. To borrow a classic example, if all men are mortal and Socrates is a man, then we can conclude that Socrates is mortal. In this example the first two claims ("all men are mortal" and "Socrates is a man") are the premises. The logic used is transitivity; an example of transitivity from introductory algebra is the transitive property of equality, "if $a = b$ and $b = c$ then $a = c$."

---

1. James T. Cushing, *Philosophical Concepts in Physics: The Historical Relation Between Philosophy and Scientific Theories* (Cambridge: Cambridge University Press, 1998) 5–7, 31–34.

The strengths of reason seems to be self-evident. It provides objective rather than subjective conclusions. With reason we can establish universal and eternal truths that are independent of the person making the argument. Reason is fundamentally egalitarian: neither age, power, life experience, nor any other factor can overturn the conclusions of a logical argument if the premises are true and the logic is valid. Finally, the authority of reason seems incontrovertible. To be "reasonable" is praiseworthy and "unreasonable" is, well, unreasonable. Science is understood as having authority because it uses reason, not the other way around.

As powerful and desirable as reason is, however, it also has weaknesses. First, it is not always clear how to establish the truth of the premises of a logical argument. We could say that the premises themselves are established using reason, but that just pushes the justification of the premises to some set of "first principles" that must be justified by some other means besides reason. Descartes thought these first principles could be known by intuition.[2] The framers of the Declaration of Independence began with premises justified as being "self-evident." Ultimately, this means we cannot use reason to justify reason. We need some other way of grounding reason.

Second, reason can only tell us what we already know to be true. That is to say, reason cannot reveal a truth to us that was not already latent in premises we believed to be true. As Reason, personified as a female knight in C. S. Lewis's *The Pilgrim's Regress,* says to the protagonist in response to a question, "I can bring things out of the dark part of your mind into the light part of it. But now you ask me what is not even in the dark of your mind."[3] Truly creative knowing—coming to know something that would never have occurred to you in a million years—requires more than reason.

Finally, reason is incomplete. Gödel's Incompleteness Theorem, while only properly applied to an arithmetic, suggests that for any set of premises, there are statements that are true that cannot be proved to be true.[4] Thus, the dream of choosing the perfect set of premises and, using logic, deriving all other true statements, appears to be unattainable. To access all truths, using reason, we need to use multiple sets of premises. The difficulty of justifying our ultimate premises is thus magnified to include not merely one set but multiple, if not many, sets. In this picture reason's role at knowing truth seems rather limited; all the heavy lifting seems to be in choosing and justifying the premises.

---

2. Ibid., 7.

3. C. S. Lewis, *The Pilgrim's Regress* (Grand Rapids: Eerdmans, 1992) 58.

4. See Stephen M. Barr, *Modern Physics and Ancient Faith* (Notre Dame, IN: University of Notre Dame Press, 2006) appendix C for a more detailed description of Gödel's Incompleteness Theorem.

While modern discourse generally disparages non-rational means of non-revelatory knowing, our everyday experience tells us that we know many things, often the most important things, through means other than reason. As Blaise Pascal wrote in *Pensées,* "The heart has its reasons of which reason knows nothing: we know this in countless ways."[5] The mother holding her newborn child or the groom beholding his bride on their wedding day knows Pascal's truth more clearly and intimately than all the syllogisms of the world could capture. Can we say something more about what it means to know with our hearts? What does it mean to know something through intuition and feelings?

When we exercise intuition, we apprehend the subject of our intuition directly. We connect to, understand, and relate to our subject. Our subject is not something we dissect or analyze, it is not something we reason *about* or do something *to*. We are, to appropriate C. S. Lewis's distinction, looking *along* something rather than *at* something.[6] We welcome the subject, walk alongside it, and come to it on its own terms. With our intuition, we come to know the subject we intuit by an act of creativity. By this we do not mean our intuited knowledge is "made up" but rather that it is "made." Intuited knowledge is not derived; it is born. Thus, intuition is often closely connected with imagination, metaphor, symbols, stories, and relationships.

Faith is also a kind of intuition, though it is not merely intuition. Faith is informed by other kinds of knowledge, such as reason. Christian faith, as an act of the Holy Spirit, is also a revealed faith. As an action of the will and an act of trust, faith does not just understand its object but apprehends it, like intuition. Faith is exercised in a way similar to how we exercise deep trust in those closest to us. While the trust we give our loved ones is informed by what we have seen in the past of their trustworthiness, there is an element in which our trust connects with the person in their entirety. I do not trust my wife merely because she has come through for me in the past, I trust my wife because she is herself. I do not only have faith *because,* I also have faith *in*.

Once exercised, faith itself is also a source of knowledge. The faith we have in another person itself provides knowledge of that person. My faith and trust of my wife opens the doors for connecting with and understanding her in ways that would otherwise be, not only hidden, but non-existent. That knowledge itself may be through reason, intuition, or feeling. We see echoes of the knowledge-source dynamic of faith in John 6:69. In the verses prior, Jesus has given a hard teaching,

---

5. Blaise Pascal, *Pensées*, rev. ed., translated by A. J. Krailsheimer (London: Penguin, 1995) 127 [Fragment 423].

6. C. S. Lewis, "Meditation in a Toolshed," in *God in the Dock: Essays on Theology and Ethics,* ed.ited by Walter Hooper (Grand Rapids: Eerdmans, 1979) 212–15.

resulting in many of his disciples abandoning him. Jesus asks the Twelve whether they too will leave and Peter answers, where else would they go? Then, in v. 69, Peter explains, "We have come to believe and to know that you are the Holy One of God." (NIV) While most of us usually think of knowledge coming first, then belief, here Peter seems to suggest the opposite. These are the "eyes of faith." There are some things that we can only come to know if we first believe.[7]

The strength of intuition is that some subjects are really only able to be apprehended or understood as a complete whole, on their own terms. For those subjects, reason and analysis do not work. For instance, ideas that are "self-evident," to borrow the Declaration of Independence's phrase, are "self" justified. The whole truth itself provides its own truthfulness. One can critique whether or not the rights to "life, liberty, and the pursuit of happiness" are really self-evident truths, or grounded on other justifications, but if they are self-evident, there is no way of apprehending them except by intuition.

The weaknesses of intuition are related to its strength. First, if an intuited truth is, in some sense, self-justified, then on what basis do we critique (or corroborate) knowledge gained from intuition? Examining the "fruit" of the intuition (similar to Jesus's teaching in Luke 6:43–45) and "counting noses" to see whether others have a similar intuition are some of the ways left for those to critique the knowledge brought by intuition. Yet, everyday we experience situations where our intuition has led us astray (for instance, the rate of fall of very small objects versus moderately sized objects). Second, it is difficult to separate when we know from intuition versus feeling. While the two are similar and are resistant to external critique, they are not the same. Intuited knowledge has staying power, unlike knowledge from feelings, but before the passage of time, it is not always clear whether a given piece of knowledge comes from intuition or feelings.

The second non-rational, non-revelatory form of knowing, feelings, is often disparaged as a form of knowing. As mentioned earlier, feelings are ephemeral, short-lived, and fickle. They are also immediate, intense, and, when present, dominating. Feelings are well-known by behavioral psychologists to be relatively easily manipulated (e.g., confirmation bias, the joiner effect, etc.).[8] When it comes to decision-making, wisdom tells us to distrust how we feel, recognizing its fleeting and misleading nature, and instead focus on reason and faith as ways of knowing. Proverbs 17:27 rightly reminds us that, "The one who has knowledge uses words

---

7. I owe elements of the arguments on John 6:69 to Bill Newsome, "Of Two Minds: A Neuroscientist Balances Science and Faith." 2016 Annual Meeting of the American Scientific Affiliation, Azusa, CA, delivered July 22, 2016. See http://www2.asa3.org/movies/ASA2016Newsome.mp4.

8. While this is a broadly understood idea, I owe this distillation to a series of posts by Scott Adams, *Scott Adams' Blog*. See http://blog.dilbert.com/.

with restraint, and whoever has understanding is even-tempered" (NIV) rather than a hot-head, heavy lashing out with his or her passions. If the quest for knowledge can be likened to wandering the stacks of a library, why would we ever want to play around there with gasoline and matches?

Yet, the feeling of joy when we see our spouse at the airport after a long period of separation, the feeling of anguish and pity when we see photographs of homeless children after an earthquake, the feeling of anger when we witness the injustice of civilians caught in the cross fire of a civil war: Do these feelings have nothing to teach us? Is their only value to us as a means of releasing excess psychic energy, the mechanical effects of biochemical changes, or a challenge to and test of our endurance?

I suggest that for all the weaknesses feelings have as a form of knowing, feelings still have a role in knowing. First, the attributes of feelings that make them unreliable as a teacher are the same attributes that make them effective as a herald. Feelings have the power of grabbing our attention, of alerting us to danger, and motivating us to act in response. Feelings thus can provide a part of the truth as well as prime us to be ready to accept knowledge gained through other means. Feelings can even provide, in some sense, knowledge of what might not yet be but could be. As an example of this kind of knowledge, consider the love a man and a woman have for each other at the beginning of their relationship. This love is, of course, a mixture of many kinds of love: unconditional *agape* love, friendship, and *eros*. The will is involved but so is feeling. The ardor of that feeling, at least partly, opens each person to see their beloved, not only as who they currently are, but also for who they might become. By this, we do not mean that they see their beloved in terms of potential, but rather that because of their feeling of being in love, they see *more* of their beloved, a "moreness" that others do not see. This "moreness," when joined with *agape* love, can be a glimpse of a more blessed beloved. When we talk about love being blind, we refer to the negative side of this kind of knowing. The feeling of love can blind us to the shortcomings of the beloved. At the same time, this can also be a glimpse of what could be, of what that person would be like if they overcame their shortcomings. This alternate reality is dangerous if it is a false reality, and many, many hearts have been led astray by this false knowledge the feeling of love gives. However, when it is prophetic, it represents true knowledge and enables a self-giving that would otherwise be difficult to offer. Thus, we might say that feelings have the ability to lift the corner of the curtain behind which lies the truth. It does not have the ability to do much more than that, and sometimes (often?) it lifts the corner of the wrong curtain. Still, the power feelings possess is almost never matched by reason and intuition.

A second way feelings can provide knowledge is as a good. While we could conceive of revelation, reason, and intuition as goods in and of themselves, we seldom do so. Feelings, however, are often considered as both consequences of a good (e.g., happiness we feel from the practice of generosity) as well as goods in and of themselves (e.g., happiness by itself). While the ancients would not have been supportive of feelings playing the role of a primary good, in modern society, at the very least feelings play the role of a very strong secondary good. Thus, in many everyday decisions having fun or enjoying the outcome is usually considered positively. The presence or absence of a feeling as a good or harm can possess evidentiary value.

How and What do Science and Religion Know

Revelation, reason, intuition, and feelings: given these four ways of knowing, which of these ways are used by science and which are used by religion, and what kind of knowledge can science and religion obtain? Regarding the first question, conventional wisdom tells us that science makes use of reason while religion makes use of revelation, intuition, and feelings. Science knows, faith believes. This conventional wisdom is, well, conventional, having been taught starting from grade school lessons on the scientific method and hypothesis-testing to intellectual defenses of science that appeal to peer review and Karl Popper's falsification hypothesis.[9]

Critiques of this conventional wisdom argue that such a definition of science and religion is too narrow. First, these critiques point out that religion makes extensive use of reason, as can be seen in any theology text. While theology and philosophy have historically made limited use of retroductive reasoning, which modern science has used at least since Newton, theology and philosophy nonetheless have a rich history of the use and development of deductive and inductive reasoning. Revelation can also work through reason, as well as intuition and feeling. Thus, while religion as a way of knowing does differ from science in that the former commonly admits direct, supernatural revelation, it is a stretch to conclude religion eschews the use of reason.

Second, critiques of the conventional wisdom understanding of scientific and religious knowing argue science is fundamentally a human endeavor and as such makes use of the range of ways of knowing that humans use. For instance, science makes use of human creativity and intuition; the chemist Kekulé's discovery of the ring structure of the benzene molecule was inspired by a dream of a snake biting its own tail.[10] Scientific discoveries are not merely mechanical derivations from prior knowledge but leaps built on both data, intuition, and feeling. As physicist Boris

---

9. Cushing, *Philosophical Concepts in Physics*, 30, 32–36.
10. Robert H. McKim, *Experiences in Visual Thinking*, 2nd ed. (Boston: PWS Engineering, 1980) 11.

Castel and philosopher Sergio Sismondo point out, such "reasoning" (versus mere logic) involves extra-logical ideas such as simplicity and elegance. "Logic," say Castel and Sismondo, "while very pretty, is by itself quite useless. Logic is self-contained, and doesn't by itself hook onto the material world."[11] Finally, critiques of the conventional wisdom argue that science even utilizes revelation. At the very least, the vast majority of scientific knowledge is accepted on the basis of authority. For instance, few, if any, students re-derive physical first principles (such as $F=ma$) on the basis of raw data; we accept the laws of motion because experts tell us they are correct. Others have argued that it is important for science to develop in a culture shaped by a worldview like the Christian worldview that is supportive of the concepts of causation and regularity in nature.

For the purposes of the present work, where does this dichotomy between the conventional wisdom view of scientific and religious knowing and the critiques of that view leave us? On the one hand, it would appear that if we hold the conventional wisdom view, we would want to rely on scientific knowledge more than religious knowledge, because the former utilizes reason while the latter does not. Yet, our analysis of reason in the previous section suggested that reason itself has weaknesses; there are serious reasons to question whether reason deserves a reputation of epistemic omnicompetence. On the other hand, if we question the conventional wisdom view, we find the differences between how science and religion know to be more differences in emphases, rather than an apples/oranges difference in how we know. They are differences not in kind but in proportion. Thus, in terms of making everyday decisions, we conclude that, at the very least, we have reason to ask for ways of knowing besides reason.

Given our analysis of how science and religion know, what can we say about what those methods tell us? Science and religion can, of course, tell us what revelation, reason, intuition, and feelings can access. To say more, however, requires an understanding of our worldview, that is, what we see when we see the world. To know what science and religion can reveal, we need to know both *how* science and religion gain knowledge as well as what *kind* of world science and religion are trying to describe. For instance, if we believe the universe is mere matter in motion (as in a materialist neo-Enlightenment notion) we can know nothing about the universe except for phenomena describable in terms of material causes. If we have a monist conception of the universe, where existence is ultimately all there is (as in a Buddhist conception) what science and religion can reveal will be radically different, as materiality as a different kind of existence is an illusion. If we have a Christian conception

---

11. Boris Castel and Sergio Sismondo. *The Art of Science* (North York, ON: Higher Education University of Toronto Press, 2008) 71.

of the universe, which has both material and non-material qualities and where God sustains the universe both within and without natural law, what science and religion can say will be yet different still.

Let us unpack the Christian worldview (or at least one common version of it) and what it says about what knowledge science and religion can give us. First, the Christian worldview understands reality as having hybrid natures in a number of areas. Nature is made of matter but is not merely matter. The material is intertwined or interacts with the non-material, whether that be the supernatural (angels, God) or the natural (transcendentals such as truth, beauty). Thus, methods of knowing that only address the material will give an incomplete understanding of the universe, as will methods of knowing that do not address the material. To the extent that science addresses only the dynamics of matter, science cannot (whether through reason, intuition, or feeling) fully address non-material phenomena (such as values). To the extent that science addresses only dynamics of nature that are knowable through regularities (e.g., natural laws) science cannot fully address non-regular phenomena (e.g., miracles, free will).

The reverse situation for religion is not quite as straightforward as the case for science. Unlike the common understanding of science as focusing on material phenomena, religion is understood as addressing both material and non-material phenomena, as well as both natural and supernatural phenomena. Thus, religion is not *a priori* limited to studying only a subset of the phenomena extant in the universe; science is limited to studying material facts while religion can study material facts and values. The questions then become, first, whether religion or science does better in studying material phenomena, and second, whether the knowledge religion provides regarding non-material phenomena is reliable and accurate. With regard to the first question, the current dominant opinion is that science provides a more accurate and productive description of the material world than religion. That opinion echoes Galileo's claim that the Bible teaches, "how one goes to Heaven, not how the heavens go."[12] The predictive abilities of the natural sciences also suggest science does better in studying merely material phenomena, but this is an important restriction as to the epistemic authority of science, as many of the most important material systems are not merely material but instead interact with non-material phenomena (e.g., the mind). With regard to the second question, the reliability of religious knowledge of non-material phenomena is beyond the scope of the present work. For the purposes of this paper, we will accept Peter's testimony of Jesus that, "You have the words of

---

12. Charles E. Hummel, *The Galileo Connection: Resolving Conflicts between Science and the Bible* (Downers Grove, IL: InterVarsity, 1986) 106.

eternal life" (John 6:68b, NIV) as justification that knowledge from Jesus about both material and non-material life is trustworthy.

Second, the Christian worldview understands reality as fundamentally relational in nature. God did not merely create the world, nor does he merely sustain the world; he also loves the world. As a result, the most important aspects of reality are those involved with relating to God and relating to others. Jesus told us, all the law and the prophets hang on the commands to love God and love our neighbor (Matt 22:37–40). The kind of knowledge the Christian religion will tend to access will be relational. Revelation, reason, intuition, and feelings can all provide relational knowledge, but we should expect the Christian worldview to emphasize the parts of each way of knowing that more naturally connect to relationships than other worldviews which lack the relational emphasis.

Scientific and Religious Knowledge and the Importance, Goals, and Practice of Everyday Decisions

How then does the knowledge associated with science and religion inform the importance, goals, and practice of everyday decisions? In this section I will first describe the kinds of characteristics of knowledge we need to examine to analyze their impact on everyday decisions. This is different from enumerating the strengths and weaknesses of each form of knowledge, as any given strength or weakness may or may not bear on answering the question how that knowledge matters. Once we understand how knowledge matters, I will analyze the various ways of weighing different kinds of knowledge, particularly given the constraints of everyday decisions. Finally, I will draw implications for understanding the importance, goals, and practice criteria with regard to everyday decisions.

Earlier, I described the four ways of knowing—revelation, reason, intuition, and feeling—and how science and religion can be considered buckets describing various ways of collecting these ways of knowing. Here I consider three questions we should ask of any given way of knowing to determine how that way may affect the importance, goals, and practice of everyday decisions. First, we can evaluate the *applicability* of the knowledge. Does the way of knowing address the "kind" of question addressed by a given criterion? Does the way of knowing tell us something that applies to the specific decision being considered? (Here, I use "way of knowing" not only to represent the four general ways of knowing but also different ways of knowing that are of the same general type. Thus, deontological and consequentialist ethics are both exercises in reason, but their scope of applicability is different.) For instance, if the way of knowing has little to tell us regarding the values or ethics involved with the decision, that way of knowing will have little to say regarding the importance or goals of the decision. Thus, to the extent science is concerned merely with describing material states, it will not have much to contribute regarding the goals of our decision. As another example, the applicability of deontological knowledge will differ from prudential knowledge because the former has a much narrower range than the latter; there are fewer ways of thinking about which laundry detergent to buy in terms of rights as compared to thinking in terms of wisdom.

A second question we can ask concerns the coverage or *scope* of the way of knowing. Does the way of knowing provide "enough" of the range of issues that one needs to evaluate a criterion? For instance, feelings, while powerful, are generally rather limited in the topics they cover and their subject. We are more apt to feel deeply about a very small set of people—family and close friends—rather than the broader population. In a decision that requires understanding values, revelation may be applicable but the scope of what has been revealed may be limited, requiring us to use reason and other sources of knowledge to help us in the decision. As an example of the latter case, revelation tells us nature has value but does not necessarily tell us how to balance the value of nature against other values (e.g., economics, politics, etc.). As a final example of the importance of scope, many everyday decisions are not only data-constrained but also imagination-constrained. The problem is not merely that we do not know enough but also that we do not know enough about what we do not know, as well as what to do with what we do know. We need both facts and creativity. Reason or revelation or intuition or feeling alone (or one kind of reason, one kind of intuition, etc.) will not do; we need all the sources of knowing.

A third question we should ask of any given way of knowing with regard to everyday decisions concerns the *reliability* and certainty of the knowledge. This question is a function of the strengths and weaknesses of each form of knowing and what knowledge science and religion provide. The strengths and weaknesses of each form of knowing include different levels of reliability. As we discussed earlier, the different ways of understanding scientific and religious knowledge can result in different conclusions about the reliability of scientific and religious knowledge. I will comment more on the reliability of different ways of knowing when I discuss how to weigh different kinds of knowledge against each other. As an aside, this third question encapsulates what we normally mean by "truthfulness" in the sense of correspondence to reality. Reliable knowledge likely tells us the truth.

Finally, as another aside, with scientific and religious knowledge we often need to consider the *apparent* applicability, scope, and reliability of the way of knowing. With science and religion, there is the applicability, scope, and reliability of the knowing mechanisms themselves, and then there are what we *think* are the applicability, scope, and reliability of the knowing mechanisms. This distinction is important because both science and religion in our culture have an inherent authority that exists independently of how science and religion actually function as knowledge systems. Put another way, there is science and religion and then there is the "PR" for science and religion. We see this when appeals to either science or God suggest there is no room for thought or debate. Phrases like "scientists say" and "God says" carry with them more than the authority of revelation but an epistemic authority that implies decision-making is straightforward and that shuts down the need for further knowledge. In order to consider properly the knowledge science and religion do provide, we need to guard against unknowingly using this aura of epistemic privilege prematurely to short-circuit the processing of all the knowledge available for decision-making.

Once we know how knowledge matters—its applicability, scope, and reliability—we can consider different ways of weighing different kinds of knowledge against one another. What or which knowledge matters (science, religion, or another collection of the four ways of knowing) for this particular decision, when, and how? This involves using the results of our previous analysis—what are the strengths and weaknesses of each kind of knowing, what kinds of knowing are important to science and religion, and what does each say about the world, given our worldview? How does each form of knowing apply to a given decision? Does the scope of the form of knowing span the issues for a given decision, is the form of knowing reliable, and does it adjudicate the issues with wisdom? We can, however, make three additional observations regarding how to weigh different kinds of knowledge against one another in the light of everyday decisions.

First, as has been suggested in my earlier arguments, there are multiple ways of connecting values and science in making decisions and policies. One way of connecting values and science to decisions and policies is to ignore values altogether and assume science prescribes what we should do. This approach is termed the "policy prescriptive" approach. Another way of making the connection is through the "fact-value dualism" approach which connects science with values. Science determines the facts that are in turn integrated with values by decision and policy makers to create policies. A third way is termed the "supporting role: science is neutral" model, where science combines with various values, but with different roles and statuses. A fourth way is termed the "supporting role: science may not be neutral" model. In this model, science and values are on equal footing, with neither possessing epistemic privilege. A fifth way of connecting science and values is the "honest broker of policy alternatives model" (proposed by Roger A. Pielke, Jr.),[13] in which science functions

---

13. Roger A. Pielke, Jr., *The Honest Broker: Making Sense of Science in Policy and Politics*

to expand rather than narrow the list of policy options. Chapter 5 of my book *The Nature of Environmental Stewardship*[14] describes in more detail these five ways of connecting science with values for the purposes of policy making. For the purposes of the present work, I note merely that there is a spectrum of ways of connecting values and science to obtain policy, and thus we should not assume that one approach fits all decisions. Indeed, with regard to environmental issues, science-policy research suggests the policy prescriptive approach is effective for only the most trivial of environmental problems. Other approaches are needed for more complex and controversial issues. We would expect the same to be the case for everyday decisions.

Second, an integral element of the process of deciding between different sources of knowledge is deciding how to account properly for uncertainty and risk. All sources of knowledge have potential weaknesses and uncertainties. On one level, dealing with those uncertainties means dealing with risk. Chapter 7 of *The Nature of Environmental Stewardship* notes that strategies of dealing with risk can be categorized into three ways: strategies to prevent any harms from occurring from the uncertainty, strategies to limit the extent of harms that may result, and strategies that accept an intrinsic level of risk and seek to mitigate the effects of, or compensate for, those harms. An example of the first kind of strategy is the precautionary principle, which places the burden of proof on those who would take an action if the action might result in an irreversible or catastrophic harm. An example of the second kind of strategy is to use large safety margins in the design of systems affected by the uncertainty. An example of the third kind of strategy is fire insurance. The use of one or more strategies to alter one's risk exposure will also affect how one integrates different sources of knowledge with each other.

Finally, everyday decisions are time and resource constrained. Whether the decision is important ("should I ask this woman to marry me") or trivial ("should I choose an aisle or window seat") we have only so much time and energy to analyze, make, and carry out the decision. We cannot write a PhD thesis about every possible decision. These constraints put a premium on the value of the knowledge based on general, flexible principles. For instance, consider the difference between the ethical theories of deontology (duty) and virtue ethics. While the commands from deontology have high levels of authority, there are relatively few commands or categorical imperatives we can define. There are no direct commands regarding whether one should buy a popsicle or an ice cream. How then, using a deontological framework, do we make many everyday decisions? Virtue ethics, in contrast, while lacking the level of authority a right or duty possesses, focus on the formation of a

(Cambridge: Cambridge University Press, 2007) 17–18.

14. See p. 143 above.

particular kind of person, a virtuous person, and in so doing, equips the person with general tools one can apply to specific decisions. For many everyday decisions then, the knowledge reason provides through virtue ethics will be more useful than the knowledge reason provides through deontological ethics.

The burden of time and resource constraints in everyday decisions also makes it easy to avoid using multiple forms of knowing in decision-making, instead depending on only one form of knowing. For those who tend towards rationality, it can be easy to discount intuition, feelings, and revelation. For those of us who believe the truths of Scripture, it can be easy to use revelation when God is actually calling us also to exercise our reason and intuition. Also the immediacy and power of emotion can make feelings a tempting form of knowing to rely on (consciously or unconsciously) when making decisions, as the advertising industry certainly recognizes. We have seen, however, that each form of knowing has its strengths and weaknesses. While time and resource limits are real and constrain what forms of knowledge we can bring to bear on our everyday decisions, the spectrum of ways of knowing presents a *prima facie* case against relying on only one form of knowing in making decisions.

With this consideration of how knowledge matters and how to weigh different forms of knowledge in everyday decision-making, how then do we understand the importance, goals, and practice criteria with regard to everyday decisions? The arguments presented so far directly answer that question. We start with the four forms of knowledge (revelation, reason, intuition, and feelings) enumerate what they say, ascertain the applicability, scope, and reliability of what they say, and wisely weigh what the knowledge says about the importance, goals, and practice of the decision.

As we analyze and ponder, we should recognize that every form of knowledge has strengths and weaknesses and that both science and religion have descriptive power regarding importance, goals, and practice—not just science alone—particularly regarding topics that involve more than physical systems. We expect science will have much to say about the merely material elements related to our decision, particularly regarding practice but also regarding the context of importance and goals. We should choose ways of knowing that apply to the decision, have a scope that covers the breadth of issues related to the decision, and whose uncertainties are properly considered. We should combine the fruits of multiple forms of knowledge using wisdom and creativity, realizing there is more than one way of combining science and religion when making decisions. Further, we should adopt knowledge processing strategies to help us minimize the effects of the time and resource constraints inherent in everyday decisions.

However, before examining in the next section examples of using scientific and religious knowledge in specific decisions, one additional implication of our analysis must be drawn about understanding the importance, goals, and practice criteria with regard to everyday decisions: the primacy of values in determining the importance and goals of a decision. To the extent science has little to tell us about values, religion and other sources of knowledge about values must take the lead in determining importance and goals. As mentioned above, science provides context and background to importance and goals, but science cannot provide much more. With regard to importance, this distinction appears reasonable. Most of us recognize priorities and prioritizing as value judgments, but why should goals also be defined mainly by values? *The Nature of Environmental Stewardship* addresses in some detail the inadequacy of science or other descriptions of nature to prescribe goals, independent of values. One reason is the inability of science to provide the meaning of what it describes. For instance, science can tell us the five-year survival rate of lung cancer, but this description, in and of itself, does not tell us the value of such a five-year survival rate nor the meaning of that rate for the purposes of decision-making. Both of these questions require value judgments such as "an increase in survival rate is a good" or "a rate of 50 percent means even highly invasive treatments are worthwhile" in order for us to determine the meaning of what science tells us. Without religion and other sources of values, we cannot determine the importance and goals of a decision.

Examples of Applying Our Framework

As described at the beginning of this paper, the framework just defined outlines topics for questions we can use to analyze how science, religion, and other forms of knowledge affect everyday decisions. The framework, however, is not fleshed out enough to provide straightforward guidance regarding specific decisions. That is to say, it is still inadequate to give us a checklist for decision-making. The framework, however, is adequate to help us analyze specific examples of everyday decisions as well as to draw out general conclusions regarding the roles of scientific and religious knowledge in such decisions. Three examples will be considered. First, I will revisit my experience of buying a new minivan. Second, I will consider a more contentious question, one that contains built-in appeals to science: the decision of whether or not to vaccinate a child. Finally, I will consider a question that appears to have no connection either to science or religion, an issue of taste such as whether we should wear checks with stripes.

Buying a New Minivan

When my wife and I bought our minivan, we used all four ways of knowing, through science, religion, and other groupings of ways of knowing. Religion and other determinants (ethical theories, politics, economics, etc.) were the foundation for our metrics for analyzing and for understanding the purchase. Using information from these sources of knowledge (e.g., a particular Western evangelical understanding of the nature of waste and monetary stewardship) long before we ever planned the purchase, we had adopted efficiency ("bang for buck") as one metric for this kind of decision. Other metrics preconditioned by our values also included the "necessity" of the convenience of having a car that can hold our entire family, avoiding appearing ostentatious or vain, and an acceptance of some limited "right" to enjoy our purchase. Again, these metrics came partly from religion and partly from other determinants. For both the primary and secondary metrics, science really did not play a role in determining these metrics, though science did contribute descriptive input into some of them (e.g., the efficiency metric but not much to the vanity metric).

These metrics specified our understanding of the importance and goals of the decision. For instance, our metrics told us it was more important to purchase this car than save the money for missions and rely on public transportation. Our metrics told us that one goal of our purchase was to gain the utility the car could give us. In terms of practice, science, in a general sense, provided the descriptions of our options and the "bang" and "buck" around each of our options. Religious knowledge did not play much role in describing or defining the practice of the decision, once the importance and goals were set.

From this description of our decision process, we see that our framework covering scientific and religious (and other) ways of knowing and the importance, goals, and practice criteria gives us a way of analyzing our decision. At the same time, this framework gives us a tool for evaluating and critiquing our decision. We see that other importance, goals, and practice criteria were possible, and that a different mix of knowledge and ways of knowing could be more applicable, have greater scope, and be more reliable, leading to a different set of criteria. For instance, we could have placed a greater emphasis on the relational aspect of God and his universe and brought a greater focus on prayer to our decision-making that may have led to a different understanding of the goal of the purchase (e.g., a greater emphasis on glorifying God and communing with him both during and after the decision versus on obtaining the utility the car would bring). We could have exercised more of the relational intuition that comes through approaches Brother Lawrence describes in his classic *Practice of the Presence of God*. Alternately, we could have focused entirely on feeling as a source of knowledge—specifically the feeling of thrill—in specifying our goals and ditched the minivan altogether in favor of a Porsche Cayenne Turbo SUV (0–60 in 4.6 seconds; not that it matters, of course).[15] Thus, what we count as knowing and knowledge and the importance, goals, and practice they prescribe, could lead to a very different decision.

Second, from our description of this decision, we find that our core metrics of analyzing the purchase were decided on years, if not decades, before we ever needed to make the decision. In a very real sense the general outcome of the decision occurred years before the actual decision, through the setting of the metrics. The specific decision to buy an Odyssey was merely an unrolling of those metrics. Major changes then to the decision will come not so much from more or more accurate data but rather from altering those metrics.

Finally, all the time we did researching and the copious amount of information we collected gave the impression we had made a very rational, data-driven, "scientific" decision, and thus that we had made a "better" decision with greater certainty. It is questionable, however, how accurate this impression is, since the bulk of the work on the decision was done years before we collected data about minivans. In a very real way our decision has the appearance of being scientific while being, in reality, more of a religious (and ethical, etc.) decision.

Vaccination

The decision to vaccinate a child appears in some ways to be even more of a scientific decision than the decision concerning which minivan to buy. When we consider what forms of knowledge to use in this decision, it appears that scientific studies of risks—the risk of complications from the vaccine and the risk of contracting the disease the vaccine targets—determine our decision. As we saw in the minivan example, risks do not by themselves dictate the importance and goals criteria. Concerning vaccination, "for every one million doses of vaccine that were distributed, one individual was compensated [by the National Vaccine Injury Compensation Program]."[16] The importance of this risk factor will be different to a person who believes, in principle, one should not purposely introduce pathogens into an otherwise healthy person versus someone who does not hold such a philosophical position. Likewise, the meaning of the risk factor for importance and goals will be different if

---

15. Edmunds.com. "Full Edmunds Expert Review: 2013 Porsche Cayenne." See http://www.edmunds.com/porsche/cayenne/2013/review/.

16. U. S. Department of Health and Human Services, Health Resources and Services Administration. *Vaccine Injury Compensation Data*. Nov. 2016. See http://www.hrsa.gov/vaccinecompensation/data/.

one uses a highly sensitive version of the precautionary principle rather than another means of dealing with risk and uncertainty. Indeed, when we survey the reasons for and against childhood vaccination, we find they are all determined by philosophical presuppositions, such as what constitutes good parenting and right care for a child, ways of handling risk, the weight of intuition given small probabilities, the nature of individual and corporate responsibility, etc. The knowledge religion gives (and ethics, philosophy, etc.) is more important for this decision than the information that science gives.

An Issue of Taste

I will consider one simple decision of taste: deciding whether to wear checks with stripes. At first blush, this decision seems either to be trivial, not requiring the input of knowledge, or entirely dependent on personal preference, in which case only intuition and feeling are required. If we make the first response, there is nothing to know and no need to analyze the importance, goals, and practice of the decision. If we make the second response, the only sources of knowledge are intuition and feeling which tell us the importance of the decision, while heartfelt, is low, the goal is personal gratification, and the practice is to either wear or not wear those patterns. However, if we think about this decision a little more, we can identify other possible reasons for wearing checks with stripes or not. Will what we wear hurt the eyes of others? Will it offend the sensibility of others? Is choosing to wear checks with stripes good use of leftover clothing? Or is it a rebellion against fashion conformity? These possible reasons use ways of knowing beyond intuition and feeling.

More broadly, then, all the other forms of knowledge, and science and religion, come into play on matters of taste. Using psychology and sociology, taste can be studied, altered, and harnessed. The immense sums the food, entertainment, and garment industries spend each year to encourage us to have certain tastes testify to the effectiveness of reason, creative intuition, and the other tools of science when applied to taste. Religious knowledge also addresses taste; Scripture, for instance, tells us women's heads should be covered (1 Cor 11:1–16) and that their beauty should not be primarily through hairstyles and jewelry (1 Pet 3:3).

If decisions of taste involve the entire spectrum of knowing, we would expect the dynamics we identified in the present work will also extend to issues of taste. Science and the ways of knowing associated with science will be able to inform us about the context of our decision but will be unable to prescribe the meanings of the information it presents. Religion, philosophy, and other forms of knowing will be needed to explain the meaning behind what science learns. If wearing checks with stripes hurts the eyes of others, religion and ethics will tell us what we should do, not science. Intuition and feeling will also play a particularly prominent role in specifying importance, goals, and practice, as issues of taste are often highly time-constrained. Few of us have hours to spend on deciding what to wear.

There is, however, one additional comment we can make about the importance of decisions of taste. We have seen that taste is popularly understood as both unimportant and personal and thus incapable of being critiqued. While we have argued that taste can be critiqued using all the forms of knowing, we note that the popular understanding of unimportance is entrenched in a way that other "unimportant" items are not. If you question someone why they have a particular taste, they will likely respond, "I just like it." If you suggest they should *not* have such a taste, they will look at you as if you are from another planet. Why? We suggest one reason is our culture's belief in the "autonomy of personal taste." Taste is entirely created by the individual and is an expression of that individual's being. To argue against having a taste is akin to arguing against having an eye color. The taste itself may not be a categorical imperative, but the autonomy of the taste is. As a result, regarding decisions of taste, we often find that we simultaneously believe the decision is unimportant and that it is wrong for anyone else to critique it. Needless to say, this enables us, in the name of taste, to make decisions that negatively impact others without fear of the pangs of conscience.

Pastoral Implications

Based on our previous discussion, we draw out four implications for pastors. First, religion and forms of knowing besides science are often more important than scientific knowledge when it comes to the decisions that make up most of our lives. Even seemingly "science determined" decisions are actually not determined by science and instead require significant input from religion, particularly in importance and goals. Such input is not only needed regarding the "religious" or "philosophical" aspects of everyday decisions but also to understand the meaning of the science. For those in pastoral ministry, there is no reason to cede the ground of epistemic privilege to those who claim otherwise. Indeed, we need pastors to encourage us to resist the temptation of "baptizing" a decision with science when the science is not what drove that decision.

Second, given how our broader culture gives such a high value to scientific backing for decisions, we need pastors to remind us not only that science has limited value in many decisions but to encourage, challenge, and model for us how to incorporate "relational knowledge" into everyday decisions. If we believe with Heb

1:3a that "The Son is the radiance of God's glory and the exact representation of his being, sustaining all things by his powerful word" (NIV) and that the core of life is our relationship with the One who sustains everything, our life with Jesus is then connected to everything inside and outside our lives, and it would behoove us to grow in living in light of this reality. Prayer and receiving from God is foundational in this, but there is a sense too in which the ability to use relational knowledge is a capacity we can also partner with God in developing, through our actions, choices, and acts of faith.

Third, the presence of multiple sources of knowledge available to inform our everyday decisions affords an opportunity for all of us to leverage the strengths (and mitigate the weaknesses) of each source of knowledge, if we are encouraged to do so. Through pastoral instruction, whether from the pulpit or through personal counsel, pastors can help improve our decisions by asking us to look at different ways of knowing rather than relying on only a few ways. Pastors can also help us understand when our decision-making processes are misusing one form of knowing and when other forms can help clarify our thinking.

Finally, outside of a small set of specific injunctions (e.g., do not steal) and the relational knowledge we mentioned earlier, religion does not play a direct role in everyday decisions. Rather, religion plays its role through culture and framework formation, particularly given the time-constrained nature of everyday decisions. Thus, pastoral support for people with regard to everyday decisions needs to focus on forming those frameworks. The tools of virtue ethics have much to offer here. Helping people to practice virtuous living and providing exemplars on which to model their decision-making will do more to help people make good decisions than a reliance on intellectual analysis.

Conclusion

In the broader culture today it is common to consider good decision-making as using science ("data-driven solutions") in contrast with decision-making driven by bias and emotion. Religion, as putatively "non-scientific," does not fare well in this critique. In some Christian circles the opposite view is taken, where faith is understood as prescribing all decisions in detail and science is considered immaterial or misleading. In the present work I have described how the demands of science and religion on everyday decisions fits neither narrative. I examined the roles of science and religion in everyday decision-making by first categorizing the ways we know, describing the strengths and weaknesses of each way of knowing as well as describing how these ways are used in science and religion. I then introduced a framework for evaluating decisions that looks at the importance, goals, and practice of everyday decisions and described what science and religion contribute to the decision. As important as science is in describing the context of decisions and the options available for practice, it is religion, its allied disciplines, and forms of knowing not usually associated with science that give us the tools to understand the meaning of the science and to make the judgments and trade-offs inherent in any decision-making. At the same time, religion is one way of knowing that God has provided to us, with its own strengths and weaknesses. The demands of science and religion on everyday decisions, it turns out, differ markedly from the stories told by conventional wisdom. Every form of knowledge knows in part, and different choices of knowledge will lead to radically different decisions. The road to good everyday decisions will likely go through multiple forms of knowing and involve an understanding of not just the importance, goals, or practice of the decision but all three criteria.[17]

---

17. Discussions with Linda Eastwood, Karen Lin, and Matt and Mindy Worthington were helpful in my preparation. All errors and shortcomings are my own, and I do not presume the people acknowledged here agree with the arguments made in this work.

RESPONSE TO LIN

Linda M. Eastwood

I appreciate this opportunity to respond to Dr. Lin's paper and his focus on both epistemology and decision-making. As a former physicist and now theologian, I co-teach Religion and Science at McCormick Theological Seminary (as well as teaching related courses at the Lutheran School of Theology in Chicago, and at the Reformed University in Barranquilla, Colombia, South America.) Given students from a wide range of ethnic and theological backgrounds, I find some who, consciously or not, will consider either "science" or "religion" to have privileged access to "truth," just as Lin suggests.

When it comes to scientific knowledge, I introduce students, for instance, to Karl Popper's "falsification" criteria, a "soft" version of which is widely accepted by working scientists as key to the "scientific method." This "soft" version can be summed up by the idea that a theory can never actually be proven, but that we can be pretty sure, after enough experimental attempts to falsify it, that it truly represents at least some limited aspect of reality. As evolutionary biologist Stephen Jay Gould put it, "in science, 'fact' can only mean 'confirmed to such a degree that it would be perverse to withhold provisional assent.'"[1] Karl Popper would not have allowed even that much certainty. He rejected *any* inductive argument of the form (to create a trivial example): "Every Oreo cookie I've eaten so far has been non-poisonous, therefore it's safe to assume that the next one will be." Yet that is the kind of generalizing reasoning, inductive reasoning, that we use every day, and not just in science. Popper accepted *only* deductive reasoning of the form: "All cookies are good. An Oreo is a cookie. Therefore, an Oreo is good." But that conclusion does not really give us any new knowledge beyond the two premises that justified it, and what did justify those premises? Lin made something like that point when he noted that even reason—and I suggest he means specifically *deductive* reasoning—has its weaknesses. Trying to establish the truth of the premises of a deductive argument—the truth, for instance, of "all cookies are good"—merely pushes the justification to some underlying generally-accepted assumption, hardly the basis for ensuring abso-

---

1. Stephen Jay Gould, "Evolution as Fact and Theory," in *Hen's Teeth and Horse's Toes: Further Reflections on Natural History* (New York: W. W. Norton, 1980) 255.

lute truth. Popper's "deductive-reasoning-only" ideas thus create what philosopher of science Tim Lewens has called not even "a building erected on piles in a swamp, but castles in the air."[2] He fails to give us any approach to scientific near-certainty. Then there is philosopher Thomas Kuhn's concept of science moving in revolutionary jumps between paradigms that represent incommensurate worldviews, with the Copernican turn from earth-centric to heliocentric worldview being a case in point.[3] Some postmodernists have perhaps gone overboard in seeing each such paradigm, each such scientific worldview, as being *purely* a social construct with the only "truth value in its propositions [being in] the power of its exponents to enforce their own interpretations."[4] Against *this* idea, even Thomas Kuhn felt that science *does* genuinely make progress towards understanding true reality. I will admit to feeling the same. Still, even if we limit ourselves to wanting knowledge of the material world, of things of matter and energy, of those things that science can best study, then we *do* need to remember that science is never certain—indeed is *driven* by uncertainty. We need to remember the social and cultural influences on scientific knowledge and not worship such knowledge as absolute.

Lin is of course right to remind us that other ways of knowing are not *only* valid complements to scientific knowledge, but they are also *vital* to the decisions we make each and every day. Trying to use Popper's repeated attempts at falsification continually to test a spouse's love, for instance, would be pretty much guaranteed to destroy the very love it was supposed to test. We need to accept that science can tell us very little about our feelings, or about human values or ethics, even if some approaches to evolutionary psychology would suggest that it can.[5] When we come to make a decision, Lin is right in suggesting that science cannot *alone* contribute to deciding on our *goals*. Science cannot even, as Lin points out, tell us the "meaning" of what it describes. If, for instance, a particular approach to remediation of lead-levels in the water in Flint, Michigan, were to reduce brain-damage in children by 50 percent, what does that mean in human terms? Is it acceptable? Is it "worth" the economic expenditure required?

---

2. Tim Lewens, *The Meaning of Science: An Introduction to the Philosophy of Science* (New York: Basic, 2016) 24.

3. Thomas S. Kuhn, *The Structure of Scientific Revolutions* (Chicago: University of Chicago Press, 1962).

4. This is discussed, for instance, in Peter J. Bowler and Iwan Rhys Morus, *Making Modern Science: A Historical Survey* (Chicago: University of Chicago Press, 2005) 11.

5. For instance, Charles Darwin, *The Expression of the Emotions in Man and Animals* (London: J. Murray, 1890) or Edward O. Wilson, *Sociobiology: The New Synthesis* (Cambridge, MA: Belknap, 1975).

Intuition, feelings, religious revelation, and cultural and religious formation all come into play to form the values that, consciously or otherwise, shape our decision-making and guide us in determining the importance and goals of a decision.

But does Lin perhaps belabor the point? After all, we are unlikely to analyze each decision about the wearing of checks with stripes, or even the buying of a mini-van, to the level that he describes. *Still*, true as that is, there *are* times when it can be really helpful, even vital, that we step back and analyze what really *is* driving our decision-making.

I am a minister of the Presbyterian Church (USA) and I serve on a national committee, the Advisory Committee on Social Witness Policy. As we seek to guide social policies of the denomination in areas such as environmental justice, energy policy, or dignity at the end of life, we work to balance the best available science with theologically-based values. This would often lead us to the precautionary principle, one of the approaches that Lin helpfully presents to us for connecting values and science. I would, perhaps, take issue with his categorizing the precautionary principle as a strategy to prevent *any* harm. That is *one* possible definition—and indeed the one that former EPA head Christine Todd Whitman was assuming when she defined the precautionary principle as "Whatever you're doing, you've got to stop."[6] But a widely used definition is that of the 1992 Rio Declaration on Environment and Development, principle fifteen[7]: "Where there are threats of serious or irreversible damage, the lack of full scientific certainty shall not be used as a reason for postponing cost-effective measures to prevent environmental degradation"—which, of course, begs the question what is cost-effective.

What Lin most usefully reminds us is that even if we agree on all the best available scientific data, and agree on one of his categories of method in connecting values and science, we may still find that our conclusions are radically different, based on good-faith differences in underlying values of which we may not even initially be aware.

As an example, my denomination, the Presbyterian Church (USA) held its most recent General Assembly in June in Portland, Oregon. One of the hot topics was whether or not to divest the church's investments from key fossil-fuel companies. For a while it looked as if the answer would be "yes, divest," but the ultimate decision, at least for now, was a "no." Both groups agreed on the urgency of combating human-caused global warming and on the need to reduce and ideally stop fossil-fuel

---

6. Cited in Kerry H. Whiteside, *Precautionary Politics: Principle and Practice in Confronting Environmental Risk* (Cambridge MA: The MIT Press, 2006) 29.

7. This can be found at: http://www.unep.org/documents.multilingual/default.asp?documentid=78&articleid=1163

extraction. For the "yes, divest" group there was a moral imperative for the church not to hold investments in fossil-fuel extraction and a practical imperative to add the church's voice to other groups trying to stop such extraction. For the "no, do not divest" group there was the feeling that our voice as an investor could be stronger than our voice as a divestor—oh, and concern at the implied critique and potential job-loss of church members who work in the energy industry!

Lin's analysis of scientific and religious knowledge in decision-making can, I believe, not only help us to step back and think about the values we are—or are not!—applying to the decisions of our daily lives, but it can also help us peacefully and constructively analyze the different conclusions we may come to when different groups or different individuals are trying to approach the same problem. While in many cases "*you* don't have to be wrong for *me* to be right,"[8] there are also times when our conclusions do outright clash, as in the fossil-fuel divestment discussion just described. As Lin suggests, even in disagreements between church members, carefully analyzing how both our scientific understandings *and* our values affected each party's decision is an approach of respectful engagement, potentially helping to find agreement on constructive ways forward. In today's world of polarized politics and of violence by the radicalized, we may well feel that mutual understanding and respectful engagement is a path worthy of our attention.

---

8. I borrow this phrase from Rabbi Brad Hirschfield, *You Don't Have to Be Wrong for Me to Be Right: Finding Faith Without Fanaticism* (New York: Harmony, 2009).

"A ROCK OF OFFENSE": THE PROBLEM OF SCRIPTURE IN SCIENCE AND THEOLOGY

Hans Madueme

"Stop doubting and believe." Jesus uttered those words to Thomas, a man who would always be remembered as the one disciple who doubted the resurrection (John 20:27). Perhaps we should not judge him too harshly, for he came around eventually, and besides, hindsight is always 20/20. In one sense, that episode in the gospel story was a premonition of what would become a vexed and age-old tension between faith and reason. Thomas's doubts foreshadowed a struggle that has haunted the church from its very inception. What are we to do when our minds are incredulous in the face of divine things? More pointedly, how does human reason pay reverence to God's Word? It is a basic question, and yet it lies at the heart of long-standing problems in the discussion of the relation of science and theology. In this paper I examine one aspect of these issues by focusing on the doctrine of Scripture and its relationship to developments in science. My contention is that the leading participants in the field discussing the relation of science and theology have systematically marginalized, or failed to grapple with, the theological significance of Scripture.

I explore this claim in three steps. I will argue that, at least since the sixteenth century, science has shaped the doctrine of revelation and biblical interpretation in significant ways. Second, as a result of these shifts, the concept of biblical authority was profoundly transformed in both modern theology and in the dialogue over science and theology. Third, in light of these developments I sketch a proposal for how to engage scientific developments that have a bearing on Christian doctrine.

Divine Revelation and the Problem of Authority

Some have argued that new discoveries in the natural sciences pose no real threat to the faith. On this view, expressing any anxiety that there are deep conflicts between science and theology is a clue that you have bought into a flat or literalistic way of reading the Bible. Far better to recognize that modern hermeneutics discloses alternate reading strategies that do not clash with the deliverances of science.[1] In

---

1. For a version of this argument, see John Rogerson, "What Difference Did Darwin Make? The Interpretation of Genesis in the Nineteenth Century," in *Reading Genesis after Darwin*, edited by

my judgment, despite a modicum of truth, this sentiment misfires and begs the question. As we shall see, scientific developments in the past (and the present) have posed profound challenges to the traditional understanding of the Bible.

In the wake of the Reformation, acrimonious debates and religious wars between Protestants and Catholics led to a crisis of authority. Protestant confessions lined up against each other. Luther, Calvin, and Zwingli disagreed over the Lord's Supper; the Remonstrants and Contra-Remonstrants split over predestination; Arminians and Socinians interpreted the same Bible differently.[2] Such early rumblings exploded in the controversy over Copernican heliocentrism. That the sun revolved around the earth not only resonated with Aristotelian metaphysics, but it also seemed to be vindicated by the authoritative scriptural witness (e.g., Josh 10:12–13; Ps 19:6, 104:5; Job 9:7). Heliocentrism was thus considered heretical by Catholics and Protestants (including Martin Luther) not least by threatening to overturn the relationship between faith and reason.[3] The scandal was kept at bay until decisive proof emerged from Galileo's telescopic observations in 1609–1613. In the ensuing debate with the Catholic hierarchy, Galileo penned his epistle to the Grand Duchess Christina clarifying why Scripture does not have epistemic say over the dictates of science. As he put it, aphoristically, citing Cardinal Boronius, "the intention of the Holy Spirit is to teach us how one goes to heaven and not how heaven goes."[4] "Galileo's name does not appear in the history of biblical criticism," a later historian remarked, "but he was the first to formulate its basic principles."[5]

The same can be said for Isaac La Peyrère (1596–1676) a French Calvinist of Portuguese origin.[6] As the seventeenth century dawned, voyages of discovery and pagan chronologies were yielding surprising data. The New World and its Native American inhabitants, distantly removed from Europe, challenged medieval confi-

---

Stephen C. Barton and David Wilkinson (New York: Oxford University Press, 2009) 75–91. In the present article I use "science" primarily to designate *natural* science as opposed to the more holistic medieval *scientia* or German *Wissenschaft*.

2. Cf. Jitse M. van der Meer and Richard Oosterhoff, "The Bible, Protestantism and the Rise of Natural Science: A Response to Harrison's Thesis," *Science and Christian Belief* 21 (2009) 133–53, at 144–45.

3. E.g., see Maurice A. Finocchiaro, "The Biblical Argument against Copernicanism and the Limitation of Biblical Authority: Ingoli, Foscarini, Galileo, Campanella," in *Nature and Scripture in the Abrahamic Religions: Up to 1700*, edited by Jitse M. van der Meer and Scott Mandelbrote; Brill's Series in Church History 36; 2 vols. (Leiden: Brill, 2008) 627–64.

4. "Galileo's Letter to the Grand Duchess Christina (1615)," in *The Galileo Affair: A Documentary History*, ed. Maurice A. Finocchiaro (Berkeley: University of California Press, 1989) 87–118, at 96.

5. Klaus Scholder, *The Birth of Modern Critical Theology: Origins and Problems of Biblical Criticism in the Seventeenth Century*, translated by John Bowden (London: SCM, 1990) 64.

6. For more on La Peyrère, see Richard H. Popkin, *Isaac La Peyrère (1596–1676): His Life, Work and Influence* (New York: Brill, 1987); Jean-Paul Oddos, "Recherches sur la vie et l'oeuvre d'Isaac La Peyrère" (PhD diss., Université des Sciences Sociales, Grenoble, 1974).

dence that all human beings were Adam's descendants. Pagan texts uncovered from ancient civilizations like Egypt, Babylon, Ethiopia, and China revealed chronologies that far exceeded the biblical timeframe.[7] How could such findings be reconciled with the old, sacred picture of the world? Adding to this growing confusion were apparent inconsistencies in Scripture itself. For example, why did God put a mark on Cain if Adam and Eve were the only other human beings alive? Where did Cain get his wife if there were no other adults? Who lived in the city of Nod?

Who indeed! After years of internalizing these doubts, in 1642–43 La Peyrère dropped his theological bombshell, a two-part tome contending that Adam was not the first human. Adam was only one of many. La Peyrère's "pre-adamite" thesis, an attempt to integrate faith and reason, was judged a colossal heresy by almost all his contemporaries.[8] In the words of one scholar, "The humanist culture of philology, contacts with previously unknown countries, the culture of collecting exotic specimens and artifacts, the study of the histories of non-European peoples all contributed to a hermeneutic crisis."[9] La Peyrère was later arrested, forced to recant and then convert to the Catholic faith. Anthony Grafton reports: "'Strong wits' across Europe gossiped enjoyably about the origins of Cain's wife and the authorship of the report of Moses' death in Deuteronomy. The most powerful of texts had tumbled down."[10] La Peyrère had the last laugh, for his influence would extend from pioneers of historical criticism like Baruch Spinoza (1632–77) Samuel Fischer (1605–1655) Richard Simon (1638–1712) Pierre Bayle (1647–1706) and Isaac Vossius (1616–1689) all the way to English deists and later avant-garde Enlightenment thinkers—e.g., Blount, Tindal, Voltaire—who further radicalized his early biblical criticism.[11]

Galileo and La Peyrère embodied the close ties between early biblical criticism and science (natural philosophy). That both men sparked so much controversy among Protestants and Catholics is no surprise. Time-honored doctrinal beliefs,

---

7. For helpful analysis, see David Livingstone, *Adam's Ancestors: Race, Religion, and the Politics of Human Origins* (Baltimore: Johns Hopkins University Press, 2009) 1–25.

8. In *Defenders of the Text: The Traditions of Humanism in an Age of Science, 1450–1800* (Cambridge, MA: Harvard University Press, 1991) 206, Anthony Grafton notes nineteen refutations printed in 1656; according to Popkin, *Isaac La Peyrère*, 80, there were "probably hundreds of answers in print" from Jews, Catholics, and Protestants, all united against the blaspheming French heresiarch.

9. Eric Jorink, "'Horrible and Blasphemous': Isaac La Peyrère, Isaac Vossius and the Emergence of Radical Biblical Criticism in the Dutch Republic," in *Nature and Scripture in the Abrahamic Religions: Up to 1700*, edited by Jitse M. van der Meer and Scott Mandelbrote; Brill's Series in Church History 36; 2 vols. (Leiden: Brill, 2008) 429–50, at 446.

10. Anthony Grafton, *New Worlds, Ancient Texts: The Power of Tradition and the Shock of Discovery* (Cambridge, MA: Harvard University Press, 1992) 242.

11. David McKee, "Isaac de la Peyrère, A Precursor of the Eighteenth Century Critical Deists," *Publications of the Modern Language Association* 59 (1944) 456–85; Popkin, *Isaac La Peyrère*, 80–93, 115–45; Jorink, "Horrible and Blasphemous."

underwritten by Scripture, were being abandoned in the face of extra-textual evidence. To the minds of sixteenth-century theologians, this was no trivial matter, for the very Word of God was at stake. If God has spoken, then no man or angel can revoke his holy directive, yet Galileo seemed to have done just that.

Copernicanism was merely the herald; more changes were coming. As natural philosophy placed more emphasis on empirical data, the older biblical epistemology was gradually overturned. A familiar pattern established itself with each new cycle of scientific progress. Enduring theological beliefs, once anchored in holy writ, were overturned and transformed in their encounter with science. Christians developed strategies to "reconcile" the Bible with each new scientific development. These biblical interpreters assumed that past theology, advancing with each new corrective from natural science, was moving inexorably—and veridically—toward the conclusions of the then contemporary theology. The traditional understanding of Scripture necessitated *concordance* between the Bible and the findings of science. They were simply connecting the dots.

The rise of geology precipitated creative attempts to reconcile the early chapters of Genesis with the emerging geological story (e.g., the gap theory, the day-age theory, the days of revelation, etc.).[12] Scripture as God's true Word *must have* anticipated the new findings of geology. Accordingly, R. Payne Smith claimed that "the agreement of the Mosaic record with geology is so striking that there is no real difficulty in believing it to be inspired."[13] Thomas Whitelaw, equally optimistic, applauded how geology "contributes its quota to the constantly accumulating weight of evidence in support of the Mosaic narrative."[14] The presumption was that any new scientific idea would find its fulfilment somewhere in the biblical material.

Christians believed *their* theology—suitably accommodated to the relevant science—represented the goal to which earlier theologies had always been moving. Scientific developments were instrumental in moving theology to the next phase of growth. After every fresh cycle of scientific discovery in the eighteenth and nineteenth centuries, Christians tended to adopt this Whiggish theology.[15] Their con-

---

12. Similar patterns unfolded with other disciplines like archeology, history, anthropology, psychology, etc.

13. R. Payne Smith, "Genesis," in *An Old Testament Commentary for English Readers*, ed. Charles J. Ellicott, vol. 1 (London: Cassell and Company, 1897) 13.

14. Thomas Whitelaw, *Genesis, The Pulpit Commentary*, edited by H. D. M. Spence and Joseph Exell, 5th ed. (London: C. Kegan Paul & Co., 1881) 5. For a classic critique of nineteenth-century Genesis commentators and their geological demons, see Charles W. Goodwin, "On the Mosaic Cosmogony," in *Essays and Reviews*, 2nd ed. (London: John W. Parker & Son, 1860) 207–53.

15. According to Herbert Butterfield, "Whig history" is "the tendency in many historians to write on the side of Protestants and Whigs, to praise revolutions provided they have been successful, to emphasize certain principles of progress in the past and to produce a story which is the ratification if not

cordism implied the Bible would always be consistent with the science, but with the later rise of historical criticism and the rejection of a traditional account of Scripture, liberal theologians no longer attributed inerrancy to Scripture. Contradictions between the Bible and science posed no problem since liberals by then had abandoned the concordist project.[16] Conservative theologians, on the other hand, still assumed biblical inerrancy and continued to operate with Whiggish theological assumptions. Charles Hodge at Princeton was representative when he argued: "The proposition that the Bible must be interpreted by science is all but self-evident. Nature is as truly a revelation of God as the Bible, and we only interpret the Word of God by the Word of God when we interpret the Bible by science."[17] Scripture's ability to accommodate shifts in science (e.g., Hodge) or its capacity to circumvent the problem entirely (e.g., Driver) governed the shape of theology through the nineteenth century and beyond.

It is difficult to overestimate the far-reaching influence of science on theology. Scripture was like plasticine, shaped and molded by then-current notions of science. One might infer that general revelation was helping correct mistaken interpretations of special revelation, yet it would be naïve to suppose that this was always what was happening. The deeper worry was that science had become *the* defining epistemic authority, despite the fact that Christian orthodoxy had always reserved that status to Scripture alone as God's Word. Almost all biblical scholarship and theology today is an attempt to clarify the meaning of Christian faith given the methodological problems laid down by the sixteenth and seventeenth centuries. This dialectic between science and theology was no mere historical artifact; it was woven into the fabric of modern theology and the discipline treating the relation of science and theology.

---

the glorification of the present" (*The Whig Interpretation of History* [London: G. Bell & Sons, 1951], v). By applying the term here, I mean that past theology was often interpreted in light of the scientific assumptions of the present. I do not mean to prejudge the question by using the term "Whiggish"; *all* Christians during the period thought they possessed theology at its truest form.

16. In his interpretation of Gen 1, Samuel R. Driver rejected the harmonizing impulse and conceded that the scientific facts contradicted the biblical narrative: "Read without prejudice or bias, the narrative of Gen. i. creates an impression *at variance with the facts revealed by science*: the efforts at reconciliation which have been reviewed are but different modes of obliterating its characteristic features, and of reading into it *a view which it does not* express" (*The Book of Genesis* [London: Methuen & Co., 1904], 26).

17. Charles Hodge, "The Bible in Science," *New York Observer* (March 26, 1863) 98. That Hodge conflated "revelation of God" and "science" is a telling error; the two are not co-extensive.

The Loss of Biblical Authority[18]

The crux of the matter was that Christians repeatedly deployed new ways to defuse any real conflicts between Scripture and emerging science. At stake was the very nature of divine revelation and how readers were to understand its claims about the extra-textual world.

The Rise of Modern Theology

Prior to the nineteenth century, religious doctrines were widely understood to be literal truths, matters of fact. Christian doctrine, explained Langdon Gilkey, "was thought by all—clerics, theologians, scholars, artists, philosophers, even scientists—to include 'facts' about the age of the world, about how the world came to be, about early events (such as the Fall) and about the early history of the human race."[19] Such doctrines were thought to include facts because Scripture was inspired by God, which guaranteed the inerrancy of the biblical text.[20] Doctrines were taken as propositions which included "divinely revealed 'information' on almost any topic of interest."[21] Note, for example, that Martin Luther in his *Commentary on Genesis* tried to identify the rivers that flowed out of the Garden of Eden.[22] Gilkey comments:

> With all their debates about reason and revelation, neither the Reformers, nor most of the Enlightenment theologians, ever doubted that revelation was composed of objective propositions concerning matters of fact, that it could therefore tell us what had happened in space and time, and provide authoritative descriptions of the character, time, place, and causes of such concrete events as were crucial to the meaning of significant doctrines.[23]

In granting us the power to change our environment, science revolutionized how we understand and relate to the world. The premodern view of Scripture lost plausibility; doctrine no longer informed what most moderns believe about the universe, its origins, and our place in it, at least not in any substantive way. Science

---

18. In what follows, my analysis of modern theology draws from Langdon Gilkey (1919–2004). Gilkey was peerless in his grasp of these matters, though his constructive proposals are very different from mine.

19. Langdon Gilkey, *Nature, Reality, and the Sacred: The Nexus of Science and Religion* (Minneapolis: Fortress, 1993) 17.

20. Langdon Gilkey, *Naming the Whirlwind: The Renewal of God-Language* (Indianapolis: Bobbs-Merrill, 1969) 74.

21. Langdon Gilkey, *Religion and the Scientific Future: Reflections on Myth, Science, and Theology* (New York: Harper & Row, 1970) 4.

22. Ibid., 7. Cf. Martin Luther, *Luther's Commentary on Genesis*, 2 vols., translated by J. Theodore Mueller (Grand Rapids: Zondervan, 1958),1.48–49.

23. Gilkey, *Religion and the Scientific Future*, 7.

ruled the roost. Science, of course, is not the only important factor behind significant shifts in modern religious thinking. There were other forces at play, but none of them come close to the influence of science. The dominant approach to religious truth "has been caused more by the work of science than by any other factor, religious or cultural."[24] The changes came gradually, but inexorably.

Christian doctrine for most of church history was seen as a union of theological "symbol" and historical "fact." The symbols of creation, fall, and redemption corresponded directly to the historical facts about our universe. But with rising pressures from the emerging sciences, "this intertwining of symbol and fact . . . has come unraveled in our time, the symbolic truth about God and human destiny having been separated from the factual accompaniment of dates, places, concrete events, and so on."[25] Seeking to accommodate the new world order, liberalism transformed the meaning of Christian truth from "infallible propositions" about history, geography, science, etc., to a set of *human symbols* which opened up the "depth and mystery of existence" without contradicting the findings of secular history or science.[26] Biblical criticism was also devastating to the traditional view of doctrines as unchanging truth. Now they were only relative, human beliefs, socio-historically conditioned, mirroring local needs and customs.[27]

The same accommodation to modern science can be seen in Karl Barth's anti-liberalism.[28] Emphasizing such themes as the relation of creation to covenant and to Christology, his theology of creation was designed to avoid conflict with natural science.[29] "In this way," notes one commentator, "Barth manages to avoid the risk of a theology that has to move further back as a result of new scientific discoveries."[30] The broader "neoorthodoxy" movement displayed similar instincts. Consider its distinctive themes: denying the knowledge of God through nature; the ambiguity of history without faith; only God's revelation can witness to his special acts in history, etc. "[I]n no sense was religious language . . . derived from scientific inquiry

---

24. Ibid., 4.

25. Gilkey, *Nature, Reality, and the Sacred*, 17–18.

26. Gilkey, *Naming the Whirlwind*, 76–77.

27. Ibid., 77.

28. Cf. Langdon Gilkey, "Cosmology, Ontology, and the Travail of Biblical Language," *JR* 41 (1961) 194–205. Scholars continue to debate the value of Barth for engaging science, e.g., see Marc Cortez, *Embodied Souls, Ensouled Bodies: An Exercise in Christological Anthropology and Its Significance for the Mind/Body Debate* (New York: T & T Clark, 2008) esp. 42–45.

29. See his preface to *Church Dogmatics: The Doctrine of Creation*, III/1, ed. Geoffrey Bromiley and T. F. Torrance (Edinburgh: T & T Clark, 1958) ix–x.

30. Gijsbert van den Brink, *Philosophy of Science for Theologians* (Frankfurt am Main: Peter Lang, 2009) 225.

nor even significantly related to it."[31] While liberal theologians were unduly interested in history, cosmology, biology, and so on, neoorthodox theologians "were conspicuously indifferent to scientific theories and hostile to any of their theological implications."[32] None of them denied evolutionary theory or historical studies of the biblical era, but neither did they base any of their doctrines of creation or providence on such material.[33] As a result, Neoorthodoxy was often thought to be completely autonomous from natural science. As a matter of fact, however, nothing was further from the truth:

> For the fact is that while (with the exception of the renegades Bultmann and Tillich) the neo-orthodox did not, as the liberals had done, deliberately or consciously refashion the Biblical Word to fit into the scientific world view they themselves accepted, nevertheless in their theological work they all presupposed important aspects of this modern view of things. Despite their protests to the contrary when they discussed hermeneutical *theory*, still the scientific world they lived in massively influenced their hermeneutic in *practice*. The theology that was ostensibly constructed solely on the Bible was in actual fact built upon and around certain basic assumptions of modern science and reflected in all its aspects this grounding in the modern scientific world view, though this dependence was never admitted and often denied. In much the same way one might build a house on some great rock hidden by the house, but still determining its structure and shape, and making it very different from a house built in another kind of place.[34]

In short, modern theology is inexplicable apart from the parameters set by the scientific project. With the exception of unfashionable conservative theologians who resisted these forces, trying to preserve continuity with the premodern theological vision, modern works of theology—almost universally—transmuted their doctrines in light of science or, conversely, developed strategic formulations of doctrine that avoided conflict altogether.[35]

31. Gilkey, *Religion and the Scientific Future*, 24–25.

32. Ibid., 25.

33. Ibid. As Gilkey noted, Pannenberg and Moltmann were exceptions.

34. Ibid., 26, emphasis original. Gilkey was emphatic on this point: "The separation between factual propositions and religious statements, established by scientific development and liberal religion, was thus accepted and reformulated by neo-orthodoxy to express its own understanding of religious truth within the limits set by an increasingly secular culture" (ibid., 24).

35. Cf. Kirsopp Lake, *The Religion of Yesterday and Tomorrow* (Boston: Houghton, 1926) 61–62: "It is a mistake, often made by educated men who happen to have but little knowledge of historical theology, to suppose that Fundamentalism is a new and strange form of thought. It is nothing of the kind: it is the partial and uneducated survival of a theology which was once universally held by Christians.... [T]he Fundamentalist may be wrong; I think he is. But it is we who have departed from the tradition, not he, and I am sorry for the fate of anyone who tries to argue with a Fundamentalist on the basis of authority. The Bible and the *corpus theologicum* of the church is on the Fundamentalist

The Science-and-Theology Discipline

The doyen of science-and-religion, Ian Barbour, was similarly exercised about avoiding conflict between the two disciplines. In his groundbreaking book *Issues in Science and Religion*, Barbour offered constructive answers to questions of the viability of religious faith given the rise of science in the seventeenth and eighteenth century.[36] On how best to characterize the relation of Scripture to truth, he recognized biblical authority as a problem. He blamed Protestant scholasticism for the doctrine of inerrancy; that kind of biblical literalism, he argued, was no longer possible in light of Copernicus, geology, and historical criticism of the Bible.[37]

In his classic typology for how science and religion relate, he identified four positions: conflict, independence, dialogue, and integration.[38] Most interesting for our purposes are the terms in which he set the discussion. He dismissed the conflict position as "extreme," the result of an untenable biblical inerrantism. It is irresponsible to interpret the Bible literally, he said, because that approach generates conflict between the biblical witness and scientific claims. Barbour was a Christian seeking to avoid future scenarios in which science could falsify central theological beliefs; churchmen have learned the painful lessons of history from the remarkable success of science—thus his allergy to irreducible conflicts between theology and science.

This concern to avoid any real conflict between science and Scripture is a dominant motif in Barbour. Geoffrey Cantor and Chris Kenny recognize that Barbour's typology is effectively a "pilgrim's progress" that begins with conflict, briefly entertains independence, and then comes home to dialogue and integration. As they explain,

> Our pilgrim starts with the familiar conflict thesis. In an important sense the other three positions are developed out of criticism of that foundational thesis. To put the matter another way, although ultimately rejected, *the conflict thesis has set Barbour's agenda* for categorizing the ways in which science and religion interrelate. This point applies not only to Barbour but also to many other religious writers whose understanding of science-religion relationships have been forged in the furnace of their enemies.[39]

---

side." Conservative theologians, however, were not immune to these developments (e.g., see my earlier comments regarding Whig theology).

36. Ian Barbour, *Issues in Science and Religion* (Englewood Cliffs, NJ: Prentice Hall, 1966). Some years later, in *Religion in an Age of Science* (New York: Harper & Row, 1990) 3, he maintained that "Science seems to provide the only reliable path to knowledge."

37. Ibid., 96.

38. Barbour, *Religion in an Age of Science*, 3–30.

39. Geoffrey Cantor and Chris Kenny, "Barbour's Fourfold Way: Problems with his Taxonomy of Science-Religion Relationships," *Zygon* 36 (2001) 765–81, at 768 (my emphasis).

His typology and its implicit aversion to conflict is standard in the field.[40] Contemporary methodological discussions among Christians in the discipline of science-and-religion, in step with Barbour, almost universally preclude any possibility of conflict between science and Scripture. They thus preempt the serious use of Scripture in such discussions and sometimes sideline Scripture completely. The cumulative effect is the domestication of Scripture in the relationship between science and theology. This situation, more pointedly, is a reflection of the influence of scientism on our modern plausibility structures.[41] Science has a remarkable power to order and shape the way in which we conceive reality—that which is *really* real—so that it seems inconceivable that the manifest witness of Holy Scripture can stand on its own integrity with, but also sometimes *against*, the assured results of empirical science.

Historiography of Science-and-Theology

The impulse to play down the conflict dilemma in science and theology is also evident among historians of science. It is commonplace to cite John Draper's *History of the Conflict between Religion and Science* and Andrew White's *A History of the Warfare of Science with Theology in Christendom* as the source of the "warfare" metaphor.[42] A familiar trope in the public imagination, this metaphor was epitomized well by Thomas Huxley in the nineteenth century: "Extinguished theologians lie about the cradle of every science as the strangled snakes beside that of Hercules, and history records that whenever science and dogmatism have been fairly opposed, the latter has been forced to retire from the lists, bleeding and crushed, if not annihilated; scotched, if not slain."[43] Conflict, however, was far less a feature of the actual historical periods chronicled by Draper and White than it was a reflection of their own personal and social worlds.

---

40. E.g., see Robert J. Russell, ed., *Fifty Years in Science and Religion: Ian G. Barbour and his Legacy* (Aldershot: Ashgate, 2004); Holmes Rolston, "Science, Religion, and the Future," in *Religion and Science: History, Method, Dialogue*, edited by W. Mark Richardson and Wesley J. Wildman (New York: Routledge, 1996) 61–82.

41. Cf. Mikael Stenmark, *Scientism: Science, Ethics and Religion* (Aldershot: Ashgate, 2001).

42. John William Draper, *History of the Conflict between Religion and Science*, 7th ed. (London: Henry S. King & Co., 1876); Andrew Dickson White, *A History of the Warfare of Science with Theology in Christendom*, 2 vols. (New York: Appleton, 1897).

43. Thomas H. Huxley, "Darwin on the Origin of Species," *Westminster Review* 17 (1860) 541–70, at 556. For additional context on Huxley and the warfare metaphor, see Colin A. Russell, "The Conflict Metaphor and its Social Origins," *Science and Christian Belief* 1 (1989) 3–26.

The most significant critique of the conflict metaphor appears in the brilliant work by John Hedley Brooke.[44] We cannot, he says, exhaust the historical richness of the various ways in which science interacted with Christianity. Relations were never simple. They were usually complex. His book opens up "the diversity, the subtlety, and ingenuity of the methods employed, both by apologists for science and for religion"; surprises aplenty await the unbiased historian.[45] Simple theses of conflict or even harmony between science and religion serve as poor witnesses to the actual historical drama. "To portray the relations between science and religion as a continuous retreat from theological dogma before a cumulative and infallible science," warns Brooke, "is to overlook the fine structure of scientific controversy, in which religious interests intruded, but often in subtle rather than overtly obstructive ways."[46] So too the secularization thesis, the idea that science was instrumental in secularizing modern society. According to Brooke, such notions rely on the conflict thesis and are simplistic if not outright false. His many case studies showcase a different story in which religion and science were entangled in immensely complex ways (i.e., the "complexity thesis").[47] While most of his caution is leveled at those who see science as injurious to religious faith, he is also sensitive to problems in the opposite direction and forces us "to consider whether revisionist histories, structured around a critique of the conflict thesis, have not gone too far in the opposite direction."[48] Thus, the complexity thesis.

Among historians of science the complexity thesis is crucial to making sense of relations between science and Christian faith.[49] David Lindberg and Ronald Numbers review how, in reaction to the bad history of Draper and White, apologists rejoined that science could only arise out of Christian Europe, offering a counter-thesis of essential "harmony" between Christianity and science. But Lindberg and

44. John Hedley Brooke, *Science and Religion: Some Historical Perspectives* (Cambridge: Cambridge University Press, 1991). On his significance, see Thomas Dixon, Geoffrey Cantor and Stephen Pumfrey, eds., *Science and Religion: New Historical Perspectives* (Cambridge: Cambridge University Press, 2010).

45. Brooke, *Science and Religion*, 5.

46. Ibid., 6.

47. Scholars use the term "complexity thesis" to describe Brooke's conclusions in *Science and Religion*. Cf. Ronald Numbers, review of John Hedley Brooke, *Science and Religion*, Metascience 1 (1992) 35–39.

48. Brooke, *Science and Religion*, 12.

49. Even the very idea of "science" and "theology" (or "science" and "religion") is considered historically problematic. Cf. John Hedley Brooke and Geoffrey Cantor, *Reconstructing Nature: The Engagement of Science and Religion* (Oxford: Oxford University Press, 1998) 43–72. Claude Welch lamented "the hypostatization of 'science' and 'religion'" represented by Draper, White, and their disciples (cf. "Dispelling Some Myths about the Split between Theology and Science in the Nineteenth Century," in *Religion and Science: History, Method, Dialogue*, edited by W. Mark Richardson and Wesley J. Wildman [New York: Routledge, 1996], 29–40, at 29).

Numbers criticize such apologetic accounts as equally simplistic, neglecting the role of the ancient Greeks and medieval Muslims in the emergence of science. Today's historians of science and religion eschew ideological debates over conflict or harmony; they are far more interested in the complexities of the actual historical protagonists.[50] As Numbers observes, "To my knowledge, no reputable historian of science and religion now doubts the truth of this tangled view of the past."[51] Complexity is the starting point for all serious historical work in this area.

What should we make of all this? Brooke and his fellow historians have rendered an inestimable service in highlighting these matters. Much public rhetoric on science and religion needs to be disciplined by Brooke's insights. Theologians have much to learn too, not least that systematic categories often distort more than they illuminate. The history of science and theology was far richer, more ambiguous than anything we can imagine. I am grateful for these helpful correctives, but I do wonder if the cumulative effect of this new, more sophisticated historiography has had unintended consequences.

Consider the distinction between *description* and *prescription*. Historians of science and religion offer an insightful depiction of the past. They help us descriptively—the past matters, i.e., "what happened?" But the theological implications of events in the past are also important, e.g., "what *should* happen?" or "what *should have* happened?" These are normative, prescriptive questions. Interactions between religious faith and science are complex, but theologians must still reflect normatively on these matters. To be sure, theologians must give an account of how fairly, how accurately, they have narrated the past; at the same time they must try to make sense of our world and whether our lives are oriented toward or away from the living God to whom we owe our allegiance. We can therefore learn from the best insights of the complexity thesis without forsaking the theological desideratum to think more broadly and prescriptively about science and theology.

Along these lines, we can grant that the complexity thesis *should* caution us against facile polarities between "science" and "theology" and still insist that the language of "science and theology" is necessary in our own day. The reality of science and theology is woven into our lives as modern people; it is part of the air we breathe, affecting us and shaping our plausibility structures—for good and ill. "Science" and "theology" may be, in part, constructed categories; they also, in part, truly pick out aspects of reality. Those categories helpfully if imperfectly crystallize what

---

50. David Lindberg and Ronald Numbers, eds., *When Science and Christianity Meet* (Chicago: University of Chicago Press, 2003) 1–5.

51. Ronald Numbers, *Science and Christianity in Pulpit and Pew* (Oxford: Oxford University Press, 2007) 4–5.

is at stake in how scientific claims relate to the claims of Christian doctrine.[52] We make a serious mistake if we essentialize conflict between science and theology, but we also make a serious mistake if we minimize deep instances of conflict between elements of scientific understanding and central doctrines of the faith.[53] Let us then be thankful for the best historical insights about complexity, but let us also deny any inference that we cannot, or should not, make more substantive, categorical claims about those same issues. There is a danger that the complexity thesis has become a new reductionism (concerns already intimated by Brooke[54]). Thomas Dixon shows awareness of this problem when he asks: "Does that mean that conflict needs to be written out of our story altogether? Certainly not. The only thing to avoid is too narrow an idea of the kinds of conflicts one might expect to find between science and religion."[55] These are refreshing notes against the hegemony of the complexity thesis.[56]

As we review the terrain in the long shadow of Galileo and La Peyrère, it is striking the many ways in which Christians have tried to minimize or deny any significant conflicts between science and religion.[57] In light of simplistic New Atheist polemics and similarly unhelpful stereotypes, one can sympathize with Christians

---

52. Cf. Thomas Dixon, *Science and Religion: A Very Short Introduction* (Oxford: Oxford University Press, 2008) 17: "The fact that the phrase 'science and religion' names an academic field, as well as conjuring up vivid if historically debatable cultural stereotypes, is enough, I think, to justify its continued use as a category of thought.... Academics and journalists alike continue to write as if there were some ongoing general relationship between science and religion, in terms of which particular contemporary episodes might be understood. Even if that relationship really exists only in our imaginations, it is still important to try to understand how it got there." Dixon's basic insight, though overly pragmatic, is helpful.

53. For example, since the traditional doctrine of the fall is central to the Christian story—or, so I would argue—that story lies in deep tension with scientific claims that a first couple never existed, the fall is not historical, etc.

54. Brooke, *Science and Religion*, 12, 49–50.

55. Dixon, *Science and Religion*, 3. See also his comments in "Religion and Science," in *The Routledge Companion to the Study of Religion*, ed. John Hinnells, 2nd ed. (London: Routledge, 2010) 509: "[R]eligion and science share an interest in the same fundamental questions about the origins and nature of the physical universe in general, and of human beings in particular. *It is when religion and science have found themselves giving different answers to these questions, whether in Renaissance Italy or in modern-day America, that conflicts have arisen*" (my emphasis).

56. See the notable essay in Geoffrey Cantor, "What Shall We Do With the 'Conflict Thesis'?" in *Science and Religion: New Historical Perspectives*, 283–98.

57. Alvin Plantinga, the Christian philosopher than which none greater can be conceived, seems to fall uncharacteristically into that trap: "Of course there are conflicts between science and particular religious beliefs that are not part of Christian belief as such: belief in a universal flood, a very young earth, etc." (*Where the Conflict Really Lies: Science, Religion, and Naturalism* [New York: Oxford University Press, 2011], 144, n. 23). But he is begging the question. Many Christians, globally, reject his claim that a universal flood is "not part of Christian belief as such" (ditto a young earth). My point is not to defend those positions but to signal another instance where one has assumed what has not been proven. Plantinga is otherwise so exemplary that he can be forgiven the slip.

who wish to underscore a more congenial relationship between faith and science. But one might ask whether the universal castigation of Andrew White and John Draper is a curious example of straining at gnats while swallowing the whole camel. Has a picture of essentialized conflict held us captive? The stark, deeply flawed narratives of conflict generated by Draper and White may have inoculated historians from more seriously considering the possibility of *other kinds of conflict*, even conflicts that are profound and entrenched. Perhaps there is a deeper sense in which the flawed arguments of White and Draper track something true and legitimate. To wit, roughly over the past three hundred years, developments in doctrine have been impossible to understand apart from developments in science.[58] That fact raises difficult methodological questions about the relationship between science, Scripture, and theology. To those issues we now turn.

Methodological Reflections

Prior to the intense rise of nineteenth-century historical consciousness, the Christian tradition accepted its doctrines as timelessly true, eternally valid, for all people and every place. Greek philosophical givens may have influenced this static view of doctrine, but it also resonated with biblical canonicity and a faith once delivered unto the saints (Jude 3). That there was actual development, that doctrines could change, initially proved deeply threatening to many Catholic and Protestant theologians.[59] In the end, however, it was impossible to deny in light of the history of theology; and besides, it was already implicit among Protestants like the Westminster Divines when they affirmed the intrinsic fallibility of their confessions.[60]

Still, theologians who were threatened by doctrinal development had a point. If we concede that doctrines are historically conditioned and inevitably change, do we not condemn theology to be tossed back and forth by the waves and blown here and there by every wind of teaching (Eph 4:14)? Does doctrinal tradition become a fallible construct, ever learning, and never able to come to the knowledge of the truth (2 Tim 3:7 KJV)? Such questions generated theological anxiety. The very idea of development seemed to spell the death knell of any enduring confessional tradition.

---

58. Obvious examples include creation, sin, humanity, and providence; the present article is an attempt to flesh out this claim.

59. E.g., see Todd Regnan Statham, *Dogma and History in Victorian Scotland* (PhD diss.; McGill University, 2011).

60. John Henry Newman set the terms of the discussion in his *An Essay on the Development of Christian Doctrine*, 6th ed. (Notre Dame: University of Notre Dame Press, 1989) first published in 1878.

They were mistaken to reject the theory of doctrinal development, but they had a point.

When science became instrumental in shaping doctrinal development, this point was amplified all the more. Scientific consensus now sets the limits on what can and cannot be said; theologians must work within those boundaries. Biblical authority is something of a paper tiger; what can be known scientifically is the operative concept. To be sure, Galileo's defense of heliocentrism and his encounter with the Catholic church instigated a *favorable* development of doctrine. Since Galileo, however, the traffic has been one-way, changes in doctrine invariably prompted by scientific claims (perhaps there are some counter-examples, but one is hard-pressed to think of clear, unequivocal cases).

Given the nature of the scientific enterprise, however, such doctrinal development consistently deployed is doomed to fail. Science is always advancing. Theology thus gains a conceptual foothold at the risk of becoming obsolete later on.[61] We have learned that lesson repeatedly in history, e.g., the marriage of the medieval church and Aristotelian natural philosophy was instrumental in the ensuing turmoil around Galileo. I am not arguing that theology should ignore natural science—far from it, but there needs to be a measure of distance, lest theology lose its core identity. Precisely how to delineate that "measure of distance" is no easy task and, as will become clear, controversial by its very nature.

Biblical Realism: A Methodological Proposal

We have a royal mess on our hands. The challenges adumbrated above have been inherited by all sides of the theological spectrum. There is much at stake, not least of which is the vexing question of theological honesty. As Joseph McKenna pointed out,

> Modern theology has always risked intellectual dishonesty and self-deception in the very act of modernizing theology. Nineteenth-century Liberal theologians and twentieth-century Revisionist theologians have reinterpreted most Christian ideas, believing that modernity's new knowledge and scholarly methodologies—in the natural sciences, social sciences, history, literature, philosophy and ethics—are largely correct and that therefore the only solution to the cognitive crisis facing modern Christianity is to revise traditional

---

61. For helpful comments, see Stephen Toulmin, "The Historicization of Natural Science: Its Implications for Theology," in *Paradigm Change in Theology*, edited by Hans Küng and David Tracy (New York: Crossroad, 1989) 233–41.

doctrines in terms suitable to contemporary learning and credible to contemporary sensibilities.[62]

Not just liberals, but conservatives as well have not always been convincing on this point. This problem of honesty is a ghost that haunts modern theology.

On the one hand, theological shifts prompted by science can illuminate how Scripture has been misinterpreted in various ways. Science comes in the guise of a theologian's friend, bringing to light those exegetical missteps. On the other hand, such shifts may reflect something more ominous, betraying a pattern of theologians disobeying God's Word in Scripture. It would be unwise to dismiss either scenario preemptively and, alas, distinguishing between them is where much of the controversy lies. Granted, contemporary hermeneutical insights have brought clarity to many of these issues, but hermeneutics is no panacea. Some arguments that privilege hermeneutical factors actually exemplify the problem of theological honesty. We find ourselves as Christians in the modern world thrown into this struggle, a struggle for life, grappling with what it means to be biblical *and* also keep faith with apostolic tradition. Biblical realism is one more attempt (!) to chart a way through this mess.[63]

Scripture and Tradition

I side with the premodern tradition in its conception of doctrine as the union of theological symbol and historical fact (to use Gilkey's language). For example, God's emancipation of his people from Egyptian captivity was a potent metaphor for American slaves, not merely because of its rich symbolism but also because of what God had actually done in Israel's history.[64] The nature of God compels me to endorse the traditional doctrine of inerrancy; the divine discourse of Scripture is wholly trustworthy.[65] I also agree with the tradition that Scripture is God's revelation of divine truths—infallible propositions—to his people.[66] Scripture, of course, is not

---

62. Joseph McKenna, "Honesty in Theology?" *Heythrop Journal* 42 (2001) 50–65, at 53.

63. I am updating an earlier discussion of "scriptural realism" in my "'The Most Vulnerable Part of the Whole Christian Account': Original Sin and Modern Science," in *Adam, the Fall, and Original Sin: Theological, Biblical, and Scientific Perspectives* (Grand Rapids: Baker Academic, 2014) 223–47, esp. 240–45.

64. *Pace* the OT minimalism of T. L. Thompson, J. Van Seters, N. P. Lemche, and others. On the African-American exodus motif, see Carl Ellis, *Free at Last? The Gospel in the African-American Experience*, 2nd ed. (Downers Grove: InterVarsity, 1996).

65. I cannot defend this claim here, but see Mark D. Thompson, "The Divine Investment in Truth: Toward a Theological Account of Biblical Inerrancy," in *Do Historical Matters Matter to Faith?: A Critical Appraisal of Modern and Postmodern Approaches to Scripture*, edited by James Hoffmeier and Dennis Magary (Wheaton: Crossway, 2012) 71–97.

66. Cf. John Baillie, *The Idea of Revelation in Recent Thought* (New York: Columbia University

limited to propositions; as the Word of God, it transforms the believer, deepens her character, nourishes her soul in song and prayer, and much, much else besides,[67] but it is not *less than* propositional. This point deserves mention in the present context because if Scripture is propositional in the way catholic tradition has always believed, naturally it can come into direct conflict with the conclusions (propositions) of modern thought, including science and history.

That verdict invites resistance, partly because it exacerbates the conflict dilemma. But, oh my friend, why let your heart be troubled? Inerrancy is inherently *Christological*. The cornerstone of our faith is the life, death, and resurrection of Jesus Christ. According to the biblical witness, Jesus was resurrected three days after his death and burial (e.g., 1 Cor 15:14 and *passim*). An absurd claim! Every elementary school student knows that resurrection is scientifically impossible. Bodily resurrection as an idea is quintessentially unscientific. If resolving conflict between science and theology is the holy grail, then why do not orthodox Christians abandon belief in the resurrection? One reason is because the entire biblical story would unravel. Without this doctrine we lose our union with Christ, the forgiveness of sins, justification, regeneration, the new heaven and new earth, and virtually all else central to orthodoxy. However, there is a *more basic* reason Christians should not relinquish their belief in resurrection. Our maximal confidence in resurrection is not grounded in the presence or absence of scientific "proof"; it rests upon the scriptural revelation of our trustworthy God. That revelation is infallible because God is infallible. As Christians encounter God's Word, the Holy Spirit instigates an abiding confidence that these words are divinely inspired, a theological confidence that cannot be invalidated by human reason—modern science being its most sophisticated form—because it has its basis in the triune God, the high and lofty One.[68] If I am right that at the very heart of Christianity lies a paradigmatic conflict between science and faith, then Christians need not be daunted when such conflicts appear more generally.[69]

Press, 1956) 3–18, who argues that the propositional view of revelation was widely assumed "throughout the greater part of Christian history" (3).

67. Some of these emphases appear, rather polemically, in Roger E. Olson, *Reformed and Always Reforming: The Postconservative Approach to Evangelical Theology* (Grand Rapids: Baker Academic, 2007).

68. As I will argue later, science *is* relevant as a potential defeater to doctrinal conviction. On defeaters more generally, see Michael Bergmann, *Justification without Awareness* (Oxford: Oxford University Press, 2006).

69. My point here is *not* a slippery-slope argument that rejecting "unscientific" positions in Scripture leaves you a short step from rejecting resurrection; instead, I am emphasizing the *epistemological warrant* for belief (and when I claim that Christ's resurrection entails a "paradigmatic conflict between science and faith," I mean "science" in a *methodologically naturalist* sense—see below). If I have strong warrant for a Christian belief—warrant that is *biblical*, then scientific claims against that belief lose force.

The infallibility of Scripture implies that Christian doctrines are infallible to the extent that they reflect the substantive teaching of the biblical canon. Since Scripture is authoritative, Christian doctrines participate in that authority. In practice that is a vital expression of biblical authority.[70] Protestants are right to distinguish special revelation from doctrinal interpretations. "Yet too much can be made of this point," cautions Paul Helm,

> for presumably the special revelation has what status it does have in the believing community because that community believes that at least some of its interpretations admit of no real debate. To suppose that all interpretations of the special revelation might be overturned would call into question the whole status of the special revelation in the community of believers, for it has this status because the community holds that at least some of the expressions of the special revelation express certain propositions.[71]

This side of Eden, however, doctrine is an imperfect distillation of Scripture. The noetic effects of sin and our post-Copernican sensibilities compel us to hermeneutical circumspection. For example, we rightly emphasize the importance of literary genre, and we recognize that Scripture is no encyclopedia or science textbook. Its main purpose is to reconcile us to the Father. We also recognize dogmatic rank as an important conceptual tool. Some doctrines are more central to the witness of Scripture, others more peripheral, less certain. Central doctrines are more clearly attested, more fundamental to Christian faith and, as a result, shape our lives at much deeper levels.[72] Such beliefs have a high *depth of ingression*. (We might say they have a *maximal* depth of ingression).[73] They are not on the periphery but at the center of my noetic structure.

Minimally, then, when our doctrinal convictions are clearly attested in Scripture, when they are central, not peripheral, to Scripture's redemptive-historical narrative, and when they are taught universally in the church catholic, then those convictions are deeply, even maximally, ingressed in our noetic structure. The Holy Spirit confirms them in our hearts and thus we are convinced of their divinity. These

---

70. As Martin Chemnitz argued in *Examination of the Council of Trent, Part I*, trans. Fred Kramer (St. Louis: Concordia, 1971) 249: Christians should accept doctrinal traditions that "are not set forth in so many letters and syllables in Scripture but are brought together from clear testimonies of Scripture by way of good, certain, firm, and clear reasoning."

71. Paul Helm, *Divine Revelation* (Westchester: Crossway, 1982) 113.

72. This is a theological correlate of the clarity of Scripture.

73. Alvin Plantinga, "Reason and Belief in God," in *Faith and Rationality: Reason and Belief in God*, ed. Alvin Plantinga and Nicholas Wolterstorff (Notre Dame: University of Notre Dame Press, 1983) 16–93, at 50.

doctrines are true on the basis of God and his word in Scripture and therefore need no extra-textual warrant from scientists.[74]

A Fallibilist Science

The doctrine of creation implies that, as God's creatures, we are able to examine empirically the beauty, elegance, and structure of God's wonderful creation. Science is a glorious, magnificent, almost miraculous activity, one of the most notable achievements of the human race, a gift of God's common grace and evidence of our role as his image-bearers. Still, this astonishingly complex set of activities that we call science is undertaken by fallen (and finite) men and women. In view of the noetic effects of sin, we only see through a glass darkly (1 Cor 13:12).[75] The devil himself and the powers of darkness brilliantly and systematically influence how intellectual, institutional, and societal structures fall short of the divine blueprint (cf. 1 Pet 5:8; Rev 12:9). Science aims at true descriptions of the world (*realist*) but always imperfectly (*fallibilist*).[76]

The epistemic fallibility of science is heightened in light of methodological naturalism, the notion that genuine science should only appeal to naturalistic explanations. This means *as* a believer, supernatural causal realities are fair game; *as* a scientist, you must be agnostic. Supernaturalists are accused of committing the God-of-the-gaps fallacy, stifling the progress of science, and so on. Christian methodological naturalists are not motivated by anti-supernaturalism *per se* but by

---

74. This needs far more conceptual development than I can offer here. E.g., while the formulation is rather idealized—there are relatively few doctrines that, in their particulars, are "taught universally in the church catholic"—important doctrines can still be seen to have greater or lesser approximation to this ideal. In addition, disagreement will invariably arise about which doctrines are "central" vs. more "peripheral"; of course, adjudicating such differences is a tricky business and will often require scrutinizing basic beliefs and fundamental assumptions. For an insightful analysis of these matters, see Benno van den Toren, "Distinguishing Doctrine and Theological Theory: A Tool for Exploring the Interface between Science and Faith," *Science and Christian Belief* 28 (2016) 55–73. My main reservation lies in his post-foundationalist take on doctrine; my own approach is closer to the moderate foundationalism of Alvin Plantinga.

75. The noetic effects of sin vary widely across different scientific disciplines. As Graham Cole writes, "Every discipline presupposes some doctrine of the human. In some disciplines that doctrine is very much on the surface and potential conflict between the Christian and others will be more to the fore. One might suggest that there is a principle of proximity to the anthropological" ("Scripture and the Disciplines: The Question of Expectations," *Zadok Papers* 142 [2005] 1–8, at 5). The noetic effects of sin on chemistry and physics are less than on biology and, even more so, on psychology. Cf. Stephen K. Moroney, *The Noetic Effects of Sin: A Historical and Contemporary Exploration of How Sin Affects Our Thinking* (Lanham: Lexington, 2000).

76. There is overlap at this point between "biblical realism" and the more common "critical realism" (e.g., see John Polkinghorne, *Science and Theology: An Introduction* [Minneapolis: Fortress, 1998], 16–17).

a fidelity to genuinely empirical science. Appeals to supernatural explanation will miss the detailed *natural* explanations that illuminate the intricate wonders of God's creation.

However, the difficulty with methodological naturalism is that Scripture assumes a robust, biblical supernaturalism.[77] Science investigates the world of biblical supernaturalism. Alvin Plantinga thinks Christians should practice a theistic or Augustinian science "that takes into account what we know *as Christians*."[78] Methodological naturalism artificially constrains the evidence base that Christians use when engaged in scientific theorizing; supernatural explanations are *verboten*. But why restrict the evidence base only to natural entities? Instead, Plantinga proposes we pursue "science using *all that we know*: what we know about God as well as what we know about his creation, and what we know by faith as well as what we know in other ways."[79] According to biblical supernaturalism, science investigates secondary causes that God sustains and concurs in moment by moment, even though this divine presence is not physically detectable.[80] In the actual practice of science there is often no difference between the conclusions of supernaturalism and methodological naturalism, but the two part ways in noteworthy instances such as creation, incarnation, resurrection, ascension, regeneration, miraculous divine action, and many answers to prayer. One option is just to stipulate that science limit itself only to secondary causes; it must therefore consistently plead ignorance about *any* supernatural realities. Another option is to adopt a more expansive definition of science inclusive of everything that is part of our evidence base, both natural *and* supernatural.[81] Methodological naturalism rules out the second and—since it often yields *anti*-supernatural conclusions from its naturalistic premises—falls short of the first.

Given the long and enormously complex process in which our current, naturalistic scientific culture has developed, there is no reason to think that something like Plantinga's "Augustinian science" will emerge in a robust way anytime in the near future. For all its theological faults, non-Augustinian establishment science has plenty

---

77. E.g., see C. John Collins, *The God of Miracles: An Exegetical Examination of God's Action in the World* (Wheaton: Crossway, 2000).

78. Alvin Plantinga, "Methodological Naturalism?" in *Facets of Faith and Science*; Vol. 1: *Historiography and Modes of Interaction*, edited by Jitse M. van der Meer (Lanham: University Press of America, 1996) 177–221, at 192, my emphasis.

79. Plantinga, "Methodological Naturalism," 213–14, emphasis mine. See also his "When Faith and Reason Clash: Evolution and the Bible," *Christian Scholar's Review* 21 (1991) 8–32.

80. Alan Padgett who seems sympathetic to methodological naturalism has an apt description: "Science is the rigorous and empirical investigation of secondary causes" (*Science and the Study of God: A Mutuality Model for Theology and Science* [Grand Rapids: Eerdmans, 2003], 82).

81. Plantinga calls these two options, respectively, "Duhemian" and "Augustinian" science. Cf. Alvin Plantinga, "Science: Augustinian or Duhemian?" *Faith and Philosophy* 13 (1996) 368–94.

to offer by God's common grace. It is also worth remembering that Augustinian science or something close to it once reigned in the history of science. Many godly Christians, without losing their faith, gradually adopted methodological naturalism as the best way to study God's creation. As Numbers argues, "Virtually all scientists (a term coined in the 1830s but not widely used until the late nineteenth century) whether Christians or non-Christians, came by the later nineteenth century to agree that God talk lay beyond the boundaries of science."[82] Repeatedly we find pious believers promoting the naturalizing of meteorology, medicine, physics, chemistry, geology, evolution, and more. Christians, ironically, were among the first to endorse methodological naturalism.[83]

While the future prospects for a robust Augustinian science are slender, its theological rationale remains essential as a *negative* criterion. Specifically, a Christian's evidence base should include everything she believes about reality, *all* the doctrines that testify to the creative, providential, and redemptive-historical work of the triune God. Any scientific theory should therefore be assessed critically in light of those doctrines. Call this approach *tacit supernaturalism*—"tacit" because the realities to which these doctrines attest are always assumed during the empirical investigation of history and nature. That kind of supernaturalism need not violate the scientific investigation of secondary causes; at the same time, however, if divine revelation has genuine and specific relevance to the reality on view, then tacit supernaturalism can—and should—turn explicit.[84]

An Eclectic Approach

Christians have traditionally approached the Bible with concordist assumptions. Given their commitment to Scripture as God's Word, they expect what it says about nature to harmonize with the way the world really is. However, when scientific investigation undermines those expectations, a familiar pattern results:

> Those who employ [concordism], at first, resist the implications of new research that conflict with their concordist expectations, often deferring a

---

82. Ronald Numbers, "Science without God: Natural Laws and Christian Beliefs," in *When Science and Christianity Meet*, edited by David Lindberg and Ronald Numbers (Chicago: University of Chicago Press, 2003) 265–85, at 272.

83. They were wrong to do so, though I cannot argue the case here. In my view, perhaps with the benefit of hindsight, methodological naturalism was inconsistent with their deepest beliefs about the nature of reality.

84. I am well aware that I may be accused of mere hand waving—"concrete example, please!" The limits of this paper preclude me from developing these points more fully. As a quick example, for the sake of argument suppose that substance dualism is the sober truth. A methodologically naturalistic neuroscience *cannot* in principle understand the deepest dimension of human being; the method excludes the possibility of an immaterial soul.

decision on the claim of insufficient evidence. However, if contrary evidence continues to mount against their position, eventually such an individual may concede the point, discard the specific concordist expectation in question, and "ratchet" over to the next available position that retains the balance of their expectations.[85]

Instead, some argue, it is anachronistic to think biblical narratives were intended to harmonize with modern science, for they were penned by fallen, historically conditioned human authors. We should simply cut the Gordian knot; God's Word, they insist, was accommodated to the original audience and takes for granted their ancient, unscientific, mistaken beliefs.[86]

This neo-accommodation theory prompts two concerns.[87] In the first place, concordism at some level is implied in the gospel story. It is true that Scripture does not usually answer the kinds of scientific questions that interest modern people; it is also true that responsible Bible reading should attend to literary genre, avoid imposing foreign concerns onto the text, etc., but the Bible *does* address material concerns that have a direct bearing on the claims of scientists. Since Scripture is God's Word, those propositions will truthfully correspond to the extra-textual world. The Bible after all is not a compilation of religious or "spiritual" truths that float free of historical, physical, and/or cosmological reality. God made the heavens and the earth (Gen 1:1) his redemptive actions were—and are—*within* history, for us and for our children (Deut 29:29; Jer 32:38–44) and his gracious Word to us addresses all spheres of life. Science will ultimately harmonize with theology, since the reality explored by science is the same reality disclosed in Scripture. Biblical realism therefore distinguishes "soft" vs. "hard" concordism. Soft concordism supports the *ultimate* harmonization of science and theology. Full harmony awaits the eschaton; premature attempts to harmonize are thus misguided. Hard concordism is a more rigorous tendency to find concordance between biblical interpretation and assured scientific results.[88] Despite such good intentions, and while many have been drawn

---

85. Dennis Venema, "Genesis and the Genome: Genomics Evidence for Human-Ape Common Ancestry and Ancestral Hominid Population Sizes," *Perspectives on Science and Christian Faith* 62 (2010) 166–78, at 176. Venema describes the pattern as "ratcheting concordism."

86. Venema defends this conclusion, as does Denis Lamoureux, *Evolutionary Creation: A Christian Approach to Evolution* (Eugene, OR: Wipf & Stock, 2008).

87. The classical doctrine of accommodation should be distinguished from its Socinian sibling (Venema and Lamoureux defend the latter—call it "neo-accommodation"). Cf. Glenn Sunshine, "Accommodation Historically Considered," in *The Enduring Authority of the Christian Scriptures*, ed. D. A. Carson (Grand Rapids: Eerdmans, 2016) 238–65; and Martin I. Klauber and Glenn Sunshine, "Jean-Alphonse Turrettini on Biblical Accommodation: Calvinist or Socinian?" *Calvin Theological Journal* 25 (1990) 7–27.

88. "Hard concordism" corresponds roughly with the examples of concordism criticized in John R. Schneider, "Recent Genetic Science and Christian Theology on Human Origins: An 'Aesthetic

to it, science exercises too much control over hard concordist exegesis. Theology married to science will be widowed sooner or later.

In the second place, the neo-accommodation doctrine entails a specific understanding of the science-theology relationship. When God communicates through Scripture, we are told, he preserves erroneous ideas in the inspired text to meet the original audience at their level. The ancient beliefs of the biblical authors have no bearing on the content of modern science. Scripture and science then are independent projects that complement each other without concord or conflict (see Barbour's original typology). This neo-accommodation approach imposes undue limits on the epistemic reach of Scripture and too quickly assumes that modern science has the corner on truth. Christian theology, I argue, should engage scientific theories *eclectically* and on a case-by-case basis. Different theories will invite different theological attitudes and responses.

If soft concordism is true, this side of the eschaton there can be genuine conflicts between science and theology. Sometimes that will mean scientific consensus—human reason at its finest, most glorious—will be rejected, especially when the offending doctrine has explicit biblical warrant, sits central to the gospel story, and enjoys catholic consensus. In principle, however, any doctrine, even when it is central, can be defeated by new scientific evidence (cf. 1 Cor 15:12–19). When and how would that happen? That is a hard question.[89]

Heliocentrism is a clear historical case of science offering a successful defeater; there was real-time telescopic evidence. Most other cases are more ambiguous. The doctrine of original sin faces scientific challenges to a historical Adam and Eve, a literal Garden of Eden, monogenism, inherited sin, and so on. The main lines of evolutionary theory, paleoanthropology, and population genetics are quite compelling, but much of the scientific reasoning is speculative and inferential, lacking epistemic certitude.[90] Most excellent scientific theories have such credentials, thus rejecting them is not necessarily irrational or obtuse. Tacit supernaturalism has access to a wider evidence base that includes the witness of Holy Scripture and a range

---

Supralapsarianism," *Perspectives on Science and Christian Faith* 62 (2010) 196–212.

89. For related analysis, see Alvin Plantinga, "Games Scientists Play," in *The Believing Primate: Scientific, Philosophical, and Theological Reflections on the Origin of Religion*, edited by Jeffrey Schloss and Michael J. Murray (Oxford: Oxford University Press, 2009) 159–67.

90. I am not saying *any* scientific claim lacking "certitude" can be casually set aside. (Such extreme epistemic strictures were the Achilles heel of classical foundationalism!). The point, rather, is how to proceed when a central doctrine that is warranted by a wider Christian evidence base is ruled out by a specific scientific interpretation. The latter can lead us to revise or relinquish the doctrinal belief, but I would argue that the epistemic threshold in such cases should be high. Depending on the doctrine on view, believers will disagree about how high the threshold should be; therein lies the rub. Cf. Madueme, "Most Vulnerable Part of the Whole Christian Account," 245–46.

of Christian doctrines. Furthermore, a doctrinal belief may be *properly basic* with "a lot of warrant on its own"; even if improbable with respect to the reduced evidence base of mainstream science, it may enjoy an "intrinsic warrant" far stronger than any potential scientific defeater.[91]

Conclusion

Some conflicts between science and theology should not be alleviated by theological revision. Our warrant for Christian doctrines lies in the scriptural witness. With or without any evidential support from science, Christians can have full confidence in those doctrines and the realities they depict. Pastorally speaking, however, the existential power of doctrinal truth can be diminished when it conflicts with well-established scientific claims. In our secular age, this clash of plausibility structures prevents many believers from embracing and living out the faith in a full, transformative way. Some within the believing community will thus have a special calling to explore such conflicts and offer fresh articulations of Christian doctrine in new contexts. For example, this might happen by giving a compelling explanation for why there is conflict, or sometimes, by using the tension with science as a catalyst for new existentially meaningful theological conceptualizations. At other times it may mean remaining agnostic about *why* there is conflict or what specific aspects of the scientific theory are in error. While this kind of reflection usually takes place in academic settings, the church as a result will be mutually built up, receiving pastoral comfort and intellectual fortitude in the faith.

As a methodological proposal, biblical realism is limited in its abstraction and needs to be worked out more concretely in relation to specific doctrines.[92] No doubt, that is a worthy project, but alas, one that must await another day.[93]

---

91. See Plantinga, "Games Scientists Play," 166–67.

92. I try to do that with reference to the doctrine of sin in my *The Evolution of Sin? Sin, Theistic Evolution, and the Biological Question—A Theological Account* (Grand Rapids: Baker Academic, forthcoming).

93. I am grateful to Jonathan King and Keith Plummer for their incisive comments on an earlier draft of this paper.

RESPONSE TO MADUEME

Matthew Maas

Dialogue about the intersection of science and religion often resembles politics rather than scholarly inquiry. Intellectual tribalism, cultural affinities, and personal history exert great influence and are mixed with logic and fact. In popular culture dispassionate analyses are crowded out by punditry, with sarcasm and straw-man arguments that betray contempt for both ideas and the people who advance them. Appropriately then Madueme's treatment of the problem of scriptural authority and science flows from historical context into epistemological critique and seeks a method of productive engagement. The result is a proposal for "biblical realism."

While many scholars have worked to develop an epistemology that engages science and religious beliefs, the outcome of those efforts has been particularly unsatisfying for believers who hold a traditional, literalistic reading of Scripture. Pointing to Ian Barbour's proposed typologies of engagement (conflict, independence, dialogue, and integration) Madueme argues that ideological conflict has been unfairly dismissed as untenable. Western culture is perceived to have embraced a naturalistic paradigm that is incompatible with the traditional Christian narrative. The result, it is argued, is an unjust marginalization of conservative doctrinal beliefs whose incongruence with scientific principles is not easily resolved.

The essay's first section makes a forceful argument to interpret the history of science and religion as a conflict narrative. Given the great influence of Christianity on European and American societies, even secular students of history with little exposure to religious history will be familiar with the narrative arc. From Copernicus and Galileo to the Scopes Monkey Trial, skirmishes over the intrusion of uncomfortable scientific ideas occurred regularly in Christian societies. The existence of public controversies pitting science against religion is not in doubt.

The essay's historical narrative, however, is both intensely Eurocentric and grounded in a Great Man theory paradigm, essentially a recounting of theological-scientific clashes between renowned European and American clerics, scholars and statesmen. We are left to wonder whether the conflict among social elites is a fair representation of how typical Christian believers have navigated the marketplace of scientific and doctrinal ideas over time. If political discourse is an apt comparison to religious-scientific engagement, one striking similarity is the degree to which strident conflict is magnified at the level of public voices compared to conversations in the community. Is it plausible that Christians of different theological persuasions regularly achieve greater peace between doctrinal and scientific ideas than the "fundamentalists," "liberals," and "militant atheists" with loud voices?

Restricted to the scholarly sphere, the historical narrative presented is a compelling backdrop for the erosion of respect for scriptural authority. Moreover, it provides context for the schism through which philosophy segregated into distinct spheres of academic theology, humanities, and the natural sciences. Growing esteem for science, spurred by the obvious advances in productivity, health, and quality of life made possible by scientific discovery, has increasingly counterweighted the balance of tension with Christian thought. Arguing in support of contradictory, traditional doctrines has become a harder sell to students in the classroom and believers in the pews. As Madueme says, "With the exception of unfashionable conservative theologians who resisted these forces, trying to preserve continuity with the premodern theological vision, modern works of theology—almost universally—transmuted their doctrines in light of science or, conversely, developed strategic formulations of doctrine that avoided conflict altogether."

Where does that leave the conservative scholar and traditional believer? Madueme's formulation is that theological liberals "have argued that new discoveries in the natural sciences pose no real threat to the faith." The suggestion is that scientific claims are literal truths, and Scripture interpretation is revised to accommodate emerging scientific worldviews. For conservative theologians, however, "We make a serious mistake if we essentialize conflict between science and theology, but we also make a serious mistake if we minimize deep instances of conflict between elements of scientific understanding and central doctrines of the faith." Scripture is authoritative, so conflict with science is inherent and unavoidable. As usual, the true disagreement is not with scriptural authority per se, but the degree to which certain Scriptures must be read and interpreted literally.

As a result, fealty to scriptural authority and a particular method of literal interpretation paints conservative religious scholars into a corner. Biblical realism is Madueme's search for the common ground. Biblical realism consists of sorting all circumstances in which Christian doctrine and science appear to conflict into two piles. One category consists of situations in which overwhelmingly certain science seems to overturn peripheral doctrine, with heliocentrism as the given example. In contrast, the other category comprises central Christian dogma (e.g., Jesus's resurrection) so integral to mainstream Christian theology that it must stand whether supported by science or not. As simply stated, biblical realism is a least common denominator that could conceptually welcome a wide spectrum of Christian beliefs. Unfortunately, it is descriptive rather than prescriptive and, as a result, offers limited potential to resolve theological disagreements. Moreover, it does little to avert unproductive conflict.

While conflicts of ideas may be inevitable between science and religion, conflict need not become the template for engagement. From the essays title,[1] through the text, and in the formulation of biblical realism, Madueme's framework calls for sharp dichotomies: believers in Jesus versus those who stumble over him as a rock of offense, liberals whose doctrine and Scripture interpretation is subservient to science versus conservatives who are compelled to reject scientific claims that contradict a literal reading of the Bible, and a biblical realism formula that relies on lumping all doctrine into two categories. A shaded view that sees both science and doctrine as potentially flawed better represents our cognitive realities and provides a more robust foundation for engagement.

It may come as a surprise to some Christians with limited scientific educations that an approach that admits limited understanding and the potential for error does not position religious doctrine at a disadvantage to science. On the contrary, at the academic levels science is a deeply skeptical discipline that is preoccupied with its own errors, limitations, and shortcomings. Publication of high quality scientific work always contains statistical estimates of the potential magnitude of error in measurements and results, and estimates of the likelihood that conclusions based on the data may have been falsely drawn, along with comments about potential methodologic shortcomings. As such, an ethos of uncertainty and self-critique is deeply entrenched within the scientific community, however imperfectly.[2] Technical jargon obscures these many caveats and doubts, which is consistently misunderstood or ignored when scientific findings are communicated in a mass media prone to reduce nuanced concepts to sound bites. The pervasive misrepresentation of an entire field is familiar turf to many Christian theologians who are accustomed to fringe positions, from Jesus Seminar gadflies to televangelist spectacles, who occupy outsized space in the public square. Breathless reporting of "breakthrough discoveries" (e.g., Harvard professor discovers proof that Jesus was married!) merit primetime specials, while their debunking occupies the quiet pages of academic journals.

---

1. An allusion to 1 Pet 2:7–8: "So the honor is for you who believe, but for those who do not believe, 'The stone that the builders rejected has become the cornerstone,' and 'A stone of stumbling, and a rock of offense.'"

2. R. Nuzzo provides an excellent overview of the scientific approach to characterizing errors and false conclusions. He describes ongoing controversies related to persistent, widespread errors in published scientific findings and suggests analytic methods may require changes to address the problem better. See R. Nuzzo, "Scientific Method: Statistical Errors," *Nature* 506 (Feb. 12, 2014) 150–52.

Scientists generally view their discipline as one of progressive revelation, in which truths are seen as though through a mirror darkly. The assumption is that portions of the scientific worldview are flawed, and the purpose of science is to discover factual information that progressively clarifies truth and reality. The evolving knowledge about the shape of the earth is an often-used example. Lacking an external source of information, most humans would conclude that the earth is flat. Aside from a few delusional souls, most living individuals with access to education reject that view. On average, the earth's surface curves eight vertical inches every horizontal mile. Obscured by our limited eyesight and the relatively massive surface contours, this deduction is not intuitive. Interestingly, many if not most modern people believe the earth is spherical, an opinion that is also wrong. The earth is an oblate ellipsoid that is "fatter" at the equator by about 13 miles. This fact has been known for a long time. Isaac Newton, for instance, described this in his treatise "Principia" in 1687, over 300 years ago.[3] Yet many, doubtlessly including some highly intelligent colleagues you respect, remain blissful in their pre-Enlightenment era scientific ignorance.

In a series of essays collected in a book called *The Relativity of Wrong*, the biochemist and science writer Isaac Asimov addressed this very error, developing the concept of "wronger than wrong": "When people thought the earth was flat, they were wrong. When people thought the earth was spherical, they were wrong. But if you think that thinking the earth is spherical is just as wrong as thinking the earth is flat, then your view is wronger than both of them put together."[4]

Believing the world is flat was wrong, but it was a reasonable and workable assumption. Broadly painting all errors equally is, however, anti-scientific because it rejects the premise of progressive revelation upon which the scientific enterprise is built.

The society and world we inhabit today is objectively increasingly abstract and complex. The great complexity of the world impacts and confounds both science and faith. As we interact with our complex world and seek to address questions, it becomes extremely difficult at times to even formulate valid questions to yield relevant answers. Perhaps nowhere has the challenge of abstract thinking been more apparent and problematic than in physics. Modern physics presents us with an unrecognizable world, where space and time are unified and curved around physical matter, and physical matter and energy are one and the same, moving as

---

3. Isaac Newton, *Philosophiæ Naturalis Principia Mathematica* (London: Joseph Streater, 1687) Prop. 19, Book 3. Print.

4. I. Asimov, "The Relativity of Wrong," *Skeptical Inquirer* 14 (1989) 35–44, subsequently published in *The Relativity of Wrong* (New York: Kensington, 1988).

both particle and wave, et cetera. It was in that milieu that the Austrian theoretical physicist and Nobel laureate Wolfgang Pauli famously commented on the work of a junior colleague, saying "That is not only not right, it is not even wrong." In other words, it contains a terminal logical fallacy or is unfalsifiable. Claims to support or refute religious doctrine through scientific discovery are often not even wrong. Supernatural phenomena are not within the scope of current scientific techniques to test, refute, or support. Modern science therefore acknowledges its current views are a mixture of truths and errors, that the scientific community is embarked upon a long journey to discover a clearer view of the truth, that refining an imperfect view of reality and truth is inherent in the scientific process, and that some questions are not amenable to a scientifically formulated answer.

So whereas the visible periphery of the science and religion dialog appears to be a contentious series of unresolvable conflicts, the great bulk of practitioners share a spirit of humility and awareness of their own limitations and propensity to error. Moreover, there is a shared awareness that the truths most easily accessed by their system are relatively impenetrable to the teachings of the other. A generous spirit that yields to the other whenever possible does not resolve all potential conflicts, but does facilitate a productive dialog.

Just prior to the "rock of offense" passage in 1 Peter is an equally pertinent statement: "For it stands in Scripture: 'Behold, I am laying in Zion a stone, a cornerstone chosen and precious, and whoever believes in him will not be put to shame.'" The lived experience of conservative believers with respect to the intersection of science and faith, however, is one of increasing cultural alienation and being put to shame. The need for a new approach is clear, but we should be wary of Madueme's call to embrace conflict. Moreover, the suggestion that biblical realism is a useful method that will secure conservative theologians a seat at the table of cultural-scientific-religious dialog is unconvincing. It is true that noisy figureheads of "militant atheism" have not sought to understand and respect the intellectual framework of conservative doctrine, which leads to a scholarly stalemate. Maybe biblical traditionalists will break the logjam by embracing laudable characteristics of the scientific worldview that will facilitate engagement.

"I BELIEVE; HELP MY UNBELIEF!" MARK 9:14–29

Kirk Wegter-McNelly

Exorcism may seem like an unlikely focus for a sermon on the relationship between faith and science. But in fact, this is just this kind of biblical passage that throws into sharp relief the difficulties involved. How are Christians to understand our Scriptures, our God, and ourselves in relation to the labors and fruits of modern science? To put it more personally: Where is the good news in a passage like this for a Christian like myself who regards the idea of exorcism with more than a little suspicion, for someone like myself who wants to be a Christian in light of science rather than in spite of it, who longs deeply for an integrated world-view? To put it less personally but perhaps more relevantly for students: How am I supposed to remain strong in my faith when I feel bombarded by unanswered questions, unresolved issues, and more than a little confusion. What does all this have to do with my faith, my belief in Christ?

I think the answer is contained in a pair of words: love and honesty. Our love for God and neighbor demands of us an attitude of care for the world, and caring for something requires serious effort to understand it. Without such understanding, attempts at care risk missing their mark and failing to manifest effectively the love undergirding them. So we Christians lean on each other as we try to understand God, ourselves, and the world better—all for the sake of expressing our care in ways that respond to the world's actual needs, rather than to what we wished the world needed. At the same time, none of us understands God, the world, or even ourselves completely. Christians also learn to lean on each other as we wrestle with the limits of our understanding, and if we are open to acknowledging our own finitude, we have the opportunity to be honest with each other about our struggles, our doubts, our fears—all in the face of a welter of ideas and emotions that can rattle us to our existential core. So with these two ideas in mind—love and honesty—let us ponder together this account of an exorcism in the Gospel of Mark.

Interpreters traditionally give this passage titles like "The Healing of the Boy with a Demon" and "The Healing of the Boy with an Unclean Spirit." Here Jesus encounters a boy who is regularly seized by convulsions, unable to speak, foaming at the mouth. You might have heard that a helpful way of understanding what Jesus is facing is to recognize the boy as suffering from what we know today as the medical condition of epilepsy: a chronic disorder characterized by recurrent, unprovoked seizures that result from excessive and abnormal electrical activity in the cortex of the brain. This invocation of the modern worldview, to the labors and fruits of medical science, may help us connect to the text and understand it more deeply relative to our own cultural context.

Ah, okay then; that explains it. This boy had epilepsy, a medical condition, the cure for which still eludes doctors today. What we see, then, is Jesus manifesting the power and love of God to cure the boy of his illness. But wait. How exactly is this explanation supposed to help us bridge the biblical world and our own? If we are to think "medical condition" instead of "spiritual warfare," is the point then that Jesus has the power to cast out medical conditions, and that by tapping into this power we can do the same? Or is the point that we should thank God for doctors and medical researchers in their ongoing search for a reliable medical cure? Or is it that, in the face of what is a still an incurable disease, scientifically speaking, we should pray for spiritual resolve to carry the burden of illness, for our spirits to be healed without necessarily having our bodies cured?

Each of these options has merit, but from my perspective none of them do much to resolve the tension I feel between the worldview informing this passage and my own, which is shaped not only by the Christian Scriptures and tradition but also by modern science. The idea of Jesus casting out a medical condition suggests to me a confused juxtaposition of two worldviews rather than their integration into one. Thanking God for those searching for a cure for epilepsy seems like a good thing to do, but that route also demythologizes the text to the point that we are only a few short steps away from rendering it superfluous. And while praying for resolve, for healing even in the absence of a cure, can in such situations be the mark of mature faith, the programmatic application of this spiritualizing kind of approach simply dissolves the tension rather than resolving it, leaving us with nothing to integrate, nothing to reassemble, nothing to leverage for the sake of deeper theological understanding. So I would like to suggest that we might be better off, at least for the purposes of this particular sermon, taking an oblique rather than direct route into this text. I have in mind, as you may have surmised from my title, turning our attention away from the boy and toward his father.

As a character in this story, the father shows potential for being our link or liaison to the biblical worldview, for he seems both to share the Bible's sensibilities regarding the possibility of the miraculous, what we might label the "supernatural," and at the same time to have some doubts that might resonate with our own. It is not clear who this man is. He is "someone in the crowd," so presumably not one of

Jesus' inner circle. He clearly believes in spirits that can take over our human bodies, prevent them from speaking, and make them grind their teeth and foam at the mouth. He has already taken his son to Jesus' disciples in hopes that they would be able to cure the boy. They tried but were unsuccessful. Now he has worked up the courage to speak to Jesus himself.

When Jesus asks him how long the boy has suffered, he responds, "From childhood. It has often cast him into the fire and into the water, to destroy him; but if you are able to do anything, have pity on us and help us." Here is a man who, I think, has little hope of his child being cured, but whose parental love will not let him give up. He is looking for something that might provide his son with relief, even if that something is not a full-blown, knock-your-socks off miracle. It seems as though he would be grateful if Jesus could offer his son even the slightest bit of relief, perhaps lessening the intensity or frequency of the attacks.

I admire this man's refusal to let go of his thin thread of hope. His request seems honest, heart-felt, and entirely appropriate to me, given what he and his son have been through and the impotence he had witnessed in Jesus' disciples. But Jesus, apparently indignant at the paltry nature of the request, lashes back at him: "If you are able?!" As if to say, "What? Do you not know who I am?" "All things can be done for the one who believes" (9:23). As I see it, this poor man has just unknowingly taken one for the team. Jesus may be venting his anger at the father, but in the first instance Jesus appears to be angry with his disciples, who were unable to do what he had sent them out to do. He responds to the man's story not with "You unbelieving man," but rather with "You unbelieving generation" (9:19).

How does this man respond to Jesus' stinging rebuke? Here is where the story cracks open, where it departs from the expected script and lays bare, if only for a moment, what looks to me like an honest portrayal of the human condition. At first, the man responds confidently, crying out: "I believe! I believe!" Which of us would not shout this on behalf of our own children, if we thought their welfare was at stake? But then comes an amazing moment, a moment of honesty on the part of this beleaguered man that I can hardly fathom.

Even as he cries, "I believe!" I imagine his mind going a million miles an hour as he thinks to himself, "Now wait a minute. That is not entirely true. Jesus' disciples could not do anything. My son has been burdened with this spirit for most of his life. No one else has ever been able to help him. How is Jesus going to be any different than all the others? What can he possibly do?" Of course, this imagined internal dialogue would have happened in the blink of an eye. For the father goes directly from exclaiming "I believe!" to "Help my unbelief!"

What a courageous and risky thing to say! In the presence of Jesus, who is clearly angry, the father corrects himself and admits that he doubts anything can be done. Because he loves his son, he is standing there before Jesus. Yet in that moment he makes himself vulnerable before Jesus, possibly dooming his son's future by speaking honestly about his doubts: "Help my unbelief."

Help my unbelief. I do not presume to know your thoughts, but I can say on my own behalf that more than a few times I have pulled into the church parking lot on Sunday morning in a similar frame of mind. I believe; help my unbelief. Have pity on me, Lord, despite the fact that I am a man not infrequently drained of hope and hanging on by a few threads. I do not know what my being here can do for me or for my family, but here I am, hoping against hope, that something, even if it is only a small thing, might be possible. The father's love for his child and his honest admission of doubt is where I find my way into this story, where I find myself inhabiting its vision: wanting healing and not entirely believing it is possible.

The tradition subordinates the father's admission of his lack of faith to the idea that Jesus' power is not limited by his doubt. It makes the point of the story to be that having faith is the goal, even if it is not the reality. The air surrounding Jesus as he confronts the man is heavy with judgment against unbelief. Then, after the father's admission, he simply disappears from the story. Jesus heals his son, and the focus shifts back to the disciples and their own troubles. Presumably the father goes away emboldened, propelled to new heights of faith by a miraculous cure.

Yet the fact that he disappears, that we do not see his faith emboldened or secured, strikes me as an opening to consider the possibility that he walks away amazed, thankful, filled with appreciation and wonder, still not knowing quite what to think. The fact that this story even permits the mind to wander in such a direction is, I think, remarkable. This is one of the things I love about Scripture: that it has the power to surprise and upend itself as we encounter and wrestle with it.

So is this good news, that the loving parent of a sick child can find the strength to be honest with Jesus, doubting his power even when the stakes are so high? I for one do see this as good news. I fully grant that this may not be what Mark intended to convey, and it certainly is not the lesson drawn from this text by the church across the ages. But I am also confident that neither Mark nor the church is in control of what messages God can convey to us through this text. To put the point in more traditional language, the Holy Spirit who lives in us also guides us in uncontrollable and unlikely ways as we attempt to hear the gospel in Scripture. As Jesus says to Nicodemus in John's Gospel, the Spirit of God "blows where it chooses, and you hear the sound of it, but you do not know where it comes from or where it goes" (3:8).

For those of us who do not know, this is indeed good news. For those of us who want to live out our spiritual calling in light of science rather than in spite of it, this is good news. If there is room in Mark's Gospel for Jesus' power to touch even someone who is willing to admit his unbelief, then perhaps there is room in the church for those of us with unbelieving belief in our hearts to feel and experience that power too, even if we cannot say we know where it comes from or where it goes. Perhaps there is room for those of us whose scientific study and training have formed us into the kind of people who cannot *not* ask the impolite, awkward questions and who want the kind of faith that seeks to live and grow in the midst of doubt rather than in spite of it.

I believe; help my unbelief! Amen.

Benediction

Now go out into the world that God loves, loving it not as we might wish it to be but as it actually is in all of its complex beauty and brokenness, that world which we do understand, that which we may yet understand, and that which may forever lie beyond our understanding. May the grace of the Lord Jesus Christ, the love of God, and the fellowship of the Holy Spirit be with you all. Amen.

ANNOTATED BIBLIOGRAPHY ON SCIENCE AND RELIGION

Bagir, Zainal Abidin. "The 'Relation' Between Science and Religion in the Pluralistic Landscape of Today's World." *Zygon: Journal of Religion and Science* 50 (2015) 403–17. This article asks whether the current trend toward pluralism begs the question whether the categories of "Science" and "Religion" need to be deconstructed and reconsidered. The author uses case studies of indigenous Indonesia to address this question.

Barbour, Ian G. *Religion and Science: Historical and Contemporary Issues*. San Francisco: HarperCollins, 1997. This book is the classic text concerning the historical and conceptual relation between science and religion. Ian Barbour is regarded as the godfather of the science-religion dialogue. One strength of Barbour's approach is that while he adopts a view of God and reality based on process philosophy, this does not negatively affect the rich and well-written description of the relation of science and religion.

Barr, Stephen M. *Modern Physics and Ancient Faith*. Notre Dame: University of Notre Dame Press, 2013. Many Christian apologetic works defending the faith against materialism set up straw men to topple. Barr, a physicist at the University of Delaware and a Catholic, sets up a strong, convincing, and fair argument for materialism before contending that modern science, rather than supporting such a worldview, instead argues against that worldview. Barr covers not only cosmology but also the mind.

———. *The Believing Scientist: Essays on Science and Religion*. Grand Rapids: Eerdmans, 2016. Both an accomplished theoretical physicist and a faithful Catholic, Stephen Barr in this book addresses a wide range of questions about the relationship between science and religion and provides a beautiful picture of how they can coexist in harmony.

Barrow, John D. *The Book of Nothing: Vacuums, Voids, and the Latest Ideas about the Origins of the Universe*. New York: Vintage, 2002. Barrow takes readers on a journey through mathematics, theology, philosophy, particle physics, and cosmology to explore the enduring hold that nothingness has exercised on the human imagination. He combines utter speculation with a treasure-trove of references, and the result is a fascinating expedition to the vanishing point of modern scientific theory.

Benz, Arnold. *The Future of the Universe: Chance, Chaos, God?* New York: Continuum, 2000. Benz, a celebrated astrophysicist, provides his commentary on religious issues from his context of astronomical and cosmological studies. Benz demonstrates how he holds faith and his research together.

Brooke, John Hedley. *Science and Religion: Some Historical Perspectives*. Cambridge: Cambridge University Press, 2014. This seminal volume is arguably the most important book in the field of science and religion. Brooke crushes the widely held myth that science and faith are and have always been mortal enemies. His analysis is brilliant, illuminating, and insightful throughout.

Brooke, John, and Geoffrey Cantor. *Reconstructing Nature: the Engagement of Science and Religion*. Cambridge: International Society for Science and Religion, 2007. Brooke and Cantor examine the historical and contemporary relationship between science and religion; specifically in terms of what nature signifies for each. They demonstrate the impossibility of seeing the science and religion debate as a single narrative, for neither can be reduced to some timeless essence. They also reject the adequacy of the conflict paradigm

Burton, Robert. *A Skeptic's Guide to the Mind: What Neuroscience Can and Cannot Tell Us about Ourselves.* New York: St. Martin's Griffin, 2014. Burton brings together clinical observations, practical thought experiments, personal anecdotes, and cutting-edge neuroscience to interpret what neuroscience can tell us about human behavior and action, and frankly what it cannot. Burton also proposes a new revelation on how to think about what the mind may be and how it works.

Cannon, Walter B. *The Wisdom of the Body: How the Human Body Reacts to Disturbance and Danger and Maintains the Stability Essential to Life.* 2nd ed. New York: W. W. Norton, 1939. Cannon gives a classic treatment of the body and biology in this work about homeostasis. His predominant thesis is that humans, characteristic of all mammals, rely less on internal physiology to create homeostasis with their environment than to regulate their internal environment within constricted boundaries. Cannon extends this phenomenon to social theory in his epilogue where he discusses the tendencies for humans to leave rather than adapt to harsh social conditions.

Carr, Bernard, ed. *Universe or Multiverse?* Cambridge: Cambridge University Press, 2011. In this collection of essays a number of active and distinguished researchers in the field—mainly cosmologists and particle physicists but also some philosophers—describe recent developments in multiverse theory. The articles represent the continuum of perspectives and provide a somewhat comprehensive overview of the subject.

Castel, B., and Sergio Sismondo. *The Art of Science.* Toronto: University of Toronto Press, 2008. One author is a physicist and the other a philosopher, and together they have written a book that argues science is more of an art than is usually acknowledged. The book is also beautifully illustrated, and the pictures convey the thesis more effectively than words alone could do.

Cavanaugh, William T., and James K. A. Smith, eds. *Evolution and the Fall.* Grand Rapids: Eerdmans, forthcoming 2017. This collection of essays by scholars from various disciplines and church traditions addresses the question of the meaning of the doctrine of the fall if there was no historical Adam. The essays deal with questions of human origins, the biblical accounts, and traditional theological explanations and propose new ways of imaging the conversation.

Clegg, Brian. *Before the Big Bang: the Prehistory of the Universe.* New York: St. Martin's Griffin, 2011. Clegg provides a somewhat skeptical look at the Big Bang Theory and other origin narratives from science and history. In asking, "What came before the Big Bang?" Clegg not only questions the theory itself but even more the philosophical impact of all origin theories on humanity.

Collins, C. John. *Did Adam and Eve Really Exist? Who They Were and Why You Should Care.* Wheaton, IL: Crossway, 2011. Collins not only argues for the importance of the historicity of Adam and Eve, but he also shows why the fall makes sense of the longing in our hearts and our deep sense that there is something wrong with the world.

Collins, Francis S. *The Language of God: A Scientist Presents Evidence for Belief.* New York: Free, 2007. Collins takes aim at the misconception that science and faith cannot coexist. Written for believers, atheists, and agnostics alike, this work offers a testament to the power of faith in the midst of suffering without faltering from its logical stride.

Crisp, Thomas M., Steven L. Porter, and Gregg A. Ten Elshof, eds. *Neuroscience and the Soul: The Human Person in Philosophy, Science, and Theology*. Grand Rapids: Eerdmans, 2016. In this collection of essays fourteen celebrated scholars grapple with current debates about the existence and nature of the soul. The essays bring together contributions from philosophy, theology, and neuroscience, and in doing so bring new nuances and significant advancement in the ongoing debate over body and soul.

Cushing, James T. *Philosophical Concepts in Physics: The Historical Relation between Philosophy and Scientific Theories*. Cambridge: International Society for Science and Religion, 2007. This is a nice introduction to the philosophy of science and scientific knowledge. Cushing starts from the very beginning, with the ancient Greeks and inductive and deductive reasoning, and goes all the way to modern times and chaos theory. Cushing's introduction, however, is not merely propositional but is instead narrative. His survey of the history of science is fun and as important as his philosophical conclusions.

Dixon, Thomas. *Science and Religion: A Very Short Introduction*. Very Short Introductions Series 189. Oxford: Oxford University Press, 2008. This is a helpful introduction to the dialogue on science and religion. While by no means comprehensive, it introduces some of the major issues and is an excellent starting point.

Dixon, Thomas, Geoffrey Cantor, and Stephen Pumfrey, eds. *Science and Religion: New Historical Perspectives*. Cambridge: Cambridge University Press, 2010. This collection of essays addresses the history and changing implications of the categories "science" and "religion." It also discusses the function of publishing and education in creating and disseminating ideas, the link between knowledge, power, and intellectual imperialism, and the motives for the conflict between evolution and creationism among American Christians and in the Islamic world.

Drees, Willem B. *Beyond the Big Bang: Quantum Cosmologies and God*. La Salle, IL: Open Court, 1990. Drees combats both the religious abuse of science and the out of hand dismissal of religious questions by the scientific community. This work asks whether belief in God is reasonable in light of modern cosmology and what, if anything, religion has to say about science.

Eisen, Arri, and Gary Laderman, eds. *Science, Religion, and Society: An Encyclopedia of History, Culture, and Controversy*. Armonk, NY: M. E. Sharpe, 2007. This work provides a unique lens by providing a multicultural and multireligious discussion of the controversies regarding religion and science. The work includes sections on creation, the cosmos, ecology, evolution, consciousness, mind, healing, death, genetics, and religion.

Farris, Joshua Ryan, and Charles Taliaferro, eds. *The Ashgate Research Companion to Theological Anthropology*. Farnham: Ashgate, 2016. This accessible volume serves as an excellent starting point for those interested in the examination of the theology of human persons/personhood. The primary topics covered are human agency and grace, the soul, sin and salvation, Christology, glory, feminism, the theology of human nature, and other major themes in theological anthropology in historic as well as contemporary contexts.

Gallagher, Shaun. *How the Body Shapes the Mind*. Oxford: Clarendon, 2013. Gallagher seeks to contribute to the formulation of a conceptual framework that will avoid both the overly simplistic scientific approaches that explain everything in terms of neuronal mechanisms, and opposite approaches that attempt explain everything in terms of Cartesian, top-down cognitive states. To do so Gallagher asks questions both of phenomenology and consciousness in order to see, to what extent, each informs the mind.

Annotated Bibliography

Gallagher, Shaun, and Dan Zahavi. *The Phenomenological Mind: An Introduction to Philosophy of Mind and Cognitive Science.* New York: Routledge, 2008. This work gives an introduction to the field of phenomenology. The book asks what role seemingly unexplainable psychological events have in the world of scientific study.

Gallese, Vittorio. "Being like Me: Self-other Identity, Mirror Neurons and Empathy." In *Perspectives on Imitation: From Cognitive Neuroscience to Social Science*, edited by Susan Hurley and Nick Chater, vol. 1, 101–18. Cambridge, MA: MIT Press, 2005. Gallese demonstrates that the same neurons fire when doing a particular action as do when watching a peer do the same action. With this being the case, Gallese concludes that much of perception in human interaction is affected by these purported mirror neurons.

Greenwood, Kyle. *Scripture and Cosmology: Reading the Bible between the Ancient World and Modern Science.* Downers Grove, IL: IVP Academic, 2015. This work is a good, recent discussion both of biblical cosmology in its ancient context and how readers of Scripture throughout history have sought to take seriously God's Word in light of new scientific discoveries.

Hanby, Michael. *No God, No Science? Theology, Cosmology, Biology.* Hoboken: Wiley, 2013. Hanby offers a long overdue critique of the philosophical meaning of Darwinian biology and attempts to reframe the dialogue between science and religion. He also delves into the complicated relationship between the church, the Bible, and the world of science with respect to the origins of the cosmos.

Haught, John F. *God after Darwin: a Theology of Evolution.* Boulder: Westview, 2000. This volume is an exceptionally clear defense of Christianity that is amenable to the theory of evolution, albeit with some significant nuances on how to understand the nature of God and God's providence.

———. *Is Nature Enough? Meaning and Truth in the Age of Science.* Cambridge: Cambridge University Press, 2006. This work looks at the philosophy of naturalism, provides a critique of naturalism, and specifically attempts to undo the efforts of naturalists to distance "nature and science" from "religion." Relying in part on Catholic philosopher Bernard Lonergan, Haught constructs an alternative way to articulate scientific knowledge that is true to both science itself and a religious way of understanding knowledge.

Herzfeld, Noreen L. *In Our Image: Artificial Intelligence and the Human Spirit.* Minneapolis: Fortress, 2002. This work is touted as the first in the field of theology to relate to Artificial Intelligence (AI). The author addresses the ever-growing interest in AI and argues that a social anthropology informs the many depictions of AI in science-fiction literature and film.

Herzfeld, Noreen L. *Technology and Religion: Remaining Human in a Co-created World.* Templeton Science and Religion. West Conshohocken, PA: Templeton, 2009. In modernity one's daily life changes more rapidly than at any other time in human history because of advances in technology. Does technology have the power to change the way one thinks about religion? Herzfeld attempts to answer this question and the result is a multifaceted look at the ongoing dialogue between these two subjects.

Howell, Kenneth J. *God's Two Books: Copernican Cosmology and Biblical Interpretation in Early Modern Science.* Notre Dame, IN: University of Notre Dame Press, 2002. This work is an analysis of how sixteenth- and seventeenth-century astronomers and theologians in Northern Protestant Europe used science and religion to challenge and support one another. The work also suggests how theological interpretation and scientific investigation should interact.

Hudson, Hud. *The Metaphysics of Hyperspace*. Oxford: Clarendon, 2008. Hudson provides an examination into why one should believe in hyperspace from a philosophical perspective. Beginning with non-theistic reasoning and then moving into theistic reasoning, this work is important in seeing how contemporary religion informs cutting-edge theoretical physics.

Hummel, Charles E. *The Galileo Connection: Resolving Conflicts between Science and the Bible*. Downers Grove, IL: IVP Academic, 1994. This introduction to faith-science issues is still frequently recommended to new students in the field. It is accessible and concise and, best of all, personal. It does not discuss issues in an abstract way; instead they are discussed as connecting to your life. The biographies of Galileo, Pascal, Kepler, and others that are sprinkled throughout reinforce the idea that science and faith are not only philosophically non-contradictory but also can thrive together in the heart and faith of a single person.

Jeeves, Malcolm A., ed. *The Emergence of Personhood: A Quantum Leap?* Grand Rapids: Eerdmans, 2015. In this collection of essays internationally acclaimed scholars such as Anthony Thiselton, Ian Tattersall, and Alan Torrance explore human evolution, the *imago Dei*, morality, and personhood. They consider both gradualist approaches to personhood and a quantum leap. This is a significant collection of essays.

———. "Neuroscience, Evolutionary Psychology, and the Image of God." *Perspectives on Science and Christian Faith* 57 (2005) 170–86. Jeeves argues that "a proper understanding of the doctrine of the image of God is an essential groundwork to formulating and understanding a proper Christian response to humanitarian, evangelistic, apologetic, and ecological concerns." He draws on modern scientific advances in neurology and neuropsychology to demonstrate how science is expanding the ways members of Abrahamic faiths can view the *imago Dei*.

Jitse, M. van der Meer and Scott Mandelbrote, eds. *Nature and Scripture in the Abrahamic Religions: Up to 1700*. Brill's Series in Church History 36. 2 vols. Leiden: Brill, 2008. This two-volume set is an important resource in the discussion of the history of science and biblical interpretation, and it is a present day resource for the ever changing and evolving questions in the relationship between hermeneutics and modern science. This work seeks to provide historical context for renewed reflection on these issues and for the issues that may come up as science and theology continue to change.

———. *Nature and Scripture in the Abrahamic Religions: 1700–Present*. Brill's Series in Church History 37. 2 vols. Leiden: Brill, 2008. This two-volume set is obviously the continuation of the historical survey begun in the previous entry.

Johnson, Elizabeth A. *Ask the Beasts: Darwin and the God of Love*. London: Bloomsbury, 2014. This volume takes the perspective of Job 12 in seeking a Christian way to ask about nature and its wisdom. Johnson centers her reflections on the confluence of the idea of self-giving love and the Nicene Creed's affirmation of God's incarnation in Jesus. She extends both ideas to incorporate the way God embraces the physical world as a whole.

Jonas, Hans. *The Phenomenon of Life: Toward a Philosophical Biology*. Evanston, IL: Northwestern University Press, 1966. Hans Jonas demonstrates how differing life forms present themselves on an ascending scale of perception and freedom of action. Jonas hypothesizes that this scale reaches its apex in a human being's capacity for thought and morally responsible behavior.

Keating, Thomas. *Invitation to Love: The Way of Christian Contemplation*. New York: Continuum, 2004. This is a practical explanation of contemplative practice. Keating answers the questions "What will contemplative practice do for one's life" and "Why are the contemplative arts important for spiritual development."

Kelly, Edward F., Adam Crabtree, and Paul Marshall, eds. *Beyond Physicalism: Toward Reconciliation of Science and Spirituality*. Lanham: Rowman and Littlefield, 2015. This collection of essays from fourteen contributors and representing various cultures uses aspects of metaphysical philosophy, empirical science, and the mystical traditions. The volume argues for a more comprehensive view of reality than physicalism. The authors attempt to reconcile science and spirituality and find an intermediary between the polarizing fundamentalisms of religion and science that often inhabit most of the public space.

Kelly, Edward F., and Emily Williams Kelly. *Irreducible Mind: Toward a Psychology for the 21st Century*. Lanham: Rowman and Littlefield, 2010. The authors systematically marshal evidence for a variety of psychological phenomena that are extremely difficult, and in some cases clearly impossible, to account for in conventional physicalist terms. Topics addressed include phenomena of extreme psychophysical influence, memory, psychological automatisms and secondary personality, near-death experiences and allied phenomena, genius-level creativity, and "mystical" states of consciousness both spontaneous and drug-induced.

Kim, Andrew. "Bernard Ramm's Scientific Approach to Theology." *Perspectives on Science and Christian Faith* 68 (2016) 155–64. Written one hundred years after Ramm's birth, this article provides insight into Ramm as one of history's great bridges between evangelicals and science. The article demonstrates how his scientific background influenced his faith and theology.

Koss-Chioino, Joan, and Philip J. Hefner, eds. *Spiritual Transformation and Healing: Anthropological, Theological, Neuroscientific, and Clinical Perspectives*. Lanham, MD: AltaMira, 2006. These essays provide a comprehensive look at spiritual transformation and healing from anthropologists, psychologists, medical doctors, biologists, and theologians. This includes the roles of religious communities and healing practitioners.

Kraay, Klaas J., ed. *God and the Multiverse: Scientific, Philosophical, and Theological Perspectives*. New York: Routledge, 2015. In the twelve essays of this volume one finds the dialogue of multiverse proponents, some of whom argue that theories of multiple universes count against arguments for the existence of God, while others claim the multiverse is further evidence of a Creator. The articles deal with everything from pantheism to incarnation.

Krishnamurthy, K. *Pioneers in Scientific Discoveries*. New Delhi: Mittal, 2002. The author provides a comprehensive overview of the sciences and technology from approximately 250 BCE to the twenty-first century. With a range of more than one hundred topics and more than two hundred scientists, Krishnamurthy discusses the differences in these discoveries, from those intentional improvements in technology to those accidental discoveries of science.

Kuhn, Thomas S. *The Structure of Scientific Revolutions: Fiftieth Anniversary Edition*. 4th ed. Chicago: University of Chicago Press, 2012. This is a classic in the philosophy of science and was one of the first to present a historically informed understanding of the epistemology of science. Kuhn argued against a gradual linear development of scientific progress and for advances outside "normal science." This edition includes a new introduction by Ian Hacking which provides explanation and context.

Lewis, C. S. "Meditation in a Toolshed." In *God in the Dock: Essays on Theology and Ethics*, edited by Walter Hooper, 212–15. Grand Rapids: Eerdmans, 1983. In this short essay Lewis ponders the difference between looking at versus along something. This is a nice introduction to the idea that the way we know something very much influences what we can know about what we are investigating.

Lilley, Christopher, and Daniel J. Pedersen, eds. *Human Origins and the Image of God*. Grand Rapids: Eerdmans, forthcoming 2017. The fourteen chapters in this book are written by scholars from various disciplines and address the question whether humans are unique or not. The chapters are organized around Wentzel van Huyssteen's work in human rationality, embodiment, and evolutionary history.

Lin, Johnny Wei-Bing. *The Nature of Environmental Stewardship: Understanding Creation Care Solutions to Environmental Problems*. Eugene, OR: Pickwick, 2016. Lin provides a survey of ethics, science epistemology, science-policy studies, and risk and uncertainty. While the focus of the book is on solving environmental problems, the topics covered are useful for decision-making in general.

Lindberg, David C., and Ronald L. Numbers, eds. *God and Nature: Historical Essays on the Encounter between Christianity and Science*. Berkeley: University of California Press, 1986. The eighteen essays in this volume are by an international team of historians and survey the period from early Christianity to the twentieth century. The essays argue against the warfare imagery as a way to discuss science and religion.

———. *When Science and Christianity Meet*. Chicago, IL: University of Chicago Press, 2008. The twelve articles collected in this volume treat items as broad-ranging as the Scopes trial, the flood, pre-Adamic races, and Galileo. The essays seek to treat each question in its own right and not as part of a larger agenda concerning the relation of science and religion.

Livingstone, David N. *Adam's Ancestors: Race, Religion, and the Politics of Human Origins*. Baltimore: Johns Hopkins University Press, 2011. Livingstone traces the historical adventures of the idea that Adam had pre-Adamic ancestors. He shows how this idea, which is as early as the Middle Ages, has had interesting political, social, and theological implications, not the least of which relate to racism and white supremacy. It was also used as a way to reconcile evolution and religion.

Mann, Robert. "Inconstant Multiverse." *Perspectives on Science and Christian Faith* 57 (2005) 302–10. While one of the primary tasks of theology has historically been to explain why there is something rather than nothing, in light of modern multiverse theory a new question of theology is born—Why is there something rather than everything? Mann provides his reflections on this topic and explains why he believes multiverse theory to be incompatible with Christian theology.

Manning, Russell Re, and Michael Bryne, eds. *Science and Religion in the Twenty-First Century: the Boyle Lectures*. London: SCM, 2013. This work is a collection of lectures given between 2004–2013 by scientists, philosophers, and theologians such as John Polkinghorne, Malcolm Jeeves, and Jürgen Moltmann. The essays present an important overview of the modern dialogue of science and religion and provide a more complex description of the relationship rather than simply reducing the relationship to one of conflict and strife.

Martin, Dale B. *The Corinthian body*. New Haven: Yale University Press, 1999. Martin hypothesizes that many of the issues which arise in Paul's Corinthian letters stem from their disharmony in the philosophy and theology of the human form. For a biblical interpreter this context is key in having a comprehensive theology of bodies and their anatomy in modernity.

McGrath, Alister E. *The Science of God: an Introduction to Scientific Theology*. Grand Rapids: Eerdmans, 2004. This is an introduction and guide to McGrath's three volume *A Scientific Theology* in which he emphasizes the natural sciences as a dialogue partner for Christian thought.

McMullin, Ernan, ed. *Evolution and Creation*. University of Notre Dame Studies in the Philosophy of Religion 4. Notre Dame: University of Notre Dame Press, 1985. This book, edited by one of the academic giants in the science-religion dialogue, includes essays from leading philosophers and theologians such as Carroll Stuhlmueller, David Kelsey, William Austin, and Nicholas Lash. The essays set out a robust biblically informed response to creationism and argue for the compatibility of creation and evolution.

McNamara, Patrick. *The Neuroscience of Religious Experience*. Cambridge: Cambridge University Press, 2009. This is a fascinating study by a professor of neurology and psychiatry who is deeply interested in religion. On the basis of neuroimaging he discusses the "functionally integrated religion-related brain circuit" which involves a widely distributed set of neural regions and nearly always includes the key nodes of the amygdala, the right anterior temporal cortex, and the right prefrontal cortex. This book is important for understanding identity, the self in its various manifestations, and the role of religion.

———, ed. *Where God and Science Meet: How Brain and Evolutionary Studies Alter Our Understanding of Religion*. 3 vols. Westport, CT: Praeger, 2006. The three volumes respectively focus on "Evolution, Genes, and the Religious Brain," "The Neurology of Religious Experience," and "The Psychology of Religious Experience." An international team of experts provide essays from evolutionary, neuroscientific, and psychological approaches to explain and explore religious experience and its biological effects, part of which evidence has led to the new field of neurotheology. The ambition of the work is not to prove or disprove God or the supernatural but rather to analyze the biology of spiritual experiences.

McNamara, Patrick, and Wesley J. Wildman, eds. *Science and the World's Religions*. 3 vols. Brain, Behavior, and Evolution. Santa Barbara: Praeger, 2012. This comprehensive three-volume work features essays from a broad spectrum of scholarship. The three volumes respectively treat "origins and destinies," "persons and groups," and "religions and controversies." The essays treat a wide range of topics such as the origin of religion, good and evil, sacral kingship, the Gaia hypothesis, empathy and cruelty, sacrifice, religious experience, and much more.

Miller, Kenneth R. *Finding Darwin's God: A Scientist's Search for Common Ground Between God and Evolution*. New York: Harper Collins, 1999. Evolutionary biologist Ken Miller is a mainstay of science-religion discussions in the United States since his early appearance in a PBS debate concerning evolutionary theory several decades ago. This book contains one of the most useful critiques of intelligent design theory.

Moreland, James Porter, and John Mark Reynolds. *Three Views on Creation and Evolution*. Grand Rapids: Zondervan, 1999. This book looks at the three dominant schools of Christian thought with respect to the origins of the Earth. Proponents of young earth creationism, old earth creationism, and theistic evolution each present their views, tell why the controversy is important, and describe their understanding of the interplay between science and theology.

Moritz, Joshua M. "Does Jesus Save the Neanderthals? Theological Perspectives on the Evolutionary Origins and Boundaries of Human Nature." *Dialog: A Journal of Theology* 54 (March 2015) 51–60. What theological sense can be made of the limitations of human nature when contemplated in light of contemporary evolutionary biology and paleoanthropology? This article explores how theologians can address such a question by looking at areas where theological anthropology, evolutionary biology, and paleoanthropology intersect.

———. "Evolution, the End of Human Uniqueness, and the Election of the *Imago Dei*." *Theology and Science* 9 (2011) Humans have often found justification for superiority based on the endowment of the image of God (imago Dei) in Gen 1:26. Instead of grounding the imago Dei in human uniqueness, Moritz offers that it is best understood within the context of the ancient Hebrew framework of historical election.

Newbigin, Lesslie. *Proper Confidence: Faith, Doubt, and Certainty in Christian Discipleship*. Grand Rapids: Eerdmans, 1995. Newbigin offers a discussion of the relationship between science and Christian faith in the context of broader reflections on theological epistemology, apologetic method, and Christian discipleship.

Noble, David F. *The Religion of Technology: The Divinity of Man and the Spirit of Invention*. Harmondsworth: Penguin, 1999. Noble argues that the relationship between science and religion is a symbiotic one that dates back over a thousand years. He offers a critique, somewhat controversially, that perhaps the link between technology and religion has outlived the mutual benefit and should be severed.

Noll, Mark A. *The Scandal of the Evangelical Mind*. Grand Rapids: Eerdmans, 1994. Noll provides a comprehensive analysis of the great divorce in modernity between intellect and piety in much of North American evangelical Christianity. He calls for the recovery of respect for intellect within the reaches of evangelical Christianity.

Numbers, Ronald L., ed. *Galileo Goes to Jail: And Other Myths About Science and Religion*. Cambridge, MA: Harvard University Press, 2010. Numbers provides a lighter read in which each short chapter addresses a commonly held myth about some aspect of science and religion.

Patterson, Gary. "Theology and Thermodynamics: In Praise of Entropy." *Perspectives on Science and Christian Faith* 64 (2012) 242–49. This article presents an introduction to both classical and statistical thermodynamics and places an emphasis on the role of entropy in the description of our physical world. Thermodynamics is examined as an alternative that provides a sound basis for understanding the significance of the God-given entropy.

Peters, Ted, and Martinez Hewlett. *Can You Believe in God and Evolution? A Guide for the Perplexed*. Nashville: Abingdon, 2006. This little book is an excellent overview asking one of the seminal questions of the relationship between Christianity and science. Accessible and brief, this would be a great book for a discussion group or classroom setting.

Plantinga, Alvin. *Where the Conflict Really Lies: Science, Religion, and Naturalism*. New York: Oxford University Press, 2011. Giving a great deal of benefit of the doubt to critics of evolutionary science and materialistic physicists, Plantinga probes some of the unquestioned assumptions that guide the reconciliation between science and religion. This book is for somewhat more advanced readers who will appreciate his careful dissections of concepts such as "divine intervention" and "design."

Pielke, Roger A. *The Honest Broker: Making Sense of Science in Policy and Politics*. Cambridge: Cambridge University Press, 2014. Pielke describes four archetypal ways science and scientists can become involved in policy. He shows how our understanding of the nature of democracy and the role of science in decision-making influences how we believe science can become involved in policy.

Polkinghorne, John C. *The Faith of a Physicist*. Minneapolis: Fortress, 1996. Taking the Nicene Creed as a starting point, best-selling author and physicist/Anglican priest John Polinghorne shows how his physics and his faith are intertwined. For Polkinghorne science invariably leads to the question of faith. Unusual for this field, Polkinghorne is willing to comment on a significant number of biblical episodes and traditional doctrines in the light of contemporary science.

———. *The Polkinghorne Reader: Science, Faith and the Search for Meaning*. Edited by Thomas Jay Oord. West Conshohocken, PA: SPCK/Templeton, 2010. This reader presents some of the important work of one of the giants in the dialogue between science and religion. Polkinghorne's positions as Anglican priest and former mathematics and physics professor at Cambridge make him uniquely qualified to speak to the complexities of the relationship between science and religion.

———. *Quantum Physics and Theology: An Unexpected Kinship*. New Haven: Yale University Press, 2007. Polkinghorne's assessment of the deep connection between science and Christology shows with new clarity a common goal in the search for truth.

———. *Quarks, Chaos and Christianity: Questions to Science and Religion*. New York: Crossroad, 2005. Science and faith ought to be friends rather than enemies in the search for truth and knowledge. Polkinghorne references discoveries made in atomic physics to make reliable the claims of Christianity and answer the question whether a scientist can really believe.

Provan, Iain W. *Discovering Genesis: Content, Interpretation, Reception*. Grand Rapids: Eerdmans, 2016. Provan gives a brief introduction to Genesis, sets its opening chapters in the context of the book and of the ancient world, and discusses various aspects of the interpretation of Genesis through the ages.

———. *Seriously Literal Interpretation: Protestant Hermeneutics in the Twenty-First Century*. Waco: Baylor University Press, forthcoming 2017. This is a comprehensive examination of the viability of Protestant hermeneutics in our contemporary times, in the context of the history of biblical interpretation to this point—including a great amount of attention to questions of biblical exegesis and science.

Reeves, Josh A., and Steve Donaldson. *A Little Book for New Scientists: Why and How to Study Science*. Little Books Series. Downers Grove, IL: IVP Academic, 2016. This concise introduction to the study of science provides both advice and encouragement for Christians entering or engaged in scientific careers because their presence in science is a vital component of the church's witness in the world.

Rovelli, Carlo. *Reality is Not What It Seems: The Elementary Structure of Things*. New York: Riverhead, 2017. This is an extension of Rovelli's most popular work *Seven Brief Lessons on Physics* and goes into greater depth with the concepts introduced there. Equally accessible to all readers, *Reality is Not What It Seems* is a great read for someone interested in a survey of the modern work being done in the field of theoretical physics but without extensive background or time to devote.

———. *Seven Brief Lessons on Physics*. New York: Riverhead, 2016. This little volume provides a very basic introduction and description of the fundamental theories that inform modern physics. At fewer than 100 pages and extremely accessible, this is a great starting place for anyone interested in engaging the topic of physics.

Ruse, Michael. *Evolution and Religion: A Dialogue*. 2nd ed. Lanham: Rowman and Littlefield, 2016. Ruse, a leading expert on Charles Darwin, presents a fictional dialogue regarding the tensions between science and religious belief. He portrays stereotypical caricatures of varying types waged in a fierce battle for the truth concerning the narratives of origin offered by science and religion.

Russell, Robert J., and Joshua M. Moritz, eds. *God's Providence and Randomness*. West Conshohocken: Templeton, forthcoming 2017). This book is the collection of papers written for the SATURN (Scientific and Theological Understandings of Randomness in Nature) project of the Center for Theology and the Natural Sciences. The SATURN project was a study of the scientific warrants for and theological implications of randomness, propensities, and indeterminism in nature (i.e., natural phenomena such as the self-organization of the rings of Saturn out of apparently random processes and gravitational interactions). Two of the symposium presenters, Joshua Moritz and Gerald Cleaver, have contributions in this work.

Scholder, Klaus. *The Birth of Modern Critical Theology: Origins and Problems of Biblical Criticism in the Seventeenth Century*. Translated by John Bowden. London: SCM, 1990. This translation from a German publication in 1966 is a provocative analysis of controversies in the seventeenth century and how they shaped the present relationship between science and faith. Among other things Scholder treats the relation of Scripture and reason, the credibility of the biblical worldview, and the consequences of Copernicus.

Shantz, Colleen. *Paul in Ecstasy: The Neurobiology of the Apostle's Life and Thought*. Cambridge: Cambridge University Press, 2009. Too often biblical scholars have balked at the notion of examining the Apostle Paul on the basis of his neurology. Shantz attempts to provide a look into the life of Paul from a neuroanatomical perspective and assess some of the more challenging biblical writings of the Apostle in light of her findings.

Shults, F. LeRon, Nancey C. Murphy, and Robert J. Russell, eds. *Philosophy, Science and Divine Action*. Vol. 1 of *Philosophical Studies in Science and Religion*. Leiden: Brill, 2009. One of the most contested themes between science and religion is the concept of divine action. This work brings together many of the leading voices in the field to provide insight on what, if anything, science has to say about divine action in the ancient and modern world.

Snowden, David J., and Mary E. Boone. "A Leader's Framework for Decision Making." *Harvard Business Review* 85.11 (2007) 68–76. This article specifically addresses the Cynefin framework which helps managers and leaders reach decisions. The article emphasizes the importance of context in decision-making.

Southgate, Christopher. *God, Humanity and the Cosmos: A Textbook in Science and Religion*. Harrisburg: Trinity, 1999. This volume is an accessible but comprehensive introduction to the different disciplines in the science-religion dialogue. It also includes significant sections dealing with Islam and science, biotechnology and ecology. It is highly recommended for use in college level courses or lay education in churches.

Soskice, Janet Martin. *Metaphor and Religious Language*. Oxford: Clarendon, 1987. Soskice argues that what is needed in modern dialogue is a better understanding of metaphor in biblical language. This work may help individuals to understand how many biblical theists working in the field of science reconcile their faith in the Scriptures with what they logically deem to be true about the world.

Spitzer, Robert J. *New Proofs for the Existence of God: Contributions of Contemporary Physics and Philosophy*. Grand Rapids: Eerdmans, 2010. Spitzer considers string theory,

Annotated Bibliography

quantum cosmology, mathematical thoughts on infinity, and much more in his quest to uncover evidence for the existence of God. This fascinating and stunning collection of evidence provides solid ground for reasonable and responsible belief in a super-intelligent, transcendent, creative power standing at the origins of our universe.

Stenmark, Mikael. *How to Relate Science and Religion: A Multidimensional Model.* Grand Rapids: Eerdmans, 2004. This is the best book on dissecting scientism. One of the important tasks of those in the science-religion dialogue is to address the way we make knowledge claims and what different forms of knowledge mean. This issue is one of the challenging aspects of the science-religion dialogue, but if the issues can be framed appropriately, the learning is much richer. Stenmark indicates how such insight takes place, even to the point where science can still be science while being shaped by religion.

Stolow, Jeremy, ed. *Deus in Machina: Religion, Technology, and the Things in Between.* New York: Fordham University Press, 2013. Modern voices might have one believe that technology and religion are, at worst, locked in a never-ending conflict and, at best, not related at all. This work forces readers to question both paradigms and reinterpret both genres and their connections.

Stump, J. B., and Alan G. Padgett, eds. *The Blackwell Companion to Science and Christianity.* Malden, MA: Blackwell, 2012. This reader is an excellent starting point for an overview of science and religion. While no work of this type could be truly comprehensive, this work surveys a history of the relationship between science and religion, gives an overview of the important modern figures in the discussion, and discusses many of the most popular ideological topics.

Tallis, Raymond. *Aping Mankind: Neuromania, Darwinitis and the Misrepresentation of Humanity.* London: Routledge, 2014. Tallis provides a critique of the exaggerated claims that neuroscience and evolutionary biology can explain and/or predict human consciousness. Tallis shows that humanity is infinitely more interesting and complex than it appears in the mirror of biologism.

Taussig, Michael. *Mimesis and Alterity: A Particular History of the Senses.* New York: Routledge, 1993. Taussig presents a history of mimesis (or imitation) and its complex relation to alterity. Taussig concludes that the history of mimesis is deeply tied to colonialism and has vast implications on the relationship of a diverse society.

Taylor, Daniel. *The Myth of Certainty: The Reflective Christian and the Risk of Commitment.* Waco, TX: Word, 1986. In a world (both within and without the church) that prizes certainty, what is one to do with doubt and nuance? Taylor has wise as well as practical words of encouragement for believers who are uncomfortable, not only with pat answers, but a culture that is, to borrow from Pascal, unable to know ". . . where to doubt, where to feel certain, where to submit."

Thompson, Evan. *Mind in Life: Biology, Phenomenology and the Sciences of Mind.* Cambridge, MA: Harvard University Press, 2007. Though many have tried to divorce the mind from physical life, Thompson takes a different approach and argues that in fact, mind and life are impossible to separate. Drawing on an array of scientific disciplines from molecular biology to psychology, Thomson argues where there is life there is mind and seeks to address more accurately the biology and phenomenology of the mind.

Walton, John H. *The NIV Application Commentary Genesis.* The NIV Application Commentary Series. Grand Rapids: Zondervan, 2001. This series focuses on original meaning, briedging contexts, and contemporary application. This volume on Genesis obviously must give significant attention to the kinds of issues that arise when the reader asks questions of Genesis through the lens of modern science.

———. *The Lost World of Genesis One: Ancient Cosmology and the Origins Debate*. Downers Grove, IL: IVP Academic, 2009. Walton presents and defends twenty propositions concerning a literary and theological reading of Genesis within the context of the ancient Near Eastern background, and then he explains the implications for a modern scientific understanding of origins.

———. *The Lost World of Adam and Eve: Genesis 2–3 and the Human Origins Debate*. Downers Grove, IL: IVP Academic, 2015. Walton extends his efforts from the previous entry to focus on the ancient Near Eastern background of Gen 2–3. He seeks a faithful reading of Scripture and a full engagement with science that leads to a new approach to human origins. The book includes an excursus by N. T. Wright which deals with Adam in Paul's writings.

Warners, David, Michael Ryskamp, and Randall Van Dragt. "Reconciliation Ecology: A New Paradigm for Advancing Creation Care." *Perspectives on Science and Christian Faith* 66 (2014) 221–35. This work discusses environmental stewardship in light of biblical creation and reconciliation theology. It is an excellent starting point for people interested in creation care through a biblical interpretation lens.

Weinberg, Steven. *The First Three Minutes: A Modern View of the Origin of the Universe*. 2nd ed. New York: Basic, 1993. This iconic volume explores the late twentieth-century view of how the universe began and how science was able to determine such theories.

William of St. Thierry. *The Golden Epistle: A Letter to the Brethren at Mont Dieu*. Translated by Theodore Berkeley. Cistercian Fathers Series. Collegeville, MN: Cistercian, 1971. Translated for a more modern generation, this work has been a practical guide for spiritual experience for nearly nine hundred years and can still provide great insight today.

Woollacott, Marjorie H. *Infinite Awareness: The Awakening of a Scientific Mind*. Lanham: Rowman and Littlefield, 2015. *Infinite Awareness* pairs Woollacott's research as a celebrated neuroscientist with self-revelations from her personal experiences about the mind's spiritual power. Between the scientific and spiritual worlds, she uncovers her definition of human consciousness in order to investigate the existence of a non-physical and infinitely powerful mind.

NORTH PARK THEOLOGICAL SEMINARY SYMPOSIUM ON THE THEOLOGICAL INTERPRETATION OF SCRIPTURE

SEPTEMBER 29–OCTOBER 1, 2016

Science and Religion

PRESENTERS

Paul Allen
Associate Professor of Theological Studies, Concordia University, Montreal, Canada

Gerald Cleaver
Professor of Physics, Baylor University

Susan Eastman
Associate Research Professor of New Testament, Duke Divinity School

Johnny Wei-Bing Lin
Senior Lecturer Computing and Software Systems Division, University of Washington, Bothell, and Affiliate Professor of Physics and Engineering, North Park University

Hans Madueme
Assistant Professor of Theological Studies, Covenant College, Chattanooga, TN

Joshua M. Moritz
Lecturer of Philosophical Theology and Natural Sciences, Graduate Theological Union; Adjunct Professor of Philosophy, University of San Francisco

Iain Provan
Marshall Sheppard Professor of Biblical Studies, Regent College, Canada

Michael Spezio
Associate Professor of Psychology and Neuroscience, Scripps College, Claremont, CA; Visiting Researcher, Institute for Systems Neuroscience, University of Hamburg Medical Center, Hamburg, Germany

Kirk Wegter-McNelly
    Wold Visiting Professor, Union College, New York

RESPONDENTS

A. Andrew Das
    Professor of New Testament, Elmhurst College

Linda M. Eastwood
    Adjunct Professor, McCormick Theological Seminary

Chris Lilley
    PhD candidate, Marquette University

Tyler Johnson
    Pastor, Albert City Covenant Church, Albert City, Iowa

Matthew B. Maas
    Assistant Professor of Neurology and Anesthesiology, Northwestern University

Stephen Ray
    Assistant Professor of Physics and Engineering and Director of Sustainability, North Park University

John Walton
    Professor of Old Testament, Wheaton College

Kirk Wegter-McNelly
    Wold Visiting Professor, Union College, New York

www.ingramcontent.com/pod-product-compliance
Lightning Source LLC
Chambersburg PA
CBHW081351230426
43667CB00017B/2790